MAYHEM IN MOGADISHU, SOMALIA 1991–94

By the same author

The Colonel's Table

Reveille & Retribution (as Sustainer)

Spit & Polish (as Sustainer)

Friend & Foe (as Sustainer)

On Laffan's Plain

K Boat Catastrophe

Chitrál Charlie

Valour in the Trenches

'Strafer': Desert General

Where Tom Long Roamed

Betrayal of an Army: Mesopotamia 1914–1916

The Logistics in the Vietnam Wars, 1945–1975

The Siege that Changed the World: Paris 1870–1871

In the Service of the Emperor: The Rise & Fall of the Japanese Empire 1931–1945

Hunger: Food Deprivation as a Military Weapon

Caribbean Crisis: The Invasion of Grenada 1983

Mayhem in Mogadishu, Somalia 1991–94

N. S. NASH

Pen & Sword
MILITARY

First published in Great Britain in 2026 by
Pen & Sword Military
An imprint of Pen & Sword Books Limited
Yorkshire – Philadelphia

ISBN 978 1 03613 216 3

A CIP catalogue record for this book is available from the British Library.

Typeset by Mac Style
Printed in the UK by CPI Group (UK) Ltd, Croydon, CR0 4YY.

MIX
Paper | Supporting responsible forestry
FSC® C013604

The Publisher's authorised representative in the EU for product safety is Authorised Rep Compliance Ltd., Ground Floor, 71 Lower Baggot Street, Dublin D02 P593, Ireland.
www.arccompliance.com

For a complete list of Pen & Sword titles please contact:

PEN & SWORD BOOKS LIMITED
47 Church Street, Barnsley, South Yorkshire, S70 2AS, England
E-mail: enquiries@pen-and-sword.co.uk
Website: www.pen-and-sword.co.uk
or
PEN AND SWORD BOOKS
1950 Lawrence Road, Havertown, PA 19083, USA
E-mail: uspen-and-sword@casematepublishers.com
Website: www.penandswordbooks.com

Mayhem: Violent or extreme disorder; chaos.

Oxford English Dictionary

The rains can fail, wells can dry up, pastures can turn to dust. It needs binding faith and clan loyalty to keep everyone alive.

John Drysdale, *Whatever Happened to Somalia?* (1994)

In Somalia, with the Cold War decisively over, the United States had no ostensible geopolitical or economic ambitions, faced no hidden political enemies backing direct combatants, and confronted neither a collectively, nor manipulable population.

Jonathan Stevenson, *Losing Mogadishu: Testing U.S. Policy in Somalia* (1995)

Principles of strategy should never transcend common sense.

Motto of the German Army Staff College, prior to 1914

Do not repeat the tactics by which you have gained one victory, but let your methods be regulated by the infinite variety of circumstances.

Sun Tzu, 500 BC

You're likely to have a big fight over some period of time with considerable casualties, and in the end, you're going to turn over the city to the Somalis.

Major General David Meade USA, September 1993

If we go into the vicinity of Bakaara Market, there's no question we'll win the gunfight, but we might lose the war.

Major General William F. Garrison USA, 1993

Contents

Contents

Maps

Illustrations

Abbreviations

160th Special Operations Aviation Regiment	SOAR
Armed Forces Road	AFR
Armoured personnel carriers	APC
Central Intelligence Agency	CIA
Chief Warrant Officer	CWO
Combat Search and Rescue	CSAR
Her Majesty's Government	HMG
Improvised explosive device	IED
International Committee of the Red Cross	ICRC
International Red Cross	IRC
Joint Operations Command	JOC
Médecins Sans Frontières	MSF
Night vision goggles	NVG
Non-governmental organisations	NGO
Private First Class	PFC
Psychological operations	PSYOP
Quick Reaction Force	QRF
Rocket-propelled grenade	RPG
Rules of engagment	ROE
Sea and Land (Special Forces)	SEAL
Sergeant First Class	SFC
Somali National Alliance	SNA
Somali National Front	SNF
Somali National League	SNL
Somali National Movement	SNM
Somali Patriotic Movement	SPM
Somali Salvation Alliance	SSA
Somali Salvation Democratic Front	SSDF

Somali Youth League	SYL
Special Representative of the Secretary-General	SRSG
Task Force Ranger	TFR
Tube-launched, optically tracked, wire-guided	TOW
Unified Task Force	UNITAF
United Nations Operation Somalia	UNOSOM I and II
United Somali Congress	USC
United States Navy	USN
US Joint Special Operations Command	JSOC
Western Somali Liberation Front	WSLF
World Health Organization	WHO

Acknowledgements

I was drawn to this subject having previously examined Operation URGENT FURY and the part played by US Special Forces in the invasion of Grenada in 1983. That operation was launched against a miniscule, poorly armed and unmotivated enemy and, although a victory was swiftly achieved, the operation was seriously flawed. There are similarities with the later American Operation GOTHIC SERPENT in Somalia in 1993.

In this book I have drawn on Mark Bowden's excellent *Black Hawk Down* (1999). This is the definitive work on the subject of the Battle of Mogadishu. It is very detailed and superbly researched. It was the basis for the film (2001) of the same name. The facts Bowden adduced are in the public domain; there is no copyright on fact.

I have considered any number of sources, beside Bowden, many of whom were spectators or participants to Somalia's anarchy, and among these are John Drysdale, Michael Durant, Scott Peterson and Jonathan Stevenson. All sources are duly noted.

It is suggested that, notwithstanding the excellence of Bowden's book and film, there is a case to readdress the reasons why Operation GOTHIC SERPENT was, at best, a pyrrhic victory that led to national humiliation. I suggest where the responsibility lies for that mortification.

The 'official' US history of the period is seriously flawed, and it ignores the single, critical event that contributed directly to the defeat of the United States in the Battle of Mogadishu. My hope is that this book fills some of the gaps and provides a sense of proportion.

Somali society was then, and is now, complex. In large measure, it is subject to the powerful influence of its clan system, a culture gap that third parties could not bridge. The innumerable players concerned in the chaos of Somalia in the latter part of the twentieth century with no shared national agenda added to the complexity.

In the interests of brevity and comprehension, some of the detail has been omitted in this chronicle. Where I quote an American source, I use American spelling when it is appropriate. Where $ values are given in the text, they are US dollars.

Once again, Pen and Sword have appointed Linne Matthews to edit my work. She nitpicks for England and over the last fifteen years and nine books has polished, and by so doing, enhanced my work. I have greatly appreciated her forensic and always encouraging observations. Linne is my sternest critic and greatest supporter.

Matt Jones and his production team in Barnsley have once again produced a handsome book, notwithstanding any deficiencies in the text, which are entirely my responsibility.

Tank Nash
Tetbury
July 2026

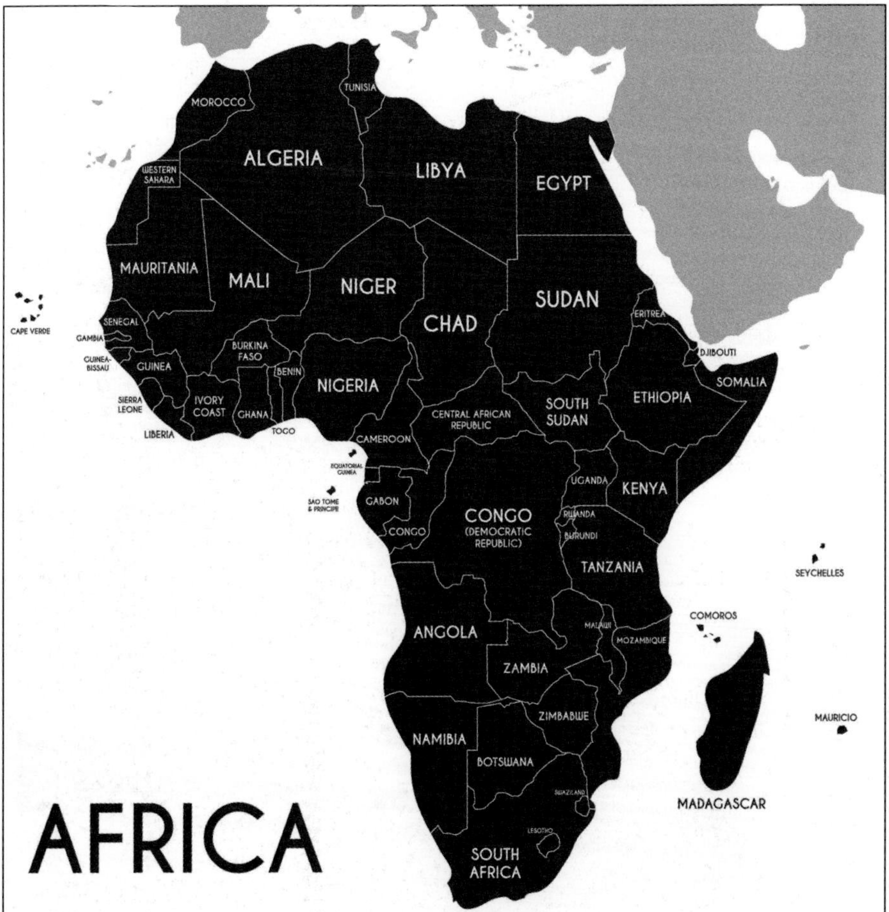

(© *Adobe Stock 152850030*)

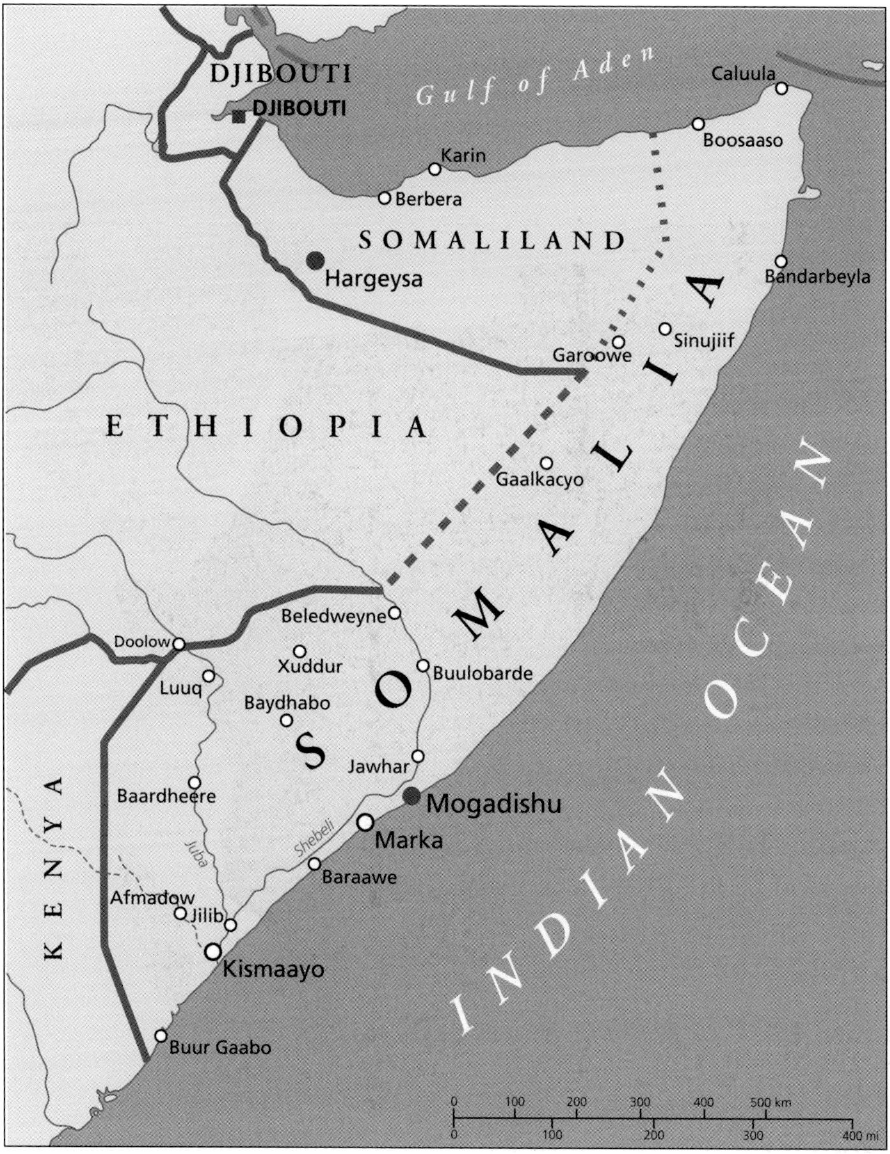

(© *Adobe Stock 45340516*)

Chapter 1

Ready to Go

The object is not the occupation of a geographical position, but the destruction of the enemy force.

General Pyotr A. Rumyantsev, 1725–96

There was a plan. On the face of it, it was simple, but then all good plans are simple.

The object of the exercise was to capture two senior members of the Somali National Alliance (SNA). The SNA was an organisation in armed conflict with the United Nations and its surrogate, the United States of America. It was American forces that were now assembled to seize the two dissidents, on that early afternoon of 3 October 1993, in Somalia, just outside the ruined and verminous city of Mogadishu.

The mechanics of the imminent operation had been carried out on six previous occasions, but they could not be implemented for the seventh time until the circumstances were ripe. However, intelligence had just been delivered that fitted the bill. All the American participants were well briefed, well trained, well armed and busting for the issue of the code word IRENE that would trigger the plan.

The operation was called GOTHIC SERPENT, and the US Task Force Ranger (TFR) was to execute it. To that effect there were four AH-6 Little Bird, two-seat, attack helicopters armed with rockets, and there were four MH-6 troop-carrying helicopters. These latter two were allocated to the cutting edge of Delta's Charlie Squadron. These high-grade soldiers, considered in American circles to be the best of the best, were the designated strike force, responsible for effecting the capture.

The follow-up Delta element, together with their ground headquarters, were mounted in two Black Hawk aircraft. A further four Black Hawks carried the Rangers of Bravo Company, 3rd Battalion, 75th Parachute Infantry

The Sikorsky UH-60 Black Hawk, a four-blade, twin-engine, medium-lift military helicopter, manufactured by Sikorsky Aircraft. It was taken into service in 1972 and played an important role in Somalia in 1991–94.

Regiment. The specialist Combat Search and Rescue (CSAR) team occupied a seventh Black Hawk and the last was allocated to the mission commanders.

The first of these was Lieutenant Colonel Tom Matthews, who was to coordinate the pilots of 160th Special Operations Aviation Regiment (SOAR), an elite group who flew the Special Forces on their, usually, secret missions. The second officer was Lieutenant Colonel Gary Harrell, the ground force commander.

> The Special Operations Aviation Regiment (SOAR) provided all the aerial support to TFR. The regiment took pride in its nickname 'The Night Stalkers'. They were so called because total darkness was their preferred environment. The technology of night vision equipment was, by 1993, so sophisticated that these pilots could fly, assault, insert and withdraw seeing all about them but remaining unseen.[1]

The background of SOAR is to be found at pages 97–8.

The helicopter force was 'burning and turning' at Mogadishu airport, where the United Nations Operation in Somalia II (UNOSOM II) had its headquarters. A ground convoy was similarly fully prepared and waiting impatiently for the signal to go. The convoy was composed of nine wide-bodied Humvees, and three 5-ton trucks. The Humvees carried Rangers,

The High Mobility Multipurpose Wheeled Vehicle (HMMWV, 'Humvee') is a class of unarmoured, light, four-wheel drive vehicles that had been used extensively in the Gulf War of 1991, where it was ideally suited to desert conditions.

additional Delta operators and four SEALs of the US Navy's Special Force. The function of the convoy was to exfiltrate the attacking force and its prisoners once the mission was complete.

The total force assembled, and waiting for the code word IRENE, was 19 aircraft (3 of which were employed for surveillance duties), 12 vehicles and 160 men.

The plan required the Rangers to fast-rope down from helicopters at four points around the target building. They were to provide a protective cordon around the Delta snatch team that would arrest the two wanted men. The convoy would then drive through the city, pick up all the participants and the prisoners and retrace its route.

It was anticipated that, from start to finish, GOTHIC SERPENT would take an hour. The US forces had complete control of the sky, overwhelming firepower and surprise on its side.

What could possibly go wrong?

Chapter 2

The Background

It would be ingenuous to suppose that the Battle of Mogadishu, described in detail later in this book, can be considered in isolation. In fact, it was the culmination of 100 years of strife, ignorance, incompetence, political ambition and anarchy. All of these elements were in constant and plentiful supply in Somalia.

The inept interference in Somali affairs by the United Nations, largely funded by the USA in the last decade of the twentieth century, was the 'blue touch paper' about to be ignited in Mogadishu in October 1993. It would be germane to consider briefly the turbulent history of this benighted country and to provide a rationale for the violent events and loss of life chronicled here.

Somalia is the easternmost country of Africa. It is located abreast of the equator and north of the Gulf of Aden. Its geography makes it strategically and economically significant, but its political potential has never been successfully exploited during its chaotic history. The recent history of Somalia has to be viewed against the historic mindset of the Somali people.

> There is practically no such thing as a Somali patriot or a Somali nationalist. By tradition Somali nomads are self-sufficient. From this heritage they developed a transcendental sense of individual superiority and the conviction that they are accountable only to God.[1]

It was the British who, in 1839, and while expanding their influence from their well-established trading post in Aden, initiated a grab for further African territory. The French and Italians joined them, determined to get their share of what seemed to be readily available. The people of Somalia then, and into the twenty-first century, have had a tribal culture. Tribal alliances have always enjoyed a priority in the matter of governance and were a factor in the events that gave rise to this book.

In 1854, Richard Francis Burton was but one explorer investigating this part of the world, while John Hanning Speke was concentrating on the Makhir coast. In the period 1846–48, Charles Guillain, captain of the brig *Ducouedid*, sailed down the Indian Ocean coast and went ashore at Mogadishu, Marca and Baraawe.[2]

In 1865, the German explorer Karl Klaus von der Decken ventured up the Jubba River, the principal river of Somalia. Originating via its headwater streams in the Mendebo Mountains of southern Ethiopia, the Jubba flows about 545 miles (875km) from Doolow on the Ethiopian frontier and enters the Indian Ocean just north of Kismayo (alternative spelling Kismaayo), one of Somalia's three main ports. Von der Decken's foray did not end well; his small steam ship *Welf* foundered in the rapids above the town of Baardheere. Soon thereafter, von der Decken was killed by Somalis, but much valuable information collected by his expedition survived.[3]

In 1883, an English group (F.L. and W.D. James, G.P.V. Aylmer and E. Lort-Phillips) penetrated from Berbera as far as the Shebelle River (or Webi Shabeelle). Between 1886 and 1892, H.G.C. and E.J.E. Swayne surveyed the country between the coast and the Shebelle area, and they reached farther east towards the Nugaaleed Valley. During 1894–95, A. Donaldson Smith explored the headwaters of the Shebelle River in Ethiopia, reached Lake Rudolf and eventually, by way of the Tana River, got to the Kenyan coast.

Somalia was probably the most extensive and united 'nation' in Africa before the arrival of the colonial powers. They all spoke the same language and shared the same faith as Sunni Muslims. Their only division was down clan lines, but the Italians, French and British all contributed to the breakdown of national homogeneity. The Berlin Conference of 1884–85 sealed the fate of Somalia for more than the next 100 years.[4]

A measure of the isolation of this country is that, deep into the twentieth century, extensive mapping surveys were still being undertaken and, not least, by J.A. Hunt between 1944 and 1950. The advance of technology eventually allowed the mapping of the county by aerial survey. The British, French and Italians carved up the bulk of the Horn of Africa into their own areas of influence. However, between 1884 and 1886, treaties of protection were drawn up with the main northern Somali tribes guaranteeing them their 'independence'. Although Somali territory was not transferred to Britain, nevertheless a British protectorate was proclaimed. For efficient governance, vice-consuls were appointed to maintain order but more importantly to control trade at Seylac, Berbera and Bullaxaar (the latter two places are not shown on the map). The bleak interior of the country held no attractions for the European powers and so was left undisturbed.

Somalia was always at risk to Ethiopian expansion, yet another predator waiting to pounce. The French had not been idle, and they had taken every opportunity to enlarge their colony. As a result, an armed confrontation with the UK seemed to be likely. However, cool heads defined mutually acceptable borders, and a treaty was signed in 1888. The following year, Italy took possession of territory in the north-east of Somalia.

At this time, Ethiopia was an independent state and clearly held sway in the vast but empty hinterland. Italy, France and Britain all recognised the powerful position of the Ethiopian Emperor Menelik and signed treaties with him in 1896–97. In accord with the provisions of the 1888 treaty, the European powers reduced their Somali possessions. Italy gave up the Somali Ogaden, and Britain released much of the western Hawd from its protectorate.

Despite the above, Italian expansion continued wherever possible. The British East India Company had leased the southern part of the Somali coast, from the sultan of Zanzibar, and soon after, sublet the territory to an Italian company. By 1905, this leased territory was in effect a colony – Italian Somaliland.

The Treaty of Wuchale (signed in the Ethiopian town of that name) was an agreement between the Ethiopian Empire and the Kingdom of Italy. The signatories were King Menelik II of Shewa, acting as *de facto* emperor of Ethiopia, and Count Pietro Antonelli, representing his monarch, on 2 May 1889. This treaty ended the hostilities between them that, over the previous two years, had caused the deaths in action of over 1,000 Italians and 400 Ethiopians.

The purpose of the treaty was to promote friendship and trade between the two countries.[5] Events were to show that this was just wishful thinking.

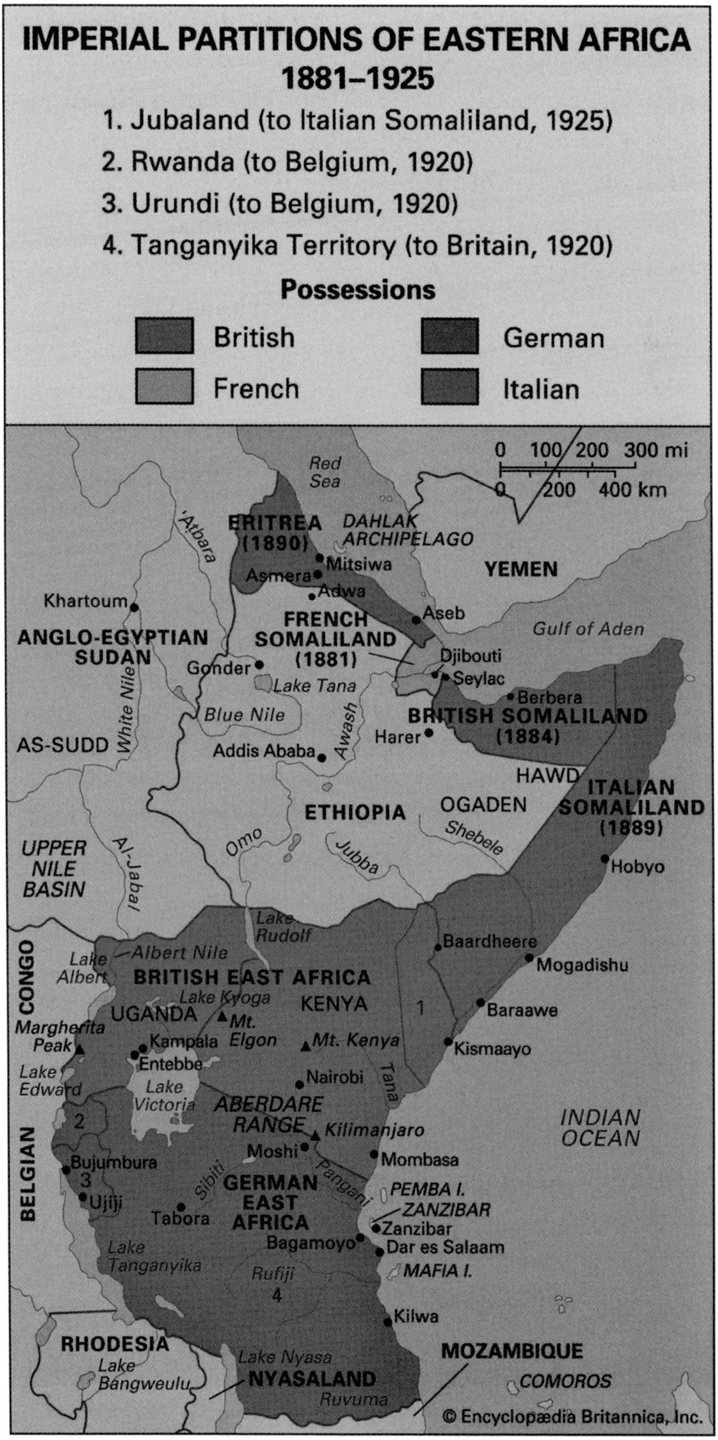
IMPERIAL PARTITIONS OF EASTERN AFRICA
1881–1925
1. Jubaland (to Italian Somaliland, 1925)
2. Rwanda (to Belgium, 1920)
3. Urundi (to Belgium, 1920)
4. Tanganyika Territory (to Britain, 1920)
Possessions
British
German
French
Italian
0 100 200 300 mi
0 200 400 km
Red Sea
ERITREA (1890)
DAHLAK ARCHIPELAGO
Mitsiwa
Asmera
Adwa
YEMEN
Khartoum
Aseb
FRENCH SOMALILAND (1881)
Gulf of Aden
ANGLO-EGYPTIAN SUDAN
Gonder
Djibouti
Seylac
Lake Tana
Berbera
Blue Nile
White Nile
BRITISH SOMALILAND (1884)
Harer
AS-SUDD
Addis Ababa
Awash
HAWD
ITALIAN SOMALILAND (1889)
ETHIOPIA
OGADEN
Shebele
Omo
Jubba
UPPER NILE BASIN
Al-Jabal
Hobyo
Lake Rudolf
Baardheere
Albert Nile
Lake Albert
Mogadishu
CONGO
BRITISH EAST AFRICA
Lake Kyoga
KENYA
UGANDA
Mt. Elgon
1
Baraawe
Margherita Peak
Kampala
Mt. Kenya
Kismaayo
Entebbe
Lake Edward
Lake Victoria
Nairobi
Tana
ABERDARE RANGE
INDIAN OCEAN
2
Kilimanjaro
Moshi
Mombasa
BELGIAN
Bujumbura
3
Ujiji
Sibiti
GERMAN EAST AFRICA
Pangani
PEMBA I.
ZANZIBAR
Tabora
Zanzibar
Bagamoyo
Dar es Salaam
Lake Tanganyika
Rufiji
4
MAFIA I.
Kilwa
RHODESIA
MOZAMBIQUE
Lake Nyasa
Lake Bangweulu
NYASALAND
COMOROS
Ruvuma
© Encyclopædia Britannica, Inc.

Somali society was then, and is now, tribal in nature. The clan is at the centre of a Somali's life. The pervading hierarchy of priorities is best expressed by a Somali proverb:

> Me and my clan against the world
> Me and my family against my clan
> Me and my brother against my family
> Me against my brother.

* * *

Any examination of Somali affairs has to include an awareness of the clan system that, in large measure, provides the backdrop to all political activity. It was, and is, a critical factor in the social, political and military landscape of the country. The clan structure, deeply rooted in Somali culture, significantly influenced the events during the last half of the twentieth century. This included the ongoing civil war and the humanitarian crisis that led to international intervention, such as Operation RESTORE HOPE and later, UNOSOM II. Further details are to be found at Annexure A on page 219.

* * *

Every Somali child knows by heart his or her genealogy more than twenty generations, back to the revered common ancestral eponym of all Somalis, Samaale. Beyond, this hero line is traced presumptuously to the Prophet Mohamed or to noble Arabian families.[6] From Samaale, the lineages divide into six clan families. Political allegiance is determined by the male line, so Somalis do not ask each other *where* they are from, but from *whom*.[7]

Somalis are a warrior race and proud to be so, and, 'Of all the races of Africa there cannot be one better to live among than the most difficult, the proudest, the bravest, the vainest, the most merciless, the Somalis.'[8] The historian Professor Ioan Lewis remarked:

> Somalis were noted for their pride in personal and later national independence. Few writers have failed to notice the formidable pride of the Somali nomad, his extraordinary sense of superiority as an individual, and his firm conviction

> that he is the sole master of his actions and subject to no authority except that of God. It is a legacy that has bedevilled every would-be coloniser. Somalis fought rule by the Italians in the late 19th century and then against British forces that tried to impose law, order and administration.[9]

These national characteristics have been highlighted because they offer an explanation as to the resolute, uncompromising and dedicated commitment to Somali sovereignty that was a feature of the political scene throughout the twentieth century. The structure and attitudes that shaped the Somali society described were essentially male. The role of women was one of subservience and they were barely second-class citizens. Commenting in 1995, Jonathan Stevenson observed:

> Somali women are the most heavily circumcised in the world – over 90 per cent have their clitorises 'clipped' sometimes at three different stages of preadolescence. In the final stage the lips of the labia are scarred and joined together, sometimes by suturing. … For young women, this cultural practice makes for an adolescence of pain and infection and a lifetime of sexual numbness.[10]

Over thirty years later, and this obscene practice continues. The United Nations Office for the Coordination of Humanitarian Affairs (OCHA) reported in 2025 that Somalia still 'leads' the world in Female Genital Mutilation (FGM):

> According to the UN Population Fund, 98 per cent of girls aged between 5 and 11 undergo the most severe form of FGM, type III infibulation. The practice has devastating consequences, including chronic pain, infections, depression, birth complications, sexual health problems, infertility, and, in the worst cases, death.

Just as the Italians and Ethiopians were at peace with each other and sweetness and light were all around, the British Somaliland Protectorate was suddenly challenged by a redoubtable opponent – Maxamed Cabdulle Xasan. He was known to the British as the 'Mad Mullah'. This man was a Somali sheikh and a member of the Ogaden clan. He assembled a force of 5,000 and issued each man with a white turban and declared a holy war.

Maxamed was a noted Islamic cleric whose preaching, termed 'messianic', attracted widespread support. His intellect made him a capable negotiator and adversary. However, it was not until he was in dispute with a Christian mission and, at the same time, at odds with the local administration that his anger developed and prompted him to head a serious Somali insurrection. Maxamed took a lead and inspiration from the Sudanese Mahdi who had been such a challenge to British rule in Sudan in the war of 1881–99.

Maxamed assumed the title of Sayyid (a descendant of the Prophet) and, in a replay of Sudan, his followers were known as Dervishes. Astutely, Maxamed was able to manipulate clan politics in his favour and, when he called for 'National Muslim solidarity against infidel colonisers', he found ample support.[11] Arms and ammunition were easily obtained and shipped in via Djibouti, to the frustration of the British. Maxamed widened his operations and fought against both the Italians and Ethiopians between 1900 and 1904.

The Italo-Ethiopian War was as brutal as any other. In May 1936, two dead, with ropes tied to their feet, lie in the street in Addis Ababa. (*Encyclopaedia Britannica*)

The British Army was ill-prepared to cope with the guerrilla tactics of Maxamed and did not adapt to meet these new conditions. The minor war dragged on until 1910, when the British decided to withdraw to the coast. They left a legacy of widespread confusion in their wake.

On the face of it, Sayyid/Maxamed had won the war. However, desultory military operations continued, albeit without an immediate conclusion. The fifth expedition of the Somaliland campaign was mounted in 1920, and it was the final British expedition against Dervish forces. The British force included elements of the Royal Air Force.[12] This application of modern technology was critical and, three weeks into the campaign, the Dervishes were defeated at Taleex (or Taleh) in the north-east. It was here that 'a combined air, sea, and land operation finally routed them'.[13] This concluded their twenty-year resistance. The Sayyid escaped from the final battle but died of influenza a few months later. After the British victory, the 'Savage and despotic Mad Mullah' was praised for:

> exacting unquestioning obedience found on fear. With the withdrawal of the British control of the interior, indescribable disorder and tribal warfare broke out, and in the holocaust that followed it is estimated that perhaps one third of the male population of British Somaliland were speared to death.[14]

The British swiftly re-established control of the protectorate under the aegis of the Colonial Office. Sayyid's territorial and political ambitions had had less impact on Italian Somaliland and the relative stability of that colony led to the appointment of the first fascist governor in 1923.

Italian settlement was encouraged, and agriculture flourished as fruit plantations were developed along the fertile Shebelle and Jubba valleys. However, the relationship between Ethiopia and Italy was always fraught, despite the agreements of 1897 and 1908 that had defined the border of Italian Somaliland with Ethiopia. There was a stretch of about 18 miles (29km) in which the border remained undefined and in dispute. In this area of Ual-Ual, more frequently known as Walwal or Welwel, was located an important complex of 359 wells used by Somalis and Italians, and by the Ethiopian nomads, who were located within the deserts of the Ogaden.

Italy had no legitimate claim on this area and its posture was at odds with the 1896 treaty. Given Italian intransigence, armed conflict was inevitable. In late 1934, the shooting started when an Ethiopian patrol clashed with

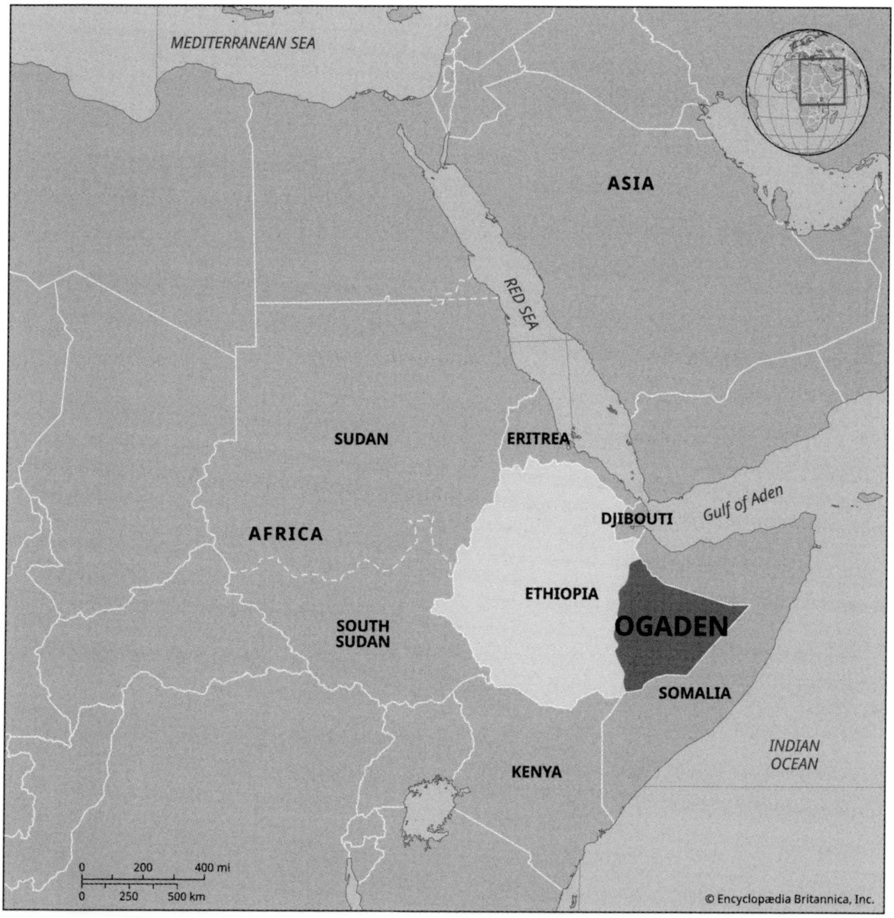

The Ogaden region of Ethiopia, home to many ethnic Somalis. (*Britannica.com*)

the well-established Italian garrison at Ual-Ual. The upshot was the deaths of 21 Italians and more than 300 Ethiopians.[15]

The Italian conquest of Ethiopia followed in 1935–36 and it resulted in the combination of Ethiopian and Italian Somali territories together in what was, briefly, the Italian East African Empire.

The Second World War caused dramatic change all over the world, Somalia included. The British reconsidered their priorities and evacuated the protectorate of Somalia in 1940. This was only temporary because the following year the territory was retaken along with Italian Somalia and Ethiopia. By the end of the war, and with the sole exception of French Somaliland, the whole of Somalia was subject to British military rule.

In 1948, the protectorate reverted to the UK Colonial Office; the Ogaden and the Hawd were gradually surrendered to Ethiopia. In 1950, the Italians returned to southern Somalia, with ten years to prepare the country for independence under a United Nations trusteeship.[16]

The Italians took note of the relatively enlightened British military management and the administrative and social improvements that had been made. The Italians followed suit and implemented, in the area under their care, a similar path of social and political advancement. However, across the whole of Somalia economic growth remained problematic.

The British protectorate became independent on 26 June 1960 as an early example of Britain's retreat from empire. The Italians granted independence to Italian Somalia a week later and the two newly independent territories combined to form the Somali Republic.

Initially, foreign aid – predominantly Western – helped in the myriad tasks facing the new republic. It was at this early stage that the two legal and judicial systems had to be combined and a communications network established across the republic. The first government was formed by a coalition of the Somali Youth League (SYL) and the Somali National League (SNL).

When Somalia gained its independence from British colonial rule in 1960, ethnic Somalis were widely distributed across the Horn of Africa. The border with Ethiopia separated a large portion of the Ogaden and the bleak Hawd western deserts. Djibouti was parcelled up by France. The south of Somalia was split by the Kenyan border. To a Somali, with his inherent warrior culture, these barriers to a unified Greater Somalia were unacceptable. The infant Somali government, faced with the opportunity to draw up a national foreign policy, saw pan-Somali unification as its priority. This issue, although addressed, was not easily resolved by diplomatic means. On that basis, Somalia chose to mount a guerrilla campaign in northern Kenya. This achieved nothing and, along the way, Somalia broke off diplomatic relations with Britain.

At the end of 1963, a Somali uprising in the Ogaden led to an armed confrontation between Ethiopian and Somali forces. At this time, the USA and other Western countries provided military support to Ethiopia and Kenya. Somalia looked elsewhere and sought military aid from, what was then, the USSR.

Chapter 3

Post-Colonial Somalia

In 1967 a new government headed by Maxamed Xaaji Ibrahim Cigaal (Muhammad Haji Ibrahim Egal) changed tack and adopted a policy of détente with Kenya and Ethiopia. Cigaal was a seasoned politician, having briefly served as the first prime minister of the Somali Republic in 1960 (for eleven days). He took up that role for a second and longer period in 1967.

In March 1969, at a national election, more than 1,000 candidates representing 64 parties (most of which were clan-based) contested the 123 seats in the National Assembly. The electoral process was chaotic, but Cigaal was re-elected and continued in post. Cigaal tried to establish order and stability against all the odds. Later, in 1969, the democratically elected president, Abdirashid Ali Shermarke, was assassinated.

In the turmoil that followed the assassination of President Ali Shermarke, Cigaal was ejected from office by an armed coup. The leader of the coup, Major General Mohamed Siad Barre, seized power.[1] Siad's government was largely composed of military acolytes, unskilled in governmental matters.

> Many who knew Siad from his boyhood and during his stint in the colonial police under the Italians were not that surprised. Siad was not a normal person; he was a psychopath whose mercurial spirit vacillated between raving hatred in one moment and words of praise and reconciliation the next moment. He was said to have witnessed the murder of his own father when he was only ten years old during the turbulent year of 1921, when the clan conflicts instigated by Mohamed Abdulle Hassan were raging across the land. Siad was reportedly forever after deeply marked by the murder of his father. He became sadistic.[2]

Siad Barre 'did not treat his people as if they were all Somalis'. He first ensured the permanence of his position by favouring his Marehan and

Darod clans. It was only members of these two clans who could aspire to hold any government position under Siad. Other clans were subject to violent persecution.[3]

Major General Mohamed Siad Barre (1909–95), the third president of Somalia, 1969–91. (*Public domain*)

Siad then invented 'scientific socialism'. This was a creed that he ruled to be compatible with Islamic teaching and practice. One of its aims was the destruction of the clan system. He held formal burial ceremonies to 'bury' the clan ideology and he caused the burning of effigies representing tribalism and misrule.[4] Despite Siad's best efforts, the clan system survived but remained under attack.

Siad Barre also placed great emphasis on the Muslim principles of social progress, equality and justice, which he argued formed the core of scientific socialism. Similarly, he prioritised self-sufficiency, public participation and popular control, as well as direct ownership of the means of production.[5] Not completely lacking a social conscience, he then pronounced a policy that would free his countrymen from poverty, disease and ignorance – a Herculean task.

Somalia has no natural resources, and its political importance was, and remains, dependent on its critically strategic location at the gateway to the Middle East and the Red Sea route to the Mediterranean and Europe. Given this gift of geography, Siad made every effort to exploit it, and his country became a player in the Cold War. In 1974, Siad signed a friendship treaty with the Soviet Union. Swiftly, 6,000 Soviet military and civilian citizens moved in and took control of the Ministries of Defence and Information, the secret police and the key military installation at Berbera.

One of the most evident results of this influx of Russians was the impact on the Somali Army. It resulted in an efficient, well-trained 25,000-strong force armed with state-of-the-art weaponry. The Somali Air Force was equipped with MiG fighters. Significantly, and with long-term consequences, Somali schools started to teach political theory. Siad was himself a committed Marxist and the indoctrination of the country's children fitted into his master plan.

Siad Barre made approaches to other socialist countries who shared his political philosophy and, inevitably, Russia and China were at the top on his target list of new friends. These new relationships flourished but at the expense of Somalia's productive relationship with Western democracies.

A personality cult was developed, and Siad Barre relished being considered the 'Father' of his people. There was a policy of 'indoctrination' of the Somali people during Siad's tenure, and slogans were produced and displayed in towns and villages proclaiming, 'Comrade Marx, Comrade Lenin, and Comrade Siad'.[6]

Siad Barre's authority was assured by the conduct of the 'Victory Pioneers', his National Security Service, conveniently headed by his son-in-law. Through this, he controlled the judicial system, which pronounced draconian punishment to those deemed to be hostile to the 'Father'. Confusingly, the millennium-old clan system was revitalised and harnessed. Regional committees composed of clan elders were established, always under the chairmanship of a state-appointed official. Nevertheless, and in a curious contradiction, 'clan loyalties were still officially outlawed, and clan-inspired behaviour became a criminal offense.'[7] The social structure of Somalia was an enigma then, and remains so.

Somalia became a site of the East/West confrontation. The USA was allied to Ethiopia, the historic enemy of Somalia. It was in Ethiopia, and specifically in the Ogaden and Hawd regions, that ethnic Somalis were persecuted. This alignment with Ethiopia was the cause of pronounced Somali anti-Americanism.

> American Peace Corps volunteers were stoned in the streets of Mogadishu, and, by 1971, they were forced to withdraw. US diplomats were spat upon, and the Embassy staff had been pared down to three by 1977. Mogadishu was plastered with posters that showed Somali peasants stomping on Uncle Sam.[8]

Any American attempt to win Somali hearts and minds had failed miserably.

Siad Barre's despotic rule did have some positives to show and one of these was his determination to improve national literacy in 1973–74. A significant product of this policy was to make Somali a written language, in Latin characters, for the first time.

After this important domestic success, Siad joined the Arab League and by so doing gained access not only to the political support of the Persian Gulf states but also to their abundant petrodollars. Somali trade with these states expanded. At this same time, he was continuing to absorb Soviet arms, now calculated to have reached a value of $270 million.

In 1974, Haile Selassie was overthrown in Ethiopia and replaced by Mengistu Haile Mariam, and the nation started to collapse. This fuelled the ambitions of the Western Somali Liberation Front (WSLF), a dissident group in the Ogaden. The WSLF sought Somali aid, which was freely given, and it sustained the attacks made on Ethiopian installations and garrisons. The Soviet Union backed Ethiopia, provided it with T-54 tanks and tried to persuade Siad to ally with Mengistu, but he was intractable. Although Somalia was now a client state of the Soviet Union, Siad covertly explored the possibilities of support from the US, UK and France. This availed him nothing. The Somali association with the Soviet Union was to the discomfort of the USA.

In July 1977, Siad made an ill-considered move. He believed that his abundant Soviet weaponry, in combination with an inherent sense of superiority, was sufficient. He directed the Somali Army to invade the Ogaden.

> By September 1977 Somalians had largely conquered the Ogaden region, and their army was at the gates of Hārer. Then the Soviet Union turned to fill the superpower vacuum left in Ethiopia by the gradual withdrawal of the United States. In the spring of 1978, with the support of Soviet matériel and [15,000] Cuban soldiers, Ethiopia reconquered the Ogaden, and hundreds of thousands of Somali refugees poured into Somalia.[9]

The war had been a catastrophe for Somalia. About 35 per cent of its regular soldiers, half of its armoured assets and half its air force had been destroyed during the war. Somalia was left with a disorganised, demoralised and weak army, and with a well-armed logistically strong and hostile neighbour.

For the next decade, the USA ignored Siad's repressive style and poured around $800 million into Somalia as aid, in one form or another. The *quid pro quo* was access to Somali ports and airports. Former colonial powers, the UK and Italy, contributed about $1 billion between 1981 and 1990. The value of foreign aid to Somalia was the highest in Africa.[10]

Just before the war, American patience with Siad had been exhausted. The American Embassy phones were being routinely tapped and its mail opened. Siad had placed stringent restrictions on Western journalists – the White House realised that Siad's actions were designed to attract further Russian support for his antagonism for Ethiopia. This exercise bore fruit and, when the USA withdrew, Russia had quickly filled the gap. In exchange for naval facilities for their Indian Ocean fleet, it furnished Siad with surface-to-air missiles. It was, however, massive Soviet intervention that had won the war for Ethiopia when it was supporting both sides!

The Siad Barre regime had become increasingly oppressive and violent in the late 1970s. Somali discontent with the Siad regime was a constant and always high. This discontent was exacerbated by the loss of the war with Ethiopia. Siad's response to this military defeat was Stalinist and he ordered the execution of eighty-two of the most senior military officers. However, the knock-on effect of these executions was to fuel further discontent, and it triggered the 1978 coup attempt.

Siad professed, inaccurately, the coup to have been the work of the Majeerteen clan and reacted swiftly by purging the government and military of Majeerteen. He carried out reprisal killings against Majeerteen civilian clan members, leaving roughly 2,000 dead.[11]

The 1980s saw the rise of opposition armed movements, the largest of which was the Somali National Movement (SNM), drawn principally from members of the Isaaq clan in north-western Somalia. The SNM developed in response to Siad's marginalisation and abuse, including the purge of Isaaq from civil service posts, confiscation of businesses, arrests, detention, and violence against Isaaq civilians.[12]

Detention and looting became a lucrative source of funding for state forces and paramilitaries, which were referred to as the 'meat market'.[13] The government employed Mobile Military Courts (MMCs) to combat opposition militants and their associated civilian populations. MMCs were superficial, judicial proceedings conducted by military officials and followed almost immediately by executions. Throughout the 1980s, the Siad Barre regime responded to opposing militias by employing increasingly violent and restrictive measures on various clan populations.

Washington viewed Siad's regime from a distance, although, in 1980, it had established its Rapid Deployment Force (RDF) in the north-western port of Berbera. From here, it engaged in exercises with Somali troops throughout the decade. In 1983, the RDF was redesignated US Central Command and it was relocated. The USA declined to get involved with the ongoing six-year friction between Ethiopia and Somalia. Despite the exit of Central Command, the USA poured a further $100 million into the enhancement of its bases at Berbera and (now) Kismayo, to accommodate its greater naval power stationed in Diego Garcia.[14]

Beginning in 1982, the Somali state imposed curfews in certain areas, and these curfews were used as a pretence for the detention and extortion of civilians. Although wholesale targeting and decimation of the Isaaq population did not begin until the SNM offensive in 1988, a confidential report from General Morgan to President Barre that was leaked in February 1987 revealed a government intention to 'liquidate the Isaaq problem' through violent tactics.[15]

Siad Barre was a monster. It was his monstrosity that hardened opposition to his regime and eventually brought about his downfall. 'Without the prospect of aggrandisement to temper Siad's ruthless grabbiness disfavoured clans clung all the tighter to historically controlled territories and ostracised interlopers.'[16]

The credibility of the 'Father' was fatally damaged. Notwithstanding the defeat of the 1978 coup, two groups opposed to Siad Barre started guerrilla operations from secure bases in Ethiopia.

Internally, inter-clan warfare broke out across the country. The numerically strong and well-dispersed Isaaq clan proclaimed the north-west of the country to be an independent Somalia with the same frontiers as the former British Somaliland. A Darod subclan turned on a fellow subclan to the north-east of Mogadishu. But probably the most significant of these inter-clan conflicts was the fighting between two Hawiye subclans for control of Mogadishu city and its port and airport. The energetic fighting reduced most of Mogadishu to ruins.

The USA put its weight behind Somalia and, as always, it gave aid generously. From 1978, and over the next ten years, even as Barre tightened his grip on the Somali people the US gave $800 million, about a quarter of which was military aid. The *quid pro quo* was access to Somali ports and airfields. Italy chipped in $1 billion between 1981 and 1990, over half of which was spent on military hardware.[17] Somalia was existing on foreign aid, which had reached a level of $80 per person.[18] By 1980, Somalia was awash with weaponry: there were copious supplies of mortars, anti-tank guns, field artillery and almost limitless small arms. Siad Barre responded to political pressure from Western supporters and moved to improve Somalia's relations with Kenya and Ethiopia. However, the formal treaty made with Ethiopia in 1988 had the unexpected effect of initiating civil war in Somalia.

The Somali National Movement was based on the Isaaq clan of the northern regions. This was one of the guerrilla groups that could see that the treaty would threaten their bases in Ethiopia. Ogaadeen (the Somali word) Somalis who had been recruited into Siad's army were effectively betrayed by the peace agreement with Ethiopia and they not only deserted, but also were actively hostile to Siad's rule.

The US Government misread the situation in Somalia, although, in 1989, the US State Department did assert that Siad's army was responsible for 'widespread systemic and extremely violent assault on unarmed civilians'.[19] However, as late as 1990, General Norman Schwarzkopf advised the US Congress that military aid to the Siad regime was critical 'to help Somalia retain its political and territorial integrity'.[20] The use of the word 'integrity' in association with anything Somali in 1990 seems to have been ill-advised.

A further US misreading of the situation in Somalia and a lack of awareness of the fragility of the Siad regime was the investment of $35 million to build the largest and most expensive US embassy in sub-Saharan Africa. This new institution was equipped with all the latest mod cons, not least a nine-hole golf course. The new embassy was opened in July 1989 and, as the Cold War drew to its bloodless close, so the strategic importance of Somalia declined. However, the product of a more stable wider world was offset by the availability of over 100,000 Soviet and American small arms to a very unstable Somalia. The situation in Somalia in early 1991 was fraught with danger on all sides. On 5 January, an amphibious unit of US Marines was diverted from Saudi Arabia, where it was to take part in Operation DESERT STORM, to Somalia, where it evacuated 272 American Embassy staff.

Siad Barre was under increasing pressure, and he recognised that his survival was at stake. Although he strengthened his grip on Mogadishu, the clan-based opposition grew and multiplied. The Somali Salvation Democratic Front (SSDF) and the SNM were the models for other resistance groups, and in combination, they proved to be irresistible. In January 1991, forces of the Hawiye-based United Somali Congress (USC), a third anti-Siad organisation, led a popular revolt that overthrew Siad Barre and drove him to seek asylum among his own clan. The *Encyclopaedia Britannica* commented:

> Outside Mogadishu, all the main clans with access to the vast stores of military equipment in the country set up their own spheres of influence. Government in the south had largely disintegrated and existed only at the local level in the SSDF-controlled northeast region. In May 1991 the SNM, having secured control of the former British Somaliland northern region, declared that the 1960 federation was null and void and that henceforth the northern region would be independent and known as the Republic of Somaliland.

During the last two years of Siad Barre's regime foreign aid dried up, money ran out and taxes went uncollected. The alleged 'Father' of the nation encouraged his army to feed on the proceeds of property theft. During this period, lawlessness was all-embracing. Young men, many of whom had had army training, acquired arms. Life, always cheap, got a lot cheaper. A general uprising against Siad Barre began on 29 December 1990. Although Barre had superiority in numbers and weaponry, his soldiers lacked the commitment to fight and die for the dictator, and they fled – some turned their coats and fought with the USC militias.[21]

> The lawlessness manifested itself in war games of extortion roadblocks, of theft and murder during the violent seizure of people's assets, of threats at the point of a gun. These and other unattractive gainful pursuits were commonplace in parts of Southern Somalia especially in Mogadishu before Barre was ousted from power on 27 January 1991.[22]

When Siad was overthrown, the country descended into total anarchy. The grandiose US Embassy had been abandoned to a mob of looters earlier in the month. They had climbed over the high walls using ladders in much the same way as, ten years earlier, there had been a comparative scenario in Saigon. Similarly, the ambassador had abandoned his post and fled by helicopter.

This organisation of the USC was a complex grouping, and it had three main components. These were USC-Rome, USC-Ethiopia and USC-Mogadishu. The organisation had originally been formed in Rome, as clearly it could not operate in a Siad Barre-led society. Its military wing, operated from Ethiopia, was led by Major General Mohamed Farrah Aidid.

The fall of Siad Barre left a vacuum. Gone overnight 'were all the instruments of repression the security service with its spies and torture, the increasingly lawless army – the fearsome glue that had held Somalia together and kept emotions in check for two decades'.[23]

A successful hotelier called Ali Mahdi Muhammad was arbitrarily selected by his clan, the Hawiye, as the interim president of the new state. The political movement that made this selection was the United Somali Congress – or at least part of it. The reality was that Aidid had a stronger claim. Thwarted in his thrust for power, Aidid directed his Habar Gidir to wage war against the Abgaal sub clan, led by Mahdi.

* * *

Aidid is central to this chronicle and a brief outline of his background will serve to personalise a key player in the mayhem that was centred on Mogadishu from 1991 onwards. Back in 1958, Aidid had taken over from Siad as chief of police but later, when Siad took control of the country, he was only too aware of Aidid's political ambition.

The emergence of Aidid's plans to mount a coup was sufficient for Siad to imprison his adversary for seven years. Aidid was released from prison in 1977, and he served in the Somali National Army during its Ogaden War with Ethiopia. He rose to the rank of brigadier and saw action again during the further Border War with Ethiopia of 1982–83. From 1984 to 1989, he was the ambassador to India for the Somali Democratic Republic. This period honed his political, social and administrative skills and complemented his military ability.

Unexpectedly, Aidid defected from his post in the embassy to India in 1989 and left the country to join the growing opposition against the Siad

Major General Mohamed Farrah Aidid (1934–96), President of Somalia 1995–96.

Ali Mahdi Muhammad (1939–2021), President of Somalia 1991–93 and 1997–2000.

Barre regime. His well-advertised defection caused the president, Mengistu Haile Mariam, to invite Aidid to create and run a USC military operation from Ethiopian soil. From base camps near the Somali–Ethiopian border, he began directing the final military offensive of the newly formed United Somali Congress to seize Mogadishu and topple the regime.[24]

Aidid's rank of major general was a legacy of his time serving Siad in the Somali Army. He liked to be addressed as 'General' as it embellished his image, which he projected as being that of a ruthless warrior.

Aidid was an adversary who deserved to be taken very seriously. He was intelligent, ambitious and multi-talented.

* * *

The short-term solution of an interim president served only to generate bitter enmity between rival Hawiye clan factions who sought power. The two aspirants were the aforementioned General Mohamed Farrah Aidid of the Somali National Alliance (SNA) and Ali Mahdi Muhammad of the Somali Salvation Alliance (SSA).

Mahdi, having been declared to be the interim president of Somalia, was, initially, unable to exercise his authority. He was obliged to contest control of southern Somalia with Aidid. Mahdi resented Aidid's participation in USC affairs and declined to recognise his rival's ambitions. In June 1990, Aidid was elected chairman of a reorganised USC at a congress in Mustahil on the Somali–Ethiopian border. Mahdi challenged the validity of the congress and all its doings.

Despite the machinations of these two men, there was a third contender for the role of president, and he was Dr Ismail Jumale Osoble, a lawyer and a well-known opponent of Siad Barre. Jumale was a member of the same clan, the Hawiye, as Mahdi and even the same subclan, the Abgaal. Aidid, although a Hawiye, was from different sub-branch, the Habar Gidir (see Annexure A). Jumale never did take post as he died of natural causes in 1990.

Aidid and people of his ilk were devoid of humanity; the only law was that of the Kalashnikov. Most adult Somali had such a weapon, which they were only too ready to use.

The situation in the Medina Hospital illustrates that point. Dr Rias Soudan, a Lebanese surgeon, worked there for Médecins Sans Frontières (MSF). He spent the bulk of his day dealing with gunshot wounds and commented, 'All my patients now keep guns with them in hospital.' Visiting relatives brought grenades and knives so that patients could protect themselves. The wards offered no sanctuary.[25] That said, they were safer than the streets, and patients who had been treated and had recovered were loath to leave the free food and a bed or mattress. In Benadir Hospital, the staff were coping with an overflowing number of patients. Some twenty of the 'recovered patients' had formed an association and refused to leave. These men were all armed and MSF had no other option but to ask Aidid for help.

The warlord responded by sending a heavily armed squad. The 'patients', realising that they were outgunned, laid down their arms and quietly shuffled out of the hospital, giving Dr Soudan the space to admit more of the wounded and sick. Aidid was dependent upon his close relationship with Osman Hassan Ali, known as 'Ato'. Ato was a gangster who made money, and lots of it, from the khat trade (see pages 31–3), which made him an estimated $1 million per month. He operated a ruthless private army and had a chain of about seven garages across the city, where his underlings converted stolen, four-wheel drive vehicles into the wagons favoured by the thugs who ruled the city.

Ato paid his henchmen $150 for each vehicle they stole, and then his mechanics installed custom-made mounts that they bolted to the chassis. To these were fitted American 106mm anti-tank guns, smaller Chinese recoilless rifles or Soviet anti-aircraft guns adapted to fire horizontally.[26] Aidid and Ato were the *de facto* government of Somalia – using the word 'government' in its widest possible interpretation.

In 1992, conditions in Somalia were at the extreme end of any scale. This was because armed looters and a vast criminal community habitually attacked food storage sites and controlled the supply routes.[27] If they were to supply food to the needy, the relief agencies had no other option but to do business with these criminals, who were described as 'technicals'. They imposed their will from the back of the heavily armed vehicles, described above, and would kill on a whim. They had to be paid in cash for safe passage through their area. The relief agencies had to account for the cash they disbursed, and their accountants termed the recipients of cash as 'technicals'.[28] 'During one week in June 1992 alone, CARE International personnel in Mogadishu were involved in twenty-one incidents of looting or gunplay.'[29]

A group of heavily armed and mobile 'technicals'. Men like these were at the heart of instability in Somalia.

In August 1992, two UN observers were shot dead. On the same day, there was massive looting at the port of Mogadishu. The band of looters were led by three tanks, a demonstration of Aidid's power and his support of the looters.[30]

The Hawiye is centred upon the central region of Somalia and provides most of the population of Mogadishu. Despite its location and size, the clan did not take best advantage of independence when it came in 1960. Instead, it deferred to an even larger clan – the Darod, which, having seized power held it for the next thirty years. Barre was a Darod.

Mahdi was the legitimate, albeit notional, president, but the conflict between him and Aidid tore Somalia apart. The forces of the two rivals brought civil war and wrought disaster on the grain-producing region between the rivers. Famine was the catastrophic result. Meanwhile, Siad Barre had consolidated his support and formed the Somali National Front (SNF). He remained a powerful and destructive element in the lives of the Somali people.

For ease of reference, herewith a list of the organisations mentioned in this last chapter:

Somali National Alliance (SNA)	General Mohamed Farrah Aidid
Somali National front (SNF)	General Mohamed Siad Barre
Somali National League (SNL)	constituent of the first government
Somali National Movement (SNM)	the Isaaq clan
Somali Republic	
Somali Salvation Alliance (SSA)	Cali Mahdi Maxamed
Somali Salvation Democratic Front (SSDF)	General Mohamed Siad Barre
Somali Youth League (SYL)	constituent of the first government
United Somali Congress (USC)	Hawiye-based
Western Somali Liberation Front (WSLF)	dissident Ethiopian group

Somalia was in a mess and the world knew it, but the UN did not get involved, although it gave no valid reason for ignoring a growing humanitarian crisis. The NGOs were working in impossible conditions.

'Trucks with food are like trucks full of money,' observed Stefan Hagelueken, a German Red Cross worker. 'But when we arrived in Giohar the eighty hired security guards mutinied, threatened to halt food distribution unless they were paid seven times the agreed amount.' Hagelueken continued, 'There was no sense of community, no sense of easing a human crisis – just *me* and what goes into my pocket. In the end, the International Red Cross had to triple their pay.'[31]

A view of Mogadishu photographed from a UNOSOM convoy. (*CT Snow-Flickr*)

Chapter 4

Famine

Famine makes greater havoc in an army than the enemy and is more terrible than the sword.

Flavious Vegetius Renatus, *The Military Intuitions of the Romans*, c. AD 378

Domestic anarchy apart, Somalia had an even more pressing need. The United Nations appreciated that Somalia was one of the most aided countries in the world and it had withdrawn after the fall of Siad Barre. The nine months that followed were chaotic and in September 1991, the UN sought to re-establish itself in Somalia,

> without consulting any of the agencies on the ground about warlord 'protocol'. The UN was seen to fête the wrong power brokers and within three days UN-hired Somali security guards were murdered in a 'political' hit. Instead of recognizing the reason for this *faux pas*, the UN headquarters in New York declared Somalia too dangerous and forbade staff from travelling there. The UN special envoy to the Horn of Africa admitted defeat at the hands of a government that did not exist: 'We were advised by the president [Ali Mahdi Muhammad] not to go back.'[1]

In peacetime, the Somali economy was fragile in the extreme. But post Siad Barre, the warring clans destroyed not just the city but the very means of sustaining life. About 75 per cent of the population were vagrant nomads who, at best, existed at a bare subsistence level. Their lives were dependent upon their livestock – sheep, goats camels and cattle. They were always at the mercy of a quixotic climate and drought was a constant threat. The provision of locally produced food was never secure or consistent. Starvation was a feature of Somali life, and it was only the activity of foreign relief organisations that kept many Somalis alive,

During the closing months of Siad Barre's regime, among the multiplicity of social, political and economic problems, there was also a dire shortage of food in Somalia.[2] These shortages had started to manifest themselves during the summer of 1990 but, on 27 January 1991, the economy collapsed as Siad Barre and the Somali Democratic Republic were swept from power.[3]

The destabilisation of the state coincided with an exceptionally harsh drought and the total absence of basic law enforcement.[4] All the constituents of a famine were in place. In the wake of Siad's overthrow, Somalia had yet to recover from the disastrous famine of 1984–85, during which about 30 per cent of the domestic livestock was lost. In addition, just short of a million refugees had fled from Ogaden and these displaced individuals placed an insuperable burden on a fragile economy that had insufficient means to feed the country.

Inflation was at 100 per cent in 1990. Somalia had sought a loan from the International Monetary Fund, but its credit was poor, with a previous $100 million loan unserviced. The IMF declined the further loan and life in Somalia became desperate.

Traditional methods to deal with a famine broke down under the pressure of the death and destruction of a civil war being waged across the fertile area between the two rivers Jubba and Shebelle. For generations, this had been the breadbasket of Somalia. Now the fields were bone dry and the people living in the riverine and bay areas, together with the multitude of people displaced by the warring factions, starved.

'No foreign diplomats remained, no businesses were open. Artillery fire kept meandering food ships from docking at the port, leaving an entire population dependent on small planes for food.'[5]

Somalia was hungry, but it was awash with weaponry.

Siad Barre may have been deposed, he was down but not out, and he gathered a three-division army. The former dictator, having formed the Somali National Front, centred it and himself in the riverine area. He had no logistic system in place and so his forces 'ravaged the grain stores of inter-riverine agricultural belt'.[6] Despite the parlous state of the country, the SNF force, with mindless enthusiasm, destroyed pumps and farming equipment, resulting in a near complete halt to agricultural production.

Little wonder that the Somali National Front is widely considered to bear primary responsibility for inducing the famine that followed in mid-1991.[7]

The food shortage caused the price of available food to soar to unprecedented heights and well beyond the reach of the mass of the starving population. In late 1991, there was intense fighting in Mogadishu and Kismayo, resulting in the closure of both ports and further limiting food supplies. Warnings of the famine conditions were voiced but largely ignored by the United Nations and the multitude of relief agencies.

Javier Pérez de Cuéllar was running to the end of his tenure as secretary-general of the United Nations and it was only at the end of 1991 that the penny finally dropped, and Pérez de Cuéllar announced his 'profound shock' that Somalia should be engulfed in a 'nightmare of violence and brutality'.

In February 1992, it was recognised that any aid that was sent to Somalia would be looted by one or the other of the warring factions. It was left to the International Committee of the Red Cross (ICRC) to grasp the nettle. This it did in March 1992 and it described the situation as a 'most urgent tragedy', warning that many would die within weeks.

It was a prescient prediction.

The famine was not nationwide, and it affected two main groups. These were the inhabitants along the Jubba and Shebelle riverine area and the people displaced by the ongoing civil war. Most of those suffering were primarily in the Bay region.[8]

The International Red Cross judged that pastoralists and townspeople had near normal levels of nutrition while farmers along the rivers and those displaced in camps outside settlements by the fighting were severely malnourished. Baidoa, capital of the Bay region, became an epicentre of the famine and was referred to, at the time, as the 'City of Death'.[9]

A principle killer during the famine were epidemic diseases such as measles and malaria.[10] Journalist and aid worker Michael Maren challenged the United Nations' claim that 4.5 million people in Somalia were on the verge of starvation, and asserted that the figure was created with the intention of galvanising an international response. According to Maren, this portrayal significantly overstated the crisis. His observations from the ground indicated that the famine was confined to specific areas, with the majority of Somalia's population remaining relatively unaffected.[11] UNOSOM advisor

John Drysdale said that media portrayals of the crisis being nationwide were devoid of reality as only about 12 per cent of the population had been affected by the famine.[12]

Nevertheless, the plight of Somalia was increasingly recognised by international relief agencies and practical assistance was forthcoming. 'By 1992, the provision of food was almost exclusively by expatriate donors and emergency aid groups.'[13] The Red Cross committed 35 per cent of its total budget to Somalia and that rose inexorably to almost 50 per cent. In August 1992, although 50,000 metric tons of food per month were needed to feed Somalia, only 32,000 tons were in the pipeline and one third of the 1.5 million people in southern Somalia were at risk of imminent death from starvation.

Although the United Nations and non-government aid organisations realised the need, they had no illusions as to the mindset of the people they sought to help. Somali behaviour was inbred, and they lacked the moral frame of reference for any degree of effective social reform. Jonathan Stevenson observed patronisingly but accurately that 'they didn't know any better'.[14] An important factor that impacted on every element of Somali life was the plant known as khat. Despite the parlous, nay desperate, conditions in Somalia, the khat trade flourished.

* * *

Khat (*Catha edulis*), alternative spelling qat, is also known as Bushman's tea. It is a flowering plant native to eastern and south-eastern Africa. For centuries, it has been cultivated, having originated in the Harar area of present-day eastern Ethiopia. Khat contains the alkaloid *cathinone*, a stimulant. Somali priorities were, by Western standards, unbalanced, not least by the khat trade. In 1993, complete rejection of khat would have released about $6 per day per user; this was calculated to equate to 20 kilograms of maize or rice and sufficient to feed six people for a week and, 'in the aggregate maybe even enough to transfuse an economy bled of currency by the khat traders themselves.'[15]

Among communities from the areas where the plant is native, khat-chewing has a history as a social custom, especially among men, dating back thousands of years. It is analogous – but slightly different – to the use of coca leaves in South America's Andes Mountains or the betel nut preparations in South Asia.[16]

In the 1990s, none of the political players in Somalia presumed to float the idea that the khat trade should be curtailed. Some, one of whom was Aidid, benefitted directly from sales. Others believed that the result of a ban on khat would be more unrest.

'Beyond the simple economics of khat versus food, the remarkable survival of the khat industry through war and anarchy demonstrates how able and cynical the Somalis can be.'[17] Back in 1995, and almost contemporaneously with the military events discussed later, Stevenson observed, 'Muslim religious leaders and devotees traditionally used to zing through marathon sessions of Koran recitation but, during this century [twentieth], it has become widely used as a recreational stimulant.'

In 1993, the chewing of khat was considered by young Somali men to be *de rigueur*. Chewing the leaves of the khat plant provides a sense of greater sociability, a degree of excitement, slight loss of appetite and mild euphoria. Its effects are not unlike those of alcohol. Another view of khat is that it is addictive and cannot be compared to cocaine because it fails to provide the same overwhelming sense of omnipotence. The user of khat undergoes changing feelings. For the initial two hours, the user feels content, warm and animated but this agreeable condition morphs into tiredness, depression and stress. Sleep is not an option. Urination is painful and it is in this phase that the user may resort to violence to appease his sense of ill-being. It makes dangerous young men even more dangerous.

One wonders why anyone of sound mind would put themselves through this uncomfortable process.

> Before Operation RESTORE HOPE gunshot wounds in Mogadishu ran at between thirty and fifty every day. These injuries peaked in the early evening when the gunmen were at the apex of their khat spree. As the day wore on, restless adolescents got more and more cranked up and less and less rational. By late afternoon, the jangled nerves and raw tempers started to show up as reckless driving, senseless arguments and what a Somali doctor called, 'just joking around'.[18]

The prospect of making easy money, and lots of it, was the motivation for the Somali merchants who kept the flow of khat coming into the country. Much of the drug came from Ethiopia, where it flourishes in the loose volcanic soil that is to be found above 3,500 feet (1,066m). In 1995, the strongest khat originated in Kenya, where it is legally cultivated, and on a daily basis, 6 metric tons were exported to Somalia by air. A weakness of khat is that it sheds its power twenty-four hours after it is picked. The need for a continuous supply is evident. In 1995, the trade was valued at $100 million annually.

In 2025, the increasing Somali dependence on Kenyan khat is illustrated by an article written thirty-two years after the events described in this book.

> Kenya's recent decision to double the price of Miraa (khat) has sent shockwaves through Somalia's already fragile economy. This policy change not only exposes the shortcomings in trade strategies and economic priorities but also lays bare the political elite's complicity in sustaining an unsustainable dependency. For decades, Somalia has been one of the largest consumers of Kenyan Miraa – *channelling hundreds of millions of dollars every year into a product that yields little economic benefit, fuels addiction, and depletes our scarce foreign reserves*. [Author's emphasis.]
>
> An analysis by the International Monetary Fund warns that such non-essential imports are undermining economic stability in fragile nations like Somalia. As noted in the IMF report, reliance on imported consumer goods – especially those that do not spur productive investment – deepens vulnerabilities and erodes the nation's capacity for sustainable growth.[19]

Since 1980, the World Health Organization (WHO) has classified khat as a 'drug of abuse'. This is because it can produce psychological dependence, although the WHO does not consider khat addiction to be a serious global problem. That was a complacent view because today it is a major problem for the still chaotic Somalia.

* * *

The United Somali Congress had led the downfall of Siad Barre. Nevertheless, the two aspiring leaders of their country, Ali Mahdi Muhammad and

Mohamed Farrah Aidid, were perforce associated with the wholesale thievery at Somalia's ports and airport. The realities of food logistics in Somalia's anarchy doused any prospects of creating a stable and legitimate food market.

Aidid was able to turn the misery of Somalis to his advantage, and in September 1991, he contrived to turn a meeting of his clan elders into a political rally, which he attended with a pistol hidden under his coat. Scott Peterson was present at this meeting, and he commented on the enthusiastic support that was given to Aidid, who clearly was not going to need his pistol. The elders predictably reported on the misery of their lives at the hands of the gangsters who ruled Somalia, perhaps unaware that many of these gangsters reported to Aidid. He listened and like every politician everywhere, Aidid promised 'free beer tomorrow' or the Somali equivalent. First, he had to complete the annihilation of Siad Barre's military force.

The SNA, led by Aidid, opened its offensive against the Somali National Front in April 1992. He strove to eject Siad Barre from southern Somalia and, near Wanie Weyn, Aidid's Somali National Alliance achieved its aim and defeated Siad Barre's SNF. The latter withdrew to the Kenyan border to lick its wounds after its destructive and now failed occupation of the 'breadbasket'.

The defeat of Siad Barre's Army of 25,000 regular soldiers had produced a bounty of captured weaponry: 20,000 M-16 rifles, 15,000 AK-47s, tanks, artillery, mines, armoured personnel carriers (APC) and a mountain of ammunition. Also taken was the air base at Baledogle by a militia group, the Somali Patriotic Movement (SPM).[20]

Welcome rain eased the environment slightly in early 1992 and by August, the famine began to recede.[21] The cost of food was reduced, not least because of a reduction in the intensity of fighting in the south of the country. This had permitted a harvest of crops, which, by happy chance was particularly productive.

It took several months but, eventually, the plight of the Somali people was being viewed on newscasts across the world. The United Nations finally responded in April 1992 and created UNOSOM I, which functioned briefly until its duties were assumed by the Unified Task Force (UNITAF) mission in December 1992. Following the dissolution of UNITAF in May 1993, the subsequent UN mission in Somalia was known as UNOSOM II.

It was in April 1992 that a defeated Siad Barre fled to Kenya, where, surrounded by a staff of twenty acolytes, he took up residence in the luxurious Safari Park Hotel. While Somalis eked out their lives beset by poverty and the constant threat of starvation, their former leader lived high on a very expensive hog. He sipped fine wine in the adjacent Hemingway's bar and ate well at a cost estimated at $1,800 per day (1992 prices).[22] Siad was granted exile in Nigeria, but the good life did not last long. He died, un-mourned, on 2 January 1995.

Starvation and epidemic diseases like measles and malaria added to the toll.[23] The UN, presumably in an attempt to generate international support, claimed that 4.5 million people were at risk of starvation. This was overstating the case, and it ignored the fact that the famine was limited to specific areas. The death toll has not been accurately measured, and estimates vary widely. At one point, 30,000 people had been dying each month. The British Broadcasting Company (BBC), usually (?) a balanced source of information, settled on a figure of 220,000 as victims of the famine. This death toll was to be exceeded by the 2010–12 famine that took 258,000 lives. Starvation is a particularly horrible way to die and at Annexure C is a brief description of what hundreds of thousands of Somalis faced and how their lives ended.

Major General Charles Wilhelm USMC summed up the situation admirably when he said, 'The people of Somalia need a friend – not just another oppressor in desert camouflage utilities.'[24] Little did he know that within months, the USA would be viewed as that very oppressor in desert camouflage.

The war between supporters of Aidid and Mahdi was unabated. During the most intense bout of fighting from mid-November 1992 until March 1993, the amount of ill-directed artillery, aimed by enthusiastic, untrained gun crews, made movement in the city of Mogadishu impossible. During any brief lull in the bombardment, the denizens emerged from cover to seek food and water. Hunger rose and insecurity deterred any relief workers from providing help. The shelling was supplemented by snipers who seemed to fire on anything that moved. During this ghastly period, about 14,000 Somali citizens were killed or died of starvation.[25] One suggestion, made by a holy man, was that 'they ought to put a 100-foot wall around this city and declare it a home for the incurably insane'.

Chapter 5

The United Nations, UNOSOM I and UNITAF

Your greatness does not depend upon the size of your command, but in the manner in which you exercise it.

Marshal of France, Ferdinand Foch,
in Major General Sir George Aston,
The Biography of Foch, 1929

On 27 December 1991, the situation in war-torn and famine-struck Somalia was so bad that the Secretary-General of the United Nations, Javier Pérez de Cuéllar, informed the Security Council that he intended to take an initiative in an attempt to restore peace in Somalia. Accordingly, and after consulting incoming Secretary-General Boutros Boutros-Ghali, he asked then Under-Secretary-General for Political Affairs, James Jonah, from Sierra Leone, to visit the area and report on the conditions and the options open to the UN.

Jonah's foray was marked by incompetence and did more harm than good. '[He] allowed his visit to be manipulated by Aidid and then issued a hasty statement on the prospects for a cease fire which only exacerbated tensions.'[1]

Following Jonah's visit, Boutros Boutros-Ghali invited all those involved in Somali affairs to meet on 31 January 1992. A significant product of this meeting was that President Ali Mahdi Muhammad and General Aidid agreed to cease hostilities. Just over a month later, on 3 March, the two warring factions signed an 'Agreement on the Implementation of a Cease Fire'. Importantly, the role of the UN to provide security for convoys bearing humanitarian aid was accepted at the same time.

The rapprochement between Aidid and Ali Mahdi could and should have settled the future of Somalia but the agreement was based on mutual insincerity, and it did not take long for the two men to be at each other's

Boutros Boutros-Ghali (1922–2016), Secretary-General of the United Nations 1992–96.

Mohamed Sahnoun (1931–2018), UN envoy to Somalia, April–November 1992.

throats again. Between them, they were responsible for the deaths of tens of thousands of their countrymen.

It was on 24 April 1992 that the UN passed what was to be the critical Resolution 751, which established a United Nations operation in Somalia. This was to be termed UNOSOM. Progress was slow but steady and, on 23 June, the Secretary-General informed the Security Council that both principal factions in Mogadishu had agreed to the immediate deployment of fifty unarmed observers to be led by Brigadier General Imtiaz Shaheen of Pakistan. He and his team arrived in Mogadishu in early July 1992.

Boutros-Ghali appointed the Algerian diplomat Mohamed Sahnoun as his envoy in Somalia and the leader of the UN force now labelled UNISOM I. Sahnoun took up his post in April 1992. He was a first-class choice: a vastly experienced diplomat, he had been his country's ambassador to West Germany, France, the USA and Morocco. He was a man with a sense of urgency and a desire to get things done. His qualities were recognised, and he quickly started to improve the situation and promising results were achieved.[2]

A factor in the UN's dealing with Somali leaders was that Boutros-Ghali was mistrusted. He was thought to be biased in favour of Ali Mahdi. In addition, it was alleged by some that, when Egypt's foreign minister, he was responsible for making a deal with Siad Barre in which he provided arms in exchange for Siad allowing 40,000 Egyptians to farm some of Somalia's most arable land. The consequence was the displacement of Somali farmers.[3] This author could find no evidence that supports the allegation.

On 12 August, the Secretary-General informed the Security Council that, after considerable delays and difficulties, Mohamed Sahnoun had been able to fashion an agreement with the principal faction leaders in Mogadishu to deploy United Nations security personnel in the capital as part of UNOSOM. The Government of Pakistan had agreed to contribute a 500-strong unit for service in Somalia for the purpose of providing security aid to the humanitarian NGOs. The first group of these security personnel arrived in Mogadishu on 14 September 1992.

By November 1992, largely owing to the leadership of Sahnoun, aid was flowing through the Mogadishu port. Instances of theft and banditry on the routes to famine zones was reduced. However, Sahnoun's peacebuilding action was limited by the lack of efficient backing from the UN and his blunt and public criticism of the UN made him few friends.[4] Sahnoun was only in post for about seven months, and he was increasingly frustrated by the ineptitude of the UN and its bureaucratic culture.

Boutros Boutros-Ghali believed that the UN should fill the power vacuum in Somalia and that the country should be the test bed for his new doctrine, which would be implemented by an international coalition. This new doctrine, based on Resolution 751, dramatically altered the priorities of the United Nations. Hitherto the absolute priority of *national sovereignty* was to give way to *universal sovereignty*. The practical effect of this change was that the UN would become a peacemaking organisation. 'Peacemaking' is a euphemism for peace enforcement and 'enforcement' implies military intervention without the consent of the local authority or government.[5] That is to say that the UN would, if need be, support a population against its government. John Drysdale, who lived and worked in Mogadishu at the time, observed:

> The UN secretariat did not appreciate the interplay of three cardinal problems that underlay every exasperating contact with Aidid and his allies.
>
> The three problems were, first, that so much damage had been done to the traditional Somali political processes through the delivery of modern weapons as 'gifts', and their subsequent misuse. Relationships between Somali politicians and elders had (as a result) become more intractable and bitter than they would have been otherwise.
>
> Second, that any attempt to disturb the symbiosis of politicians and elders when they were acting to mutual advantage was strongly resisted by the politicians concerned.
>
> Third, the early contacts by the UN Secretariat with Somali leaders in Mogadishu had unwittingly aroused grave doubts about UN neutrality in the minds of the Aidid camp, reinforced by the perception in Somalia that Boutros-Ghali had been a personal friend of Siad Barre and was thus biased against those who overthrew Siad.[6]

Intervening in the governance of a sovereign nation, in any degree, no matter how chaotic that governance is, has no guarantee of success. A 2016 study by Professor Dov Levin of Carnegie Mellon University found that the United States had intervened in eighty-one foreign elections between 1946 and 2000, the majority of these being covert rather than overt actions.[7] A 2021 review of existing literature found that foreign interventions since the First World War tend overwhelmingly to fail their purported objectives.[8] This was despite the difficulties outlined by Drysdale, who observed:

> The idea of sending foreign troops to Somalia was however lurking in UN minds not so much because of Mahdi and Aidid's penchant for fighting, but because of difficulties encountered by Non-Governmental Organisations (NGO), such as Save the Children Fund (ACF), CARE International, and the International Red Cross (IRC) the supply of relief aid to increasing numbers of displaced and starving people in the agricultural inter-riverine areas – between the rivers Juba and Shabelle.[9]

In the closing weeks of his presidency, George Bush ordered the movement of 25,000 US troops to Somalia in support of the UN, but during that same period of 1992, the situation in Somalia went from bad to worse. The warring factions were unstable and their structures, such as they were, changed daily.

Agreements made by UNOSOM I for food distribution with one party were worthless when the stores had to be shipped through the territory of another. Two hundred thousand Somalis had already starved to death, and 1.5 million remained at risk of starvation.[10]

The UN role in Somalia would be to monitor a ceasefire between the warring factions and to ensure the delivery of humanitarian aid. This ceasefire was to be implemented by UNOSOM I. It had been back in April 1992 that the first fifty unarmed blue-bereted UN observers landed in Somalia. In August, the 500 Pakistani soldiers, commanded by Brigadier General Imtiaz Shaheen, arrived 'to secure humanitarian supply lines in Mogadishu'. This token force was only accepted in Somalia with the permission of Aidid. It was ineffective and was entirely overshadowed and daunted by the 35,000 militants of mixed ability commanded by Aidid.

The Somali warlord had made it clear that he would engage any foreign troops in excess of these initial 500. Shaheen was a practical soldier, and he realised that his soldiers could not possibly secure the port, safeguard food shipments, and escort food convoys from the port and airport to the designated recipients. On this basis, his Pakistani soldiers hunkered down near the airport, stayed in their base, and did nothing to provoke any sort of response. Their presence in Somalia achieved nothing and was no more than symbolic.

Sahnoun's calm and measured diplomacy was working after a fashion and, while Shaheen kept his soldiers in their barracks, the mayhem in the streets continued unabated. Sahnoun's plan was twofold. First, he sought to deploy a force small enough not to pose a territorial threat to the warlords, but large enough to deter them from hostile action and even encourage their cooperation. Second, Sahnoun wanted to demonstrate that if food and other aid were directed in an orderly fashion, each would have sufficient to preclude their having to steal. The pious hope was that the warlords and clan chiefs would bring about a change in the mindset of the gunmen and convert them to help feed their communities rather than steal food from them.[11]

Although it was a daunting task, Sahnoun was nudging Aidid into accepting a further 3,000 UN troops. It was a delicate situation that went pear-shaped when UN headquarters, without reference to Sahnoun, suddenly made a unilateral announcement that 3,000 troops were to be sent to Somalia.

Aidid was outraged, negotiations ceased and any 'goodwill' evaporated. Sahnoun's credibility with Somalis was severely reduced. His position was untenable, and he protested very strongly. He highlighted UN incompetence, not mincing his words and by so doing angered Boutros-Ghali. He was summarily dismissed by the Secretary-General, who ignored Sahnoun's letter of resignation. The mismanagement of this effective official was a blot on the reputation of Boutros-Ghali – a blot that was embellished by his subsequent choice of a low-quality replacement.

The United Nations could not permit Aidid to dictate terms and, on 3 December 1992, the UN Security Council passed Resolution 794, approving the US-led Unified Task Force (UNITAF) to use military force to ensure humanitarian aid delivery.

The USA initiated Operation PROVIDE RELIEF in direct support of the Red Cross, to whom it provided an airlift capacity. The Red Cross had expended half of its 1992 budget on Somali relief, and it was the agency responsible for about 75 per cent of the aid reaching war-torn, hungry Somalia. The combination of USA logistic support and Red Cross activity was thought to have saved 40,000 lives.[12] That same month, Aidid's Somali National Alliance (SNA) agreed to the deployment of 500 UN troops to ensure the security of aid.[13]

The manner in which the UN conducted its relationship with Somalis in general could be the key to success. This is not original thought, because over 2,000 years ago Polybius observed: 'When we conquer our enemies by kind treatment and by acts of justice, we are more likely to secure their obedience than by victory in the field of battle.'[14] In modern parlance, this is the 'Hearts and Minds' approach. It worked for the British in Malaya, but the French and the USA failed to make it work in Vietnam. In Somalia, there existed a chance for the UN to try again.

However, and quite incredibly, some Somalis actively opposed UNOSOM I and its humanitarian aims. This was because the United Nations was not trusted. It was perceived to be at odds with an independent sovereign Somali state. This mindset is difficult to understand but, nevertheless, UN troops were fired upon, ships were denied docking facilities and aircraft bringing food and medical supplies were attacked. Mohamoud Afrah, a respected Somali journalist, witnessed his country's travails and he commented sadly that:

'Death has become too commonplace to matter. The two greatest products in Mogadishu these days are shooting and rumors: from morning to night they manufacture rumors, from night to morning they manufacture shootings.'[15]

Somalia, and Mogadishu in particular, were overrun by armed and violent gangs. By late 1991, it was estimated that there were just short of forty such lawless groups in the city alone. These bandits took anything and everything from anybody. All the copper and phone wire under the streets was excavated and electrical transformers were cut from their poles to give access to the miserable half pint of low-grade oil they contained. The corpses of anyone who presumed to thwart or challenge a gunman were left to rot in the street. At the pinnacle of the clan-based hierarchy of this mayhem were the former guerrilla leaders who had chased Siad Barre from power.[16]

By November 1992, Major General Aidid, one of those responsible, felt sufficiently well established that he went on the offensive and demanded that the UN withdraw its assets. He gilded the lily by declaring that any future UN involvement in Somalia would be treated as hostile. It was a significant statement.

The UN's efforts at humanitarian assistance were significantly less efficient than those of the relief agencies, not least because UN efforts were directed by desk-bound functionaries in Nairobi. Boutros Boutros-Ghali had previously rejected Sahnoun's trenchant criticisms of this long-range management, a factor in Sahnoun's sacking/resignation in November 1992.

The new UN envoy appointed in December 1992 was Ismat Kittani, an Iraqi Kurd, a friend of Boutros-Ghali, and a former president of the UN General Assembly during its thirty-sixth session in 1981–82. Kittani was all that Sahnoun was not, and the contrast was stark. The business of the UN never crisp became markedly less so. Kittani was a dreadful choice to represent the UN. He was blinkered, rude and most undiplomatic. He resented the warmth felt for the now departed Sahnoun and spared no effort to undo Sahnoun's achievements. He petulantly proscribed the use of Sahnoun's name in his presence. He filled his role for only five months, from November 1992 until March 1993.

It was during Kittani's tenure that, on 5 December 1992, UNOSOM I morphed into the Unified Task Force (UNITAF). This new organisation functioned for only five months, until 4 May 1993. The change came about as a result of the mounting public pressure and criticism of the ineffective UN presence in Somalia, now epitomised by the hapless Kittani.

Boutros Boutros-Ghali, alert to the severe damage being done to the standing of the UN, recommended to the Security Council that significant armed force was required if the multiplicity of armed groups in Somalia were to be quelled. He pointed out that the charter of the United Nations allowed for 'action by air, sea or land forces as may be necessary to maintain or restore international peace and security'.[17]

Boutros-Ghali was aware that this was a major deviation from the aims of UNOSOM I. He realised that solving Somalia's problems would require a multitude of troops from many countries and that the UN staff did not have the skills to control and deploy a major military force. Accordingly, he recommended that a large intervention force be constituted under the command of a member state but authorised, by the Security Council, to carry out operations in Somalia.

The goal of this deployment was 'to prepare the way for a return to peacekeeping and post-conflict peace building'. An incentive that caused Boutros-Ghali to take this line was the recent offer from the United States to make the UN a significant troop contribution with which to enhance operations in Somalia. This offer came with the proviso that these personnel would be commanded by US officers and not the UN. This caveat is at the very heart of American policy.

The USA expects to direct the armed forces of any country acting in alliance with it. As it invariably provides the logistic base, the aircraft and the bulk of the manpower, it is not an unreasonable posture. UNOSOM II was, nominally, under the command of a Turkish general but it was the Americans who controlled all the levers of military power.

Boutros-Ghali's advice was taken and the Security Council unanimously authorised the use of 'all necessary means to establish as soon as possible a secure environment for humanitarian relief operations in Somalia'. The Security Council urged the Secretary-General and member states to make arrangements for 'the unified command and control/of the military forces that would be involved'.[18]

The UN Security Council passed Resolution 794 unanimously on 3 December 1992. The practical effect of this resolution was to cede control of military operations in Somalia to the USA. In response, President George Bush, in one of the last decisions of his presidency (Bill Clinton was president elect at this time), initiated Operation RESTORE HOPE. *The Guardian* carried the following report:

> President Bush told the American people yesterday that the United States forces he was sending to Somalia to lead an international humanitarian coalition had orders to use 'whatever military force is necessary to safeguard the lives of our troops and the lives of the Somali people'. 'This is serious business,' he added, outlining what promises to be the last decisive act of his presidency.
>
> Armed with pledges of 2,000 troops each from France and from Italy, up to 900 from Canada, and with promises of soldiers from Pakistan, Zimbabwe, Kenya and Nigeria, Mr Bush has put together a credibly international force under the United Nations mandate to get relief supplies through the rival Somali militias which have been disrupting the aid effort.
>
> The operation is seen as being short-term, with responsibility handed back to UN peacekeeping forces once order is restored and the immediate emergency over, Mr Bush promised.
>
> 'The US alone cannot right the world's wrongs, but some crises in the world cannot be resolved without American involvement,' said Mr Bush. 'Only the US has the global reach.'

US Defence Secretary Dick Cheney said, on 4 December, that the 26,000 US Army and Marine troops under orders to leave for Somalia were to be deployed once the airport had been secured by the 1,800-strong Marine contingent waiting offshore. 'The Marines will land early next week to establish preliminary bases at Mogadishu and the inland town of Baidoa.'

'You are doing God's work,' President Bush told the American troops. 'We will not tolerate armed gangs ripping off their own people.' To reassure Somalia and other African countries that the US had no ulterior political motive, President Bush declared: 'We do not plan to dictate political outcomes. We respect your sovereignty and independence.'

> Britain's Minister for Overseas Development, Baroness Chalker, said yesterday that the UN must go beyond the immediate need to stave off mass starvation, and consider the need for longer-term stability and administrative structure

> after the emergency. 'Somalia needs a long-term political solution and we need to work out with the [Somali] elders the long-term civil administration. That is not the job of the American troops, that is the job of the UN,' she said, adding that British troops would not join the planned force.
>
> President Francois Mitterrand and Chancellor Helmut Kohl said after talks in Bonn yesterday that they backed the UN Security Council decision to send the US-led force to Somalia and would increase their humanitarian aid. Germany is expected to make a financial contribution.[19]

The American attitude towards Somalia, as expressed by President Bush, was positive and generous. It was the USA at its best. It was the earnest hope that, ere long, Somalia would be back on its feet. However, before Operation RESTORE HOPE had even got off the ground, the CIA had projected that it would result in the USA being ensnared in a protracted urban guerrilla war in which the enemy would be a 'ruthlessly unafraid populace'.[20] What a prescient judgement that turned out to be.

On 9 December 1992, 20,000 American troops began landing on Black Beach, close to Mogadishu. UN operations by UNOSOM I were suspended to allow the UNITAF force to establish itself. Within thirty minutes of the landing, the most senior US commanders were giving live TV interviews explaining that their role was to conduct a mission of mercy. They took possession of the moral high ground when they claimed that:

> their presence was the birth of a New World Order. The first purely benevolent use of the strongest army on the planet, the military might of the last superpower harnessed to feed people, to save innocent Somalis from the medieval predations of warlords and gunmen, to rescue a useless Third World nation in Africa from devouring itself.[21]

This mission of mercy was to be fully exploited by the American media. The top three TV anchors spoke to their audience, several thousand miles away, from comfortable studio chairs brought from New York along with all the impedimenta of a modern TV station. The audience were expecting only good news. The crushing victory in the Gulf War of 1991 was fresh in American minds, and Dan Rather of CBS set an optimistic scene.

Notwithstanding the upbeat tone of the reports of the 'invasion', some US commanders complained that journalists had 'come between us and our mission' and went so far as accusing the press of 'ambushing the incoming troops on Black Beach'. This was notwithstanding the fact that Robert Oakley, the US envoy in Somalia, had provided the press with full details of the operation and gave specific instructions on the protocol to be observed. Such instructions as 'Park your personal armed "technicals" at the upper airport', 'Keep large weapons off your vehicles' and 'Conceal Somali guards' were among Oakley's dictates.

Robert Oakley had previously been the US ambassador to Somalia in 1982–84. He was versed in Somali culture, had travelled around the country, and was an accomplished and very experienced diplomat. He had been appointed as President Bush's special envoy and, on the face of it, seemed to be the ideal man for the job. Oakley had a commanding presence, and he identified his first task as ensuring that the Marine landing did not face local hostility. Hence the heavily stage-managed invasion at Black Beach.

The removal of Mohamed Sahnoun, back in October, had quelled any possibility of an all-embracing peace deal. Nevertheless, much was expected of Oakley. The hope of many, not least the Somalis, was that he would marginalise the warlords. To general consternation, instead, he enfolded them and sought to create a warm association that would support American aims in Somalia. For a man of his experience, this was a perverse aim. He went further and encouraged American commanders *not* to pursue a policy of disarmament of the warlords and their acolytes.

Oakley talked a good game. He advertised the military strength of the USA and of the excellence of its armed forces. He readily reiterated the recent success of Operation DESERT STORM in Iraq and warned against any resistance of American aims. He said:

> They know what can happen. There is a difference between UN peacekeepers who have been here and American troops with full freedom to fire back if they think it is necessary. Anyone who approaches [the Marines] with a .50 calibre machine gun will be in peril. It is very hard for marines to determine between those gunmen with good intentions, and those with bad intentions.[22]

Initially, the atmosphere between the incoming Marines and locals was cordial, but the undisciplined and intrusive children and young men tested the good nature of the Marines. A knife fight between two children was stopped by a husky Marine. One of the protagonists refused to give up his knife. 'We were ready to shoot him, but he was ready to take us all on. He can't have been more that twelve years old,' reported one witness.[23] The culture gap became evident very quickly, and one observer wrote that:

> the most powerful military regime could direct a big missile to hit a tiny target and ferry millions of tons of equipment and supplies to a faraway land, but for most American soldiers, just saying 'hello' to a Somali was impossible.

The arrival of the American force was popular, and the general view was 'we trust the Americans, they've come to help us, and they don't want anything from us'. As the Marines drove towards the abandoned and looted embassy, cheering Somalis lined the route. The embassy was 'retaken' with a curious mixture of machismo and unnecessary aggression. The building was a ruin and had been for two years.

Oakley moved quickly and, two days after the Marine landing, he orchestrated a very public meeting between Aidid and his foe Ali Mahdi Muhammad. The two bitter adversaries embraced publicly, watched by the incredulous, international press. It all seemed too good to be true. A year before, they had made similar protestations of peace and reconciliation. Many were aware that that arrangement had not lasted for long and so there was a degree of scepticism among the spectators.

The icing on this political cake was the mutually agreed statement that Aidid and Ali Mahdi had agreed to peace between themselves. Further, that they would forbid their supporters from harassing American troops and they would dismantle the 'green line'. The *Los Angeles Times* commented:

> The two major rival clan leaders in Somalia have agreed to abolish the so-called Green Line dividing their forces in this capital and to allow US troops to occupy the entire city. Until now, US troops and other foreign forces here have been confined to the southern area of Mogadishu, with the northern section the objective of only sporadic patrols.
>
> As a result, northern Mogadishu became a zone of chaos with constant violence and general lawlessness. But in a five-hour meeting at the makeshift US Embassy that began on Saturday and lasted into the night, General

Mohamed Farrah Aidid and his chief clan rival, self-proclaimed acting President Ali Mahdi Muhammad, agreed to unify the city.

Aidid controls the southern section, while Mahdi's forces are dominant in the 20% of the capital north of the Green Line. The city was divided during two years of civil war as Aidid and Mahdi violently vied for power after having together toppled President Mohamed Siad Barre in January 1991.

The Green Line – now a no-man's-land of burned-out rubble and collapsed buildings – is scheduled to be the site of a joint demonstration by Aidid and Mahdi today to celebrate their agreement. Some Somalis liken the event to the 1989 fall of the Berlin Wall. 'We're going to tear down the Green Line; we're going to free the city,' said Mohamed Hassan Siad, a follower of Aidid.

The pact presages an increase in the presence of US forces in northern Mogadishu and a more aggressive attitude by the US-led, UN-sponsored force here toward confiscating heavy weapons. 'I think you will see in the next several days the removal of all heavy weapons from north Mogadishu and the removal of all vestiges of the Green Line,' said a senior US official who had a hand in setting up the Aidid–Mahdi talks. He based his statement on a part of the accord that re-emphasizes an earlier agreement by both sides to move all their heavy weapons, including gun-mounted pickup trucks, into compounds outside the city.

US Army Lt. Col. Steve Ritter said on Sunday that 'we are beginning day and night patrols into the area very soon.' UN spokesman Farouk Mawlawi said he was told that the US Marines will establish two permanent posts in the north. Sunday's agreement was the third pact aimed at reducing violence that the rival warlords have lent their names to since the Marines landed here December 9.

The previous two met with only partial success. The senior US official said, 'I'm not so sure this will work [any better than before], but I hope for the best.' The official said that the reason for past breakdowns, as well as the delay in removing the Green Line, was the inability of the two leaders to put aside clan disputes in favor of pragmatic political needs. The feeling now seems to be, the US official said, that 'three weeks of our presence has given them an opportunity to break out of the mould [of their old feuds]. This shows a greater willingness to settle their problems.'

He said the meeting and the plan for today's demonstration were worked out between the two leaders without US interference. 'They met for five hours without our being around,' the official said. 'We just provided a neutral meeting ground.'[24]

Responsibility for Somali operations had fallen to the United States because Boutros-Ghali had pragmatically recognised that it was only the USA that had the means to effect any sort of significant change in the political, social, diplomatic and military basket case that was Somalia. It was with UN concurrence that the nominally designed UNITAF mission (Operation RESTORE HOPE) was to be a transitional action under US control. The operation was structured into four phases.

Initially, troops were deployed to secure key harbour and airport sites in Mogadishu and Baledogle, forming the operation's base. The so-called 'security zone' was then extended to include the surrounding regions of southern Somalia. The third phase involved further, southern expansion of the security zone into Kismayo and Bardera. This was to ensure the maintenance of secure routes for humanitarian operations. Finally, in the last phase the US transferred operations to the UN and withdrew most UNITAF forces.[25]

The famine deaths had peaked during the period October/November 1991 and the most vulnerable had already expired. A US Government report postulated the theory that this intervention had saved 10,000–25,000 lives and the airlift and food distribution a further 40,000 between August and December 1992. However, the lives lost 'due to delays in undertaking earlier decisive action' were estimated at between 100,000 and 125,000.[26]

Notwithstanding the fundamental goodwill that UNITAF offered, there existed boundless opportunities for misunderstanding. US Marines, who spoke not a word of Somali, shouted their orders louder and louder to bemused Somali who had no idea what the issue was.

One afternoon, Dr Hussein Mursal, Director of the Save the Children Fund, was aggrieved to see Marines drag a man from his car and push him to the ground. Mursal intervened and asked, 'What was the problem?' The Marines explained that the man had refused to get out of his car. When advised that the man did not speak English and, incidentally, was also lame, the American apologised.

Language was the constant barrier to good relations from first to last. Before they had landed, American non-commissioned officers received language cards with a handful of basic Somali phrases. Officers were the recipients of an eleven-page pamphlet giving the background to the country and its culture. The pamphlet was hopelessly out of date as it referred to civil organisations and administrative systems that had long since been swept away.

Officers were briefed on the likely opposition and were made aware of the warlords and the clans that they led. This information did not always leak down to the soldier who manned a barrier. There was general ignorance of Somali culture and their Muslim religion. Muslim modesty was offended by UNITAF soldiers sea bathing naked in what was a fundamentalist stronghold. Although the offence was given accidently, nevertheless, Somalis were offended. Not the least of these was Abdulsamad Abdulahi, who led the militant Al-Itihaad al-Islamiya, 'The Islamic Union', which was an Islamist politico-military group, formed in 1983 through a merger of smaller Islamist groups.

Abdulsamad Abdulahi led this, the most powerful Islamic organisation in the country. He was very influential, and during the latter part of the twentieth century, he had the most widespread clan following of all the Islamist factions across the nation.[27] He aspired to create a 'Somali Islamic State'.

He announced his opinion of the bathers, saying, without any evidence, 'They will encourage prostitution like in the Philippines.' These were inflammatory words that UNITAF did not need.

If American public relations were problematic, those of the French contingent were very much worse. France had provided soldiers of the French Foreign Legion and their contact with Somalis was sufficiently abrasive to cast Americans in a warmer light. A US diplomat was moved to say, 'The Marines are doing a hell of a job. They are soft-spoken and courteous, quite a contrast to the Legionnaires who are threatening and alienating.'[28]

The Legionnaires were all non-French, noted for the ruthless application of military skills. They were rough, very tough and quite unsuited to the UNITAF mission. Peacekeeping was not in their skill set – something readily conceded by Colonel Jean-Paul Perruche, a Legion spokesman, who said, 'We are here for peace, which is an apparent contradiction, aggressive tendencies yes, criminal tendencies … I hope not.'[29]

'In early 1993, as in post-Tet Vietnam, the US military controlled only islands where its soldiers stood.'[30] Unlike General Westmoreland twenty years before him, Lieutenant General Robert Johnston, the commander of the Marine Expeditionary Force, had no delusions about the degree of his control. An incident that illustrates the atmosphere and uncertainty at the time occurred in north Mogadishu about three weeks after the Marines had landed.

Ten Somali gunmen hijacked a United Nations Children's Fund (UNICEF) car along a 150-yard stretch of road and robbed the passengers. The US Marines were at one end of the road and armed Somali UNICEF guards at the other. The Marines were unaware of what was happening, only yards away. However, the guards saw the robbery but did not raise their weapons because they feared that the Marines might fire on them, and not on the miscreants. Afterwards, the owner of the stolen car arrived at the UNICEF compound, grenade in hand, demanding compensation.[31]

On New Year's Eve and on the first day of President Bush's visit, in western Mogadishu a pitched battle was fought between rival clans. It was a bloody affair. Seventeen were killed and twenty-five were wounded. The US Marines opted out of any intervention when a Somali woman was attacked on the suspicion that she had been selling herself to French soldiers. She was stripped and beaten savagely by a ferocious crowd in front of the Sahafi Hotel. Journalists, resident in the hotel, French soldiers and US Marines were no more than interested spectators. To be fair, any intervention by US troops into a volatile situation may have had a deleterious and counter-productive effect.

It was was suggested that the provision of aircraft for Operation RESTORE HOPE generated 'the public-relations serendipity that gave President Bush an irresistible sip of painless Third World heroism with no backwash'.[32] That is the cynical, but probably accurate, view of an American journalist. The President observed that the complementary ground operations 'to get the food through is not an open-ended commitment. We will not stay one day later than necessary. We are determined to do it right.'[33]

A direct consequence was that the UNOSOM I chain of command was, effectively, redundant. There was a quickening in pace under these new arrangements, which would install 38,000 troops in Somalia. Eventually, 27,800 of these would be American. The UNITAF force would depend on the USA for logistic support, now freely given.

The US Army component of UNITAF was Task Force MOUNTAIN, initially commanded by Brigadier General Lawson Magruder III, Assistant Division Commander, Manoeuvre, of the 10th Mountain Division, based at

Fort Drum, New York. He remained in command until 22 December when the division commander, Major General Steven Arnold, replaced him. Task Force MOUNTAIN was built around the 2nd Brigade, 10th Mountain Division and, at its peak, consisted of approximately 10,000 soldiers including 2 infantry battalions, an aviation brigade, and division artillery and support assets. It was a sizable and effective military force that overawed the poorly armed Somali militia.

> Coalition forces including large components from France, Italy, Belgium, Morocco, Australia, Pakistan, Malaysia, and Canada soon joined US forces. During the course of RESTORE HOPE, some 38,000 soldiers from 23 different nations and representatives from 49 different humanitarian relief operations worked together to put food into the mouths of the starving people of Somalia.[34]

Other UNITAF contributors were: 1st Battalion Royal Australian Regiment (January–May 1993), Bangladesh, Belgium, Botswana, Canada, Egypt (one battalion), Ethiopia, France (a brigade HQ and one battalion), Germany, Greece (a medical company), India (a brigade HQ commanding three infantry battalions), Ireland (a transport company), Italy, Kuwait, Morocco, elements of 40 Squadron RNZAF, Nigeria, Norway, Pakistan, Saudi Arabia, Spain, Sweden, Tunisia, Turkey, United Arab Emirates, the United Kingdom and Zimbabwe.[35]

This miscellany was, in some cases, a purely nominal contribution and of limited practical use. However, the symbolism of their presence offset their practical deficiencies. Most of the soldiers concerned had never served outside their own country and few had ever seen active service. The behaviour of these troops was frequently overbearing and, on occasions, criminal – a matter considered in more detail on pages 64 to 68.

> Psychological operations were also used extensively to support operations in Somalia. UNITAF established a Joint PSYOP Task Force made up primarily of elements of the 4th Psychological Operations Group (Airborne) to ensure that information operations were effectively integrated into all plans and operations in theatre. PSYOP troops ran a local newspaper (called *Rajo* – 'the truth') and set up a radio broadcasting system. They also provided tactical

> loudspeaker teams to US and international forces. In addition, the task force designed, printed, and distributed more than 7 million copies of 49 different leaflets, posters, and handbills.[36]

A sample of the leaflet is below. It, and others, were well received before relations soured and became violent. UNITAF had only one aim and that was to provide protection for the humanitarian agencies. It was not intended to play any part in the governance of Somalia. It functioned during the first few faltering months of President Clinton's tenure. One of Clinton's early decisions was to drastically reduce American numbers in Somalia – from 27,800 to 1,500. Clinton's secretary of defense was Leslie (Les) Aspin Jr. He was in office for only one year from January 1993. It was a hectic year, internationally, with major issues not only in Somalia but also in Bosnia and Haiti.

The culture gap between UNITAF and Somalis was exemplified by khat. Somalis offered khat to American soldiers as a gift and in friendship. They reacted with disdain. A spokesman observed, 'It's [khat] being treated as an illicit drug, if the Marines see it, they will confiscate it.' Stevenson judged that 'American soldiers never came to appreciate fully that despite its antisocial consequences chewing khat was a perfectly respectable activity in Somali culture and did not indicate behaviour that was unacceptable in Somali terms.'[37]

The inability of US soldiers to relate to any aspect of Somali lifestyle was a replay of a similar disassociation with the Vietnamese two decades before and the result was much the same. On 4 January 1993, US Marines raided Aidid's armouries and cleared the largest gun markets in Mogadishu and Bakaara. These forays provoked a predictable and spirited response. Soon thereafter Marines broke into civilian homes and searched and seized any small arms they found. In the process, thirty Somalis were killed. This was, emphatically, not the *raison d'être* of UNITAF and someone, unnamed, exceeded his brief. The mayhem, always a feature of Mogadishu life, accelerated downhill from this point on.

On 14 January 1993, Private First Class (PFC) Domingo Arroyo Jr. had the doubtful distinction of being the first American soldier to be killed in Somalia. He was shot while on a foot patrol near Mogadishu International Airport. His untimely and pointless death was the catalyst that pointed UNITAF towards the need for the disarmament of the 'technicals' controlled by Aidid and Mahdi. There was only limited success on this front and the atmosphere had turned very much darker. Children now chanted 'Shoot the Americans' or 'Down with Bush'.

Gemmo Lodesani, Deputy Director of Operations for the World Food Programme, drew attention to the fact that in the previous year only two of his aid workers had lost their lives, and that had been an accident when they were caught in crossfire. Under this new UNITAF regime, two of his people had been murdered in the space of just fifteen days.[38] In late January 1993, jumpy US Marines responded to the fire of a sniper on a US vehicle in a Mogadishu street by firing on a crowd and killed eight Somalis.

For the soldiers operating under UNITAF rules life was relatively routine. They patrolled towns and villages with the main focus on Magadishu. There were, from time to time, confrontations with lawless or turbulent crowds. By the dawn of 1993, UNITAF had made progress in allieviating the famine. The port of Magadisgu was functioning at full capacity. Three convoys, each carrying 300 metric tons of food, were being safely escorted to Baidoa – the area suffering most. Seven other 'famine centres' had been established.

The American envoy overseeing the operation was Robert Oakley, who was at pains to protest that 'Our mission is not to take over the responsibility for the security of the country.'[39] All American participants in UNITAF were conscious of the manner in which the US had been drawn into armed conflict in Vietnam twenty years before, and were determined that there would be no replication.

UNITAF made progress and, in early 1993, fourteen disparate Somali political movements agreed on a ceasefire. Furthermore, they accepted the need to hand over all their weapons to UNITAF. Despite this undoubted success and barely a month into RESTORE HOPE, the American command chain judged that this was an operation not best suited to its soldiers. An outline plan was drafted to replace the Americans with a new force of African and Arabian troops, commanded by a Muslim. This was a view shared, in principle, by the United Nations.

Operation RESTORE HOPE, 9 December 1992. Sailors and Marines load crates of cargo onto a CH-46 Sea Knight helicopter deployed from USS *Tripoli*. (*Terry C. Mitchell*)

In mid-January, after only six weeks in station, the strength of UNITAF was reduced from 38,000 to 24,000.[40] The UN soldiers' Rules of Engagment (ROE) had been carefully drafted, and they made clear to all that this was emphatically not a wartime situation. The instruction was that every Somali with whom they had contact was to be treated with courtesy and respect. If force had to be applied, it was to be the minimum commensurate with success. However, these ROE did not in the least interfere with the individual's right to defend either himself or his comrades. Inevitably in a setting where people used different languages, misunderstanding led to confusion and sometimes anger or even violence.

The display of US military power had a deterrent effect on aggressive Somalis, notwithstanding the almost universal ownership of a Kalashnikov. They had no appetite for a pitched battle and sought only to stimulate the flow of money and materiel that the Kalashnikov provided. What Somalia needed was not an occupying army but a police force and, preferably, that police force would be Somali. In a nutshell, this had been the rationale for the CIA's earlier prediction. The Italians and Germans had combined to propose that very Somali police force, and they offered to train, pay, feed and clothe the police recruits.[41] This arrangement was anathma to Aidid, who would not tolerate a foreign-supported law enforcement agency superior to his SNA militia. The idea withered on the vine and Somalia plunged on completely unpoliced.

Deploying soldiers in this lawless place did give rise to very unfortunate incidents; one such was reported in the *Los Angeles Times.*

> A small US Army unit returning to Mogadishu surprised a band of highway robbers and, while returning fire, killed six Somalis, including one bandit and at least three of the unarmed victims of the robbery, a military spokesman said Saturday.
>
> The incident, on the main two-lane road from Mogadishu to Bela Dogle on Friday night, marked at least the second time that American forces have acknowledged killing unarmed civilians since Operation RESTORE HOPE was launched five weeks ago and it reflected growing uneasiness among the 24,500 American troops, who have been stepping up patrols in an effort to root out the gangs of bandits who prey, daily, on the citizenry and take potshots at the occupying forces.

> The Army patrol was operating without lights when it came upon the robbery in progress. The surprised gunmen, who were in the process of robbing a truck filled with passengers, opened fire first on the soldiers. When the soldiers returned fire, six Somalis were killed and five were injured.
>
> Marine Colonel Fred Peck, chief spokesman for the US-led mission in Somalia, blamed the gunmen for putting the lives of innocent civilians at risk by opening fire on a heavily armed army patrol.
>
> 'It's regrettable that civilians were killed,' Peck said. 'But when fired upon in the dark, the soldiers responded by firing at the muzzle flashes. It was rather evident that the bandits did not seem to care about the civilians. As far as we can determine, the soldiers reacted as they were trained to react,' Peck added.
>
> One of the Somalis killed was identified as a bandit, and one weapon was found at the scene. The other gunmen apparently fled into the countryside. Of the other five killed, three were family members of the truck driver. The two unidentified victims also could have been civilians, the military said. The injured were being treated at an Army field hospital.
>
> On December 10, a day after US forces arrived in Somalia, French Legionnaires and US Marines manning a roadblock in Mogadishu opened fire on a truck loaded with men, women and children that had lost its brakes. The troops said the truck had appeared to be running the roadblock. Two died in that attack, and no firearms were found on the truck.
>
> French and American commanders said that shooting was justified under the American 'rules of engagement' (ROE), which allow troops to open fire on any person showing 'hostile intent.' Under those rules, US forces have killed at least two dozen armed Somalis who either fired on – or aimed weapons at – troops.[42]

In another incident, a 12-year old boy carrying a 'suspicious object' was shot and killed when he approached an American vehicle. The sergeant who was responsible believed that the 'suspicious object' might be a bomb.

In fact, it was a toy.

Despite the tragic nature of the event, charges against the soldier were dismissed under legitimate, self-defence grounds. However, in yet another instance, a sergeant shot and killed an individual who had stolen his sunglasses. His claim of self-defence was rejected, and he was convicted at a general court martial. Clearly, there was a major culture barrier between UN/American troops and the people they were there to help, and, inevitably, there were accidents and misunderstandings like those listed above. On balance, however, US Army soldiers 'behaved with care and restraint', or so Stewart believes.[43]

In March 1993, an aid conference set up by the United Nations was held at which the international community agreed to supply over $130 million in aid. Boutros Boutros-Ghali built on this success and managed to secure from fifteen political groups an agreement for disarmament, reconstruction of the nation's infrastructure and, what was most significant, the formation of a transitional government.

Boutros-Ghali realised that there was still a long way to go, and in a report to the Security Council on 3 March 1993, he made it clear that:

> A secure environment had not yet been established in Somalia and incidents of violence continued to occur. There was still no effective functioning government in the country, no organized civilian police force and no disciplined national armed force. The security threat to personnel of the United Nations and its agencies, UNITAF, ICRC and NGOs was still high in some areas of Mogadishu and other places in Somalia.[44]

UNITAF had had its successes and some of the humanitarian aims had been met. A very fragile base of goodwill had been established in some places. A combination of skilful diplomacy and restrained military operations were needed to consolidate the UN position. March/April 1993 was the high-water mark of UN activity in Somalia. However, the Secretary-General believed that the armed force in Somalia should, by May 1993, transition into UNOSOM II. The stated aim was to establish stability in the north of the country and along the Kenya–Somali border. These were both areas where security was non-existent. The US contingent had been dramatically reduced but the majority of those remaining were airborne soldiers of Task Force Ranger.

The chain of command of American troops in Somalia was complex. It started at the very top with the President (Clinton), Secretary of State (Aspin) and Chairman of the Joint Chiefs of Staff (Powell). These three devised and then Clinton dictated the Somali strategy. This strategy 'was a carefully crafted arrangement that ensured coordination of American elements on the ground without compromising its security or US national interests'.[45] Thus, a significant UNOSOM II asset was outside UN control. Major General Garrison was obliged to coordinate the activities of TFR with Major General Montgomery, who was notionally the second-in-command of UNOSOM II and the commander of US troops on the ground.

General Bir, the commander of UNOSOM II, answered to Admiral Howe, who was a Clinton appointee, and although, ostensibly, the representative of the Secretary-General of the UN, the reality was that Howe took his 'riding orders' from Washington.

Leslie Aspin Jr. (1938–95), US Secretary of Defense, January 1993–February 1994.

Lieutenant General Çevik Bir (1939–), Commander of UNOSOM II Somalia, April 1993–January 1994.

Chapter 6

UNOSOM II

Never lose sight of your principal object: do not act contrary to your orders, do not be led astray by secondary issues.

Lieutenant General Johann von Ewald,
Treatise on the duties of Light Troops, 1790

The United Nations Operation in Somalia was designated 'Somalia II' (UNOSOM II). It was the third phase of the United Nations intervention in Somalia and took place from May 1993 until March 1995. The stated objectives were: 'To aid in relief provision and economic rehabilitation, foster political reconciliation, and re-establish political and civil administrations across Somalia.'[1]

An important military principle is the selection and maintenance of an aim. In this case, an unelected, international, civilian-led organisation had selected multiple military, domestic and administrative aims for a multinational armed force.

This was the blueprint for mayhem at best, and disaster at worst.

UNOSOM II was originally perceived to be the panacea for all of Somalia's ills. In practice, it made a bad situation worse. It cost lives and treasure, led to war crimes and severely damaged the standing of the United Nations and the United States.

The peacekeeping operation was implemented by the largest multinational force ever assembled for such a mission. UNOSOM II was very expensive and, at that time, the costliest UN operation in the history of the organisation.[2] Perhaps its most notable feature was the authority given to the commander to use the force at his disposal proactively. This was a significant step far beyond the normal constraints of self-defence.[3] The need to build on any residual goodwill was set aside; it was always, at best, a very long shot and was judged to be unlikely to be successful. The US Central Intelligence Agency (CIA) had concluded, long before RESTORE HOPE, that Somalia would eventually slip into 'a protracted urban guerrilla war waged by a ruthlessly unafraid populace'.[4]

The formation of UNOSOM II was not welcomed by the majority of Somalis and they resented the administration of their country being in foreign hands.[5] There was a view that, in the longer term, the UN aim was to establish a trusteeship.

Although the UN mandate for UNOSOM II included 'peacekeeping', local conditions were such that, by June 1993, it was inextricably locked in armed conflict with a miscellany of Somali factions. The most significant of these was the Somali National Alliance (SNA) led by General Mohamed Farrah Aidid. The consequence of the need to conduct operations against Aidid inevitably, and adversely, affected the UN's wider political aims of reconciliation, institution building and even humanitarian aid. Dr Ramesh Thakur, Emeritus Professor in the Crawford School of Public Policy at the Australian National University, observed:

> [Peacekeepers] should not … have the obligation, the soldiers, or the equipment to engage violators in hostilities. International peacekeeping forces express and facilitate the erstwhile belligerents' will to live in peace; they cannot supervise peace in conditions of war. Turning them into a fighting force erodes international consensus on their function, encourages withdrawals by contributing contingents, converts them into a factional participant in the internal power struggle, and turns them into targets of attack from rival internal factions.[6]

The multinational UNOSOM II had a complex system of command and control. Every national contingent had its own indigenous system, and the overarching UN command had to be exercised with tact and restraint. The overall political and strategic direction was vested in the Secretary-General with oversight by the UN Security Council.

Nevertheless, a Special Representative of the Secretary-General (SRSG) was appointed to provide political direction and to coordinate the actions of military and humanitarian missions.

Admiral (Rtd) Jonathan Howe, late USN (1935–), Special Representative of the United Nations Secretary-General, March 1993–February 1994.

The man selected for this role, by recently elected President Bill Clinton, was retired Admiral Jonathan Howe, late of the United States Navy. The UN agreement to the appointment of an American was indicative of the grip that the USA had on Somali operations. Howe's appointment was described as 'the miscasting of the century'.[7] Howe failed to impress, and he came under criticism for distancing himself from the military activity and 'hiding away from the action in his fortified bunker'.[8] When he did involve himself it was seen to be a personal vendetta against Aidid.[9]

Despite Howe, and to complicate matters, UNOSOM II had a military command structure headed by a force commander who in 1993 was the Turkish General Çevik Bir. He was responsible for directing the military aspects of the mission, including peace enforcement, security and support for humanitarian operations. Under Çevik Bir's command were 22,000 troops from 27 countries, including Pakistan, India, Turkey, Italy, Nigeria and many others. The second-in-command of the organisation was an American officer, Major General Thomas Montgomery.

The USA was providing significant support to UNOSOM II and the reality was that Montgomery was the power behind the throne.[10] He reported directly to the Pentagon.[11] It was on this basis that Montgomery exercised enormous influence on events and, not least, because the staff at HQ UNOSOM II were predominantly American.

After the handover from UNITAF to UNOSOM II, the United States still maintained a significant presence in Somalia. The US provided a Quick Reaction Force (QRF), which operated under US Central Command (CENTCOM). The QRF was commanded by Major General Montgomery. He was 'double hatted' and could and would act independently, especially in situations where US forces were directly involved. However, it was expected that he would coordinate operations with the UNOSOM II force commander.

The command-and-control structure faced significant challenges due to the complex and fluid nature of the conflict in Somalia. UN forces had to deal with numerous warlords and militias, some of which were not cooperating with UN efforts, and some were openly hostile. This required constant adaptation of military strategy and communication. Coordination between different nations' forces and between military and humanitarian actions was difficult, further complicated by differing national rules of engagement and political pressures. While the US forces remained under national command, they were expected to cooperate with UNOSOM II, though in practice, their autonomy led to occasional disconnects.

Given the multinational nature of the forces, the US element operated, at least notionally, under the UN flag and the force commander's orders. However, tensions sometimes arose between contributing countries. Ill-discipline was rife and the conduct of some UNOSOM troops was judged to be war crimes. This could never be a 'hearts and minds' campaign and the behaviour of a few UN troops earned them the hatred of many of the population.

UNOSOM II deservedly faced heavy criticism for countless offences contrary to international law. Murder, rape and physical assault were laid at UNOSOM's door. The conduct of UN soldiers was widely reported in the press.[12]

Chapter 7

On Ill-Discipline

It was once alleged that 'the camel is a horse designed by a committee'; if that is the case then perhaps UNOSOM II was the work of that same organisation. The previous chapter showed the comprehensive difficulties faced by this unwieldy force and the command obstacles inherent in its construction.

The troops from the twenty-seven countries contributing to the composition of UNOSOM II had a wide variety of skill and experience. For many it was their first time abroad and many had never seen active service. Serving in a foreign country where one cannot understand the local people or communicate with them produces a feeling of detachment. These cultural and language barriers between peacekeepers and the Somali population exacerbated tensions. Misunderstandings frequently led to confrontations, especially when peacekeepers interpreted civilian actions as threats, resulting in the use of force. It might be argued that this inability to communicate contributed to, but does not excuse, the rampant ill-discipline that seriously damaged the standing of the UN in Somalia.

The French and Americans had inflicted brutal criminality on the population of Vietnam in the period 1945–73. This behaviour had served to stiffen the resolve of the Vietnamese to expel these invaders and it was a major factor in the crushing defeat of two sophisticated Western armies.

The chaotic environment in Somalia, combined with cultural misunderstandings, lack of proper oversight and the stress experienced by soldiers in an unfamiliar and hostile environment, contributed to the breakdown in discipline among some contingents. These incidents also highlighted the challenges in multinational peacekeeping operations, where varying standards of military conduct and discipline could complicate efforts to maintain cohesion and professionalism.

To illustrate the impact of this behaviour it is germane to consider some specific examples, the first of which concerned the Canadian contingent. It became a major scandal in Canada, and it stemmed from the actions of the Canadian Airborne Regiment during their deployment in March 1993. The incident concerned the torture and killing of a Somali teenager named Shidane Arone.

On 16 March 1993, members of the Canadian Airborne Regiment captured Shidane Arone, a Somali suspected of attempting to infiltrate the Canadian compound in Belet Huen. Arone was taken to a bunker, where he was held in custody. Throughout the night of 16/17 March 1993, Canadian soldiers subjected Arone to severe physical abuse and torture.

Several soldiers, including Private Kyle Brown and Master Corporal Clayton Matchee, beat Arone with their fists and weapons, burned him with a cigar, and poured water on him to intensify the pain. Incredibly, photographs were taken of the abuse, some showing the soldiers posing with Arone Shidane. Arone eventually succumbed to his injuries and died.

This was murder – and by those designated as 'peacekeepers'.

Initially, the Canadian forces tried to manage the situation internally, but the severity of the incident led to broader public awareness and outrage. Journalists and media organisations began to report on the incident, bringing the death of Arone into the public spotlight.

Private Kyle Brown was court-martialled, found guilty of manslaughter and sentenced to five years in prison, which seems to be a very modest punishment for a monstrous crime. Master Corporal Clayton Matchee was also charged but did not stand trial. When he attempted suicide, it resulted in him suffering a degree of brain damage that left him unfit to stand trial.

The matter did not end there, and the incident led to a comprehensive investigation into the Canadian Airborne Regiment's conduct and culture. In 1994, the Canadian government launched a public inquiry to investigate the broader issues surrounding the deployment in Somalia, the conduct of the Canadian Airborne Regiment, and the handling of the incident by military leadership.

In January 1995, as a direct result of the scandal and a series of other disciplinary issues, the Canadian Government disbanded the Canadian Airborne Regiment. The Somalia Inquiry revealed significant failures in its leadership, command structure and oversight within the Canadian military. The inquiry's final report, released in 1997, criticised the military's handling of the incident, the lack of accountability, and the inadequate preparation and conduct for the peacekeeping mission.

The 'Somalia Affair' had a profound impact on the Canadian military, leading to substantial reforms in military practices, training, and the handling of misconduct. It also prompted a re-evaluation of Canada's role in international peacekeeping missions and the responsibilities of military personnel in such operations.

The deleterious effect of Arone's death on his community and the wider Somali population needs no emphasis. There were other incidents that had a similarly direct effect on UNOSOM II's standing.

The Italian contingent of the UN mission faced serious allegations of abuse, including physical mistreatment and sexual violence.[1] Italian peacekeepers were accused of torturing and severely beating Somali detainees. Reports included instances of prisoners being hung by their wrists and beaten with metal rods, as well as being subjected to electric shocks.

These accusations came to light through media reports in Italy, where disturbing photographs and testimonies emerged. In one of the high-profile cases, Italian soldiers were alleged to have tied a Somali man to a tree and tortured him by shocking him with electrical wires. Valerio Ercole was identified as the individual who was alleged to be fitting electrodes to a Somali prisoner.[2] There were also reports of Somali women being raped by Italian troops.

The Italian Government launched an investigation into the conduct of its troops following media reports and disturbing photographic evidence of torture and abuse. Italian prosecutors and military authorities began formal inquiries into the actions of soldiers deployed in Somalia.

Some soldiers faced a court martial for their actions, particularly in cases where solid evidence, such as photographs and testimony, were available. However, the legal process was often slow and faced hurdles due to the challenge of gathering reliable evidence from a distant war zone.

Only a few cases resulted in convictions, and several were dismissed due to insufficient evidence. In some instances, soldiers argued that they were under extreme stress or were acting in self-defence, which complicated the legal outcomes.

The revelations about Italian soldiers' misconduct led on to a parliamentary inquiry. The inquiry published a report that highlighted the failure of military discipline and oversight. However, the report was criticised for not addressing systemic issues or holding high-ranking officials accountable.

The trials and investigations received significant media coverage in Italy, and public opinion about the deployment became sharply divided. Many Italians were shocked by the allegations, while others defended the soldiers, citing the extreme conditions they faced in Somalia.

Ultimately, while a few soldiers were convicted of crimes related to torture and abuse, many others were not held accountable. The Italian military and government faced criticism for not fully addressing the systemic issues that allowed such abuses to occur, and there was little done in the way of reparations for Somali victims.

In contrast to the high-profile investigations of Italian soldiers, the allegations against Polish troops were less severe but still concerning. The accusations involved excessive force, rough treatment of Somali civilians and violent altercations. The Polish Government launched internal investigations into these allegations, but they did not attract the same level of media attention or public scrutiny as the Italian cases.

Polish authorities reportedly handled most of the incidents internally within the military justice system. Some soldiers were reprimanded, and others faced temporary suspensions or demotions, but few cases reached the level of court martial.

The Polish military justified some of the actions taken by their troops as being necessary in the context of a dangerous and chaotic environment, where soldiers frequently came under attack or felt threatened by armed civilians. This reasoning led to relatively lenient outcomes in terms of disciplinary actions.

Compared to the Italian trials, the legal consequences for Polish troops were limited, with only minor punishments issued for lower-ranking soldiers. These actions did not result in high-profile trials or any long-term legal consequences for the Polish contingent.

The relatively minor scale of the Polish misconduct, combined with the lack of graphic evidence such as the photographs from the Italian abuses, meant that the cases received far less media attention in Poland and internationally. As a result, there was little public or political pressure to pursue further investigations or trials.

The Belgian contingents were also the subject of criticism. Belgian soldiers were accused of numerous instances of abuse, including tying Somali children to military vehicles and using them as human shields. Other allegations involved beatings and acts of humiliation against Somali civilians.

Suffice it to say that the misconduct by some peacekeeping troops in Somalia contributed to a growing hostility to their presence and severely damaged the standing of the entire UNOSOM II force.

It is not acceptable to blame the chaotic environment in Somalia, cultural misunderstandings and the stress experienced by soldiers for unsoldierly conduct. The examples cited above concerned a very small group of men from civilised, First World democracies. These men were not uneducated savages. However, their savage conduct had long-term repercussions, not least that their behaviour reflected on the entire UN operation.

These incidents highlighted the challenges in multinational peacekeeping operations, where varying standards of military conduct and discipline could complicate efforts to maintain cohesion and professionalism.

Chapter 8

Escalation

Principles of strategy should never transcend common sense.

Motto of the German Army Staff College, prior to 1914

The presence of UN troops in Somalia was resisted by much of the population from the first formation of UNOSOM II in May 1993. Unlike its predecessor, UNITAF, which focused primarily on securing the distribution of humanitarian aid, UNOSOM II had a more expansive and aggressive mandate under Chapter VII of the UN Charter. This authorised UNOSOM II to use military force to disarm militias, restore order and help rebuild a functioning Somali government.

'On the alert'. An American soldier and Somali citizens. (*Jeffrey Manuszak, 1994*)

To achieve this mixed aim, the first step was to disarm the miscellany of Somali warlords and their armed organisations. The most dangerous of these was the Somali National Alliance (SNA) led by Mohamed Farrah Aidid. The chaotic conditions in Somalia in mid-1993 was in large measure the result of Aidid's activities. He enjoyed the support of the Habar Gidir clan, which predominated in Mogadishu and gave him control of the city.

Aidid was wholeheartedly opposed to the UN's well-meaning aims. These he judged, correctly, to be obstacles to his personal ambition for the control of the entire country of Somalia.

Radio Mogadishu was an Aidid asset, and an effective and valuable tool that he used to broadcast daily invective aimed at the United Nations. The radio station broadcast material that railed against the 'foreign occupiers' and it provided a popular service to the residents of the city.[1]

On 3 June, Major General Thomas Montgomery advised Admiral Howe that it was his intention to inspect SNA weapons deposited in five authorised sites, one located in the grounds of the radio station. Lieutenant General Bir was outside the country and so Montgomery was in command of UNOSOM II. Montgomery gave Howe a letter to be delivered to Ambassador Ahmed Alim, a part-time adviser to the SNA, advising him of the inspections.

The letter reached the home of Ahmed Alim in the late afternoon of 4 June, and it was read, at once, by Colonel Abdi Qeybdiid Hasan Awale. His response was immediate and very strong. 'This is unacceptable,' he protested. 'This means war.'[2] It was a prescient observation.

Nevertheless, the next morning about 100 Pakistani troops, accompanied by a group of American officers with unspecified duties, arrived at Radio Mogadishu. The SNA press release, issued after the event, gave this questionable account of what followed:

> UNOSOM II troops occupied Radio Mogadishu at 0530 hrs on 5 June, removing staff, breaking doors and damaging the FM radio. The spontaneous reaction of the Somali people to the seizure of the Radio was quick and firm. Hundreds of thousands of people from all walks of life rushed to the Radio area to demonstrate against the takeover but UNOSOM II troops opened fire on the unarmed civilians, killing several people.

> This violent action by UNOSOM II troops obviously outraged the Somalis even more and, by the time the news of this terrible incident reached the Somali authorities, the situation was beyond control. …
>
> The seizure of the Radio Station by UNOSOM II troops was seen by the Somali people as an attempt to repress their voices. … The peace and reconciliation agreement signed last Friday [4 June] in Mogadishu conforms to the charter of the United Nations, the resolutions of the Security Council, and the Addis Ababa agreements and there is no reason why one should oppose it to cause the above-described problems.[3]

The UN did not buy what it perceived to be a travesty of the truth and disputed the validity of the SNA press release, which sought to place the blame for the bloodshed firmly on the Pakistanis – twenty-four of whom were killed at the scene and a further two died of wounds. Fifty-six Pakistanis were wounded, eleven of whom were crippled for life. Three Americans were also wounded. The Pakistani party suffered about 80 per cent casualties. This is a particularly high percentage for an armed force, and especially the one initiating violence.[4]

A short time after the event it was announced that 75 Somalis had perished and 350 were wounded, so, whatever the circumstances, the Pakistanis gave a good account of themselves. This had been a major confrontation but, according to the 1994 United Nations Inquiry, in the events leading up to the Battle of Mogadishu:

> opinions differ, even among UNOSOM officials, on whether the weapons inspection of 5 June 1993 was genuine or was a cover-up for reconnaissance and subsequent seizure of Radio Mogadishu.[5]

UNOSOM II was anxious to close the SNA's Radio Mogadishu, but it was allowing the radio station of Aidid's main rival, Ali Mahdi Muhammad, to remain open, allegedly on the basis that Ali Mahdi's station was 'unofficial'. Aidid's faction saw this as biased – and part of the ongoing UN aggression against it – and had determined that any interference with the radio station was a *casus belli*.

> The Pakistanis had in fact entered the radio station, looking for weapons. They were leaving, but crowds gathered thinking the station was under attack. A later independent investigative commission called the Pakistani inspection 'highly provocative and unwise'.[6]

On that day, Pakistani soldiers had been tasked to carry out the inspection. They were attacked in a skilfully planned and executed operation by the SNA. The Pakistani soldiers had little chance and were slaughtered.

The UN could not allow this loss of Pakistani life to go by without a robust response and the following day, the UN Security Council passed Resolution 837. This required the arrest of those responsible for the death of the Pakistani soldiers. This was easy to 'resolve' but less easy to accomplish. Aidid was identified as the primary target and Admiral Howe was the prime mover in attempts thereafter to capture or kill Aidid.

During the summer of 1993, UNOSOM II forces, particularly those from the United States, intensified their activity in the Mogadishu area. Frequent raids and search operations were mounted to capture or kill Aidid and eliminate his command structure. These efforts were frustrated by a civilian population within which Aidid's forces were deeply embedded, making it difficult for UN forces to differentiate between militia members and civilians. Aidid himself remained elusive, moving frequently and using his network of supporters to avoid capture.

The US Joint Special Operations Command (JSOC), which included Delta Force and the 75th Ranger Regiment, carried out several operations, often involving helicopters and fast-moving ground forces. They resulted in frequent skirmishes with SNA militia. An unrecorded number of Somalis were killed but Aidid was never found. American forces in June 1993 numbered only about 1,500, reduced by President Clinton from a force initially 25,000 strong.

Admiral Howe was interviewed on the TV programme *Frontline* in 1994, and he commented on the command and control of UNOSOM II forces, saying:

> It was a mechanism that served the purpose of making the US comfortable with the arrangement for the forces that were left behind, the Quick Reaction

> Force and the logistic forces. It was a workable arrangement with General Montgomery, who worked very closely with General Bir. They consulted together on everything, they helped each other out, the staffs were fully integrated. So that was not a huge problem. What was a problem, however, was that those US forces had specific requirements; what they did had to be blessed in Washington or at least by the Central Command. So therefore, it wasn't necessarily a force that the commander, General Bir, could control. Even General Montgomery, if he wanted to do something, it required a lot of constant liaison back and forth with the various commands in the United States.

This interview makes clear that military activity in Somalia in 1993 was not in the hands of the UN because it was in Washington that all the levers of military power were being manipulated.

The ambush of 5 June was inevitably attributed to the Somali National Alliance (SNA).[7] It heralded the start of a war in which the level of violence escalated quickly. American AC-30 aircraft were used to strike at suspected SNA sites and were countered by mortar fire on UN garrisons, the ambushing of UN vehicles, and the assassination of UNOSOM members.[8]

Following the commencement of enhanced military operations, UNOSOM II had (via radio broadcast and propaganda leaflets dropped over Mogadishu) emphasised the point that it was not the enemy of the Habar Gidir clan, but only wanted to capture Aidid.[9] This pronouncement was ingenuous because Aidid was a leading member of that very clan which provided much of his active, armed support. A new phase of military operations against the SNA commenced on 17 June 1993. On this date, an ill-judged operation was mounted, with the inevitable aim of capturing or killing Aidid, who was thought to be in the area of Digfer Hospital. However, once again, Aidid slipped away by initiating a diversionary attack on the UNOSOM II perimeter.[10]

The UN/US force suspected that the hospital was an SNA weapons storage site and acted accordingly. It responded very robustly to sniper fire from the hospital roof and, in doing so, UNOSOM II deployed the power of USAF AC-130 gunships, which inflicted severe collateral damage. The number of Somalis killed was rising inexorably and, for every person killed, UNOSOM II gained at least another ten dedicated adversaries.

The international press was vociferous in condemning the profligate employment of devastating air power and its imprecise targeting. The operation of these aircraft served only to further damage the standing of the UN and the USA. The knock-on effect of the burgeoning outrage was the withdrawal of the gunships from the theatre.[11] This decision, taken in Washington, removed from the scene a most potent weapon system and one feared by the SNA.

The USA had backed down, and the removal of the gunships had, inadvertently, gifted a considerable military and political victory to the SNA. It was an example of a decision, with very significant military implications, being taken by people thousands of miles from the scene of operations.

The UN had long ago abandoned any 'hearts and minds' considerations and after this incident it had lost the public relations war too. There followed a further public relations misjudgement. Admiral Howe and Generals Bir and Montgomery determined to take a different approach, and they offered a reward for information leading to the capture of Aidid.[12]

Unfortunately, they fixed the reward at $25,000. This paltry sum was viewed as insultingly small, and it proved to be counterproductive as it served to further unify support for Aidid. Howe, now bereft of his most powerful weapons, lobbied the Pentagon for the deployment of US Special Forces in Somalia.

Throughout the summer, and despite UN forces conducting raids on suspected Aidid strongholds and militia compounds, the man continued to remain elusive. He was running rings around his adversaries. However, in the process there were several skirmishes in which uncounted Somali civilians were killed or injured. Every Somali casualty further inflamed tensions between UNOSOM II and the local population.

Chapter 9

Bloody Monday

Commanders must have integrity. Without integrity they have no power.

Sun Bin, *The Lost Art of War*, *c*. 350 BC

Retribution for the 5 June massacre took some time and it was more than a month before UNOSOM II found a suitable target. This was a civilian house in the Hodan district of Mogadishu. It was the residence of Abdi Qeybdiid Hasan Awale. This man was a senior member of the SNA, and he had called a meeting of leading Somalis for 12 July. Most of the invitees were senior members of the Habar Gidir clan, but they were not armed militants, quite the reverse. They were, for the most part, the intellectual opposition to Aidid and all his works; many were widely respected and admired.

Abdi Qeybdiid Hasan Awale (1948–).

There was nothing remotely clandestine about this meeting. It was widely advertised and about as secret as an Olympic 100-metre final. Had the UN asked, it could probably have sent a delegate to the meeting.

The object of the exercise was to find 'a way by which peace could be restored to Somalia and a cessation to the ruinous blood feud raging between the delegated adamantine warlord and the UN

"Peacekeepers"'.[1] Only the previous day, a group of these same clan elders had conferred with Admiral Howe, and he had endorsed their peace-seeking aim. Hussein Sanjeeh, a senior Aidid aide, commented later, 'That was a day when a peace agreement could have been achieved.'[2]

American forces, nominally under UN authorisation, were given authority to attack the meeting. This was as part of the campaign to capture or kill Aidid. The mission was given to the US Army's 10th Mountain Division of the Quick Reaction Force in Mogadishu.[3] It was termed Operation MICHIGAN.

The invitees at the conference were to meet in a large house, and on its first floor (American second floor) it had a large, carpeted room big enough to accommodate the 100 or so individuals attending. The American planning for a strike on this conference started on 7 July. At this distance, it is not possible to determine the mindset of the senior American officers who made the arrangements for the forthcoming attack, but suffice it to say that, arguably, they were hopelessly misguided and criminally culpable for what followed. To initiate their nefarious plan, they had an agent in place. He would attend the meeting and would signal the most opportune moment to strike.

The planned attack broke new ground, because it was the first military operation in which the target would be Somalis and not weapon caches or other structures. It was described by one observer to be 'the UN's first ever officially authorized assassination'.[4]

The UN position was that the meeting was nothing less than a war council. It alleged that all the attendees were hard-line SNA members, meeting in an SNA occupied house and, as such, an entirely legitimate target. The UN was unable to produce any evidence to substantiate its claim and justify the subsequent loss of life.[5]

The subject of a 'just war' has generated hundreds of books, and it is a concept debated endlessly in staff colleges around the world. It is only when a war is considered 'just' that civilised nations take up arms. Major General Thomas Montgomery, the architect of the assault, had convinced himself and his immediate subordinates that his planned response to the peace conference was 'just'. History shows that he was in a small minority.

The SNA protested that the meeting was a peace conference in which eminent elders, SNA moderates, all of whom were unarmed civilians, convened to discuss a possible diplomatic resolution to the escalating conflict between the SNA and UNOSOM II.

In an interview with journalists, Abdi Qeybdiid Hasan Awale remarked on the conference: 'Everybody was interested in stopping the fighting, to open a dialogue. It was in the interest of all.' The conference was called and advertised widely as being to discuss Howe's recent peace initiative.[6]

By now, UNOSOM II operations were, for practical purposes, American and the retribution for 5 June was planned and led by Major General Montgomery employing his QRF. The objective was to kill the participants at the conference at Abdi Awale's house on 12 July. The subsequent events of that day were to be accurately termed 'Bloody Monday'.

Just before the American attack, Abdi Awale was speaking to the assembly of prominent Somalis. His audience was a 'who's who' of Somali society. It included sheikhs, former judges, poets, professors, engineers, and

Two UH-60 Black Hawks, on Bloody Monday, on the street outside Abdi Qeybdiid Hasan Awale's house, having deployed the Assault Platoon.

representatives of several women's organisations. In a nutshell, the group were the most respected and best-educated members of Habar Gidir.

The American agent, Omar Hassan Ganay, waited until all the attendees were present, then, wearing clothes prearranged with his handler, at 1015 hrs he walked out of the house – this was signal to initiate the attack. Hussein Sanjeeh recalled the attack as an explosion of complete confusion and told Peterson, 'The first missile tore a hole in the wall, revealing a host of Cobra gunships that appeared to be at eye level.'[7]

The inhabitants of Mogadishu were well acquainted with the Cobras. For months, these potent weapons of war had been racing across the city at rooftop level to display their brute force. They were intended to intimidate the population – and this they had done for several months on a daily basis. The armament of these aircraft was awesome. The lethality of their TOW (tube-launched, optically tracked, wire-guided) missiles needs no advertisement. It is an anti-tank and bunker-busting weapon of enormous power. Bowden observed:

> It is a two-stage, forty-pound projectile with fins at the middle and back that trails a copper wire as thin as a human hair. The wire allows the TOW to be steered in flight so that it will follow precisely the path of a targeting laser. Equipped with a shaped charge inside its rounded tip, on impact it spurts a jet of molten copper, which burns through the outer layer of its target, allowing the missile to penetrate and deliver its full explosive charge within. The explosion is powerful enough to dismember anyone standing near it and it hurls deadly shard metal in all directions.[8]

In addition, the Cobras carried a 20mm cannon designed to destroy vehicles. When this weapon was turned against personnel, it was like a mincing machine: it did not just kill, it butchered its target. After the initial missile strike, a half-conscious Sanjeeh made for the stairs to get out of the building. There were no stairs as their destruction had been planned as a first priority to keep all the conference attendees confined to the upper floor and thus easy meat for the voracious Cobras.

Sanjeeh jumped down the stairwell into the sights of a Cobra gunner. The 20mm rounds 'tore off his right arm and shredded his right thigh'.[9] The Habar Gidir's most senior elder, Sheikh Haji Mohamed Iman Aden, who was over 90 years old, had been killed instantly by the first of the American TOW missiles.[10] The venerable old man died along with other elders and the walls of the conference room offered no protection against the sophisticated ordnance.[11]

> It was a slaughter. A half-dozen Cobras pumped sixteen TOW missiles and two thousand rounds of cannon fire into the house with deadly accuracy. First, they blew away the stairwell to prevent anyone from escaping. … A video taken just after the attack showed the mangled bodies literally blown apart in the attack – the religious leaders, the elders, even the women in their colourful wrap dresses who were always on hand to serve the tea.[12]

The house was destroyed, as were most of the occupants. Nevertheless, fifty-three Rangers landed nearby and accessed the remains of the house. Twenty-two gas grenades were dropped from circling Black Hawks to deter spectators. Hussein Sanjeeh survived his grievous injuries but feigned death when he saw American soldiers executing the wounded. He alleged that fifteen survivors were killed by the ground troops.

> American troops stormed in and began finishing off the survivors. They were using their pistols – they shot them in the head. The Americans always talk about human rights and democracy, so this really surprised me.
>
> They lied.
>
> They said they came to Somalia to bring relief. But they changed it to a war which had never been seen before. It was a war crime. I was very glad I was still alive, to witness. I wanted a chance to go to a war crimes tribunal or The Hague. But if there is no court then I will take revenge some other way. I will pass on to my children that the Americans have done this.[13]

This quote was published by a newspaper with a historically anti-American posture. The allegations were strongly denied by the American senior command at the time.[14] However, the reports of gunfire during the ground phase of the operation cannot be discounted as a Reuters correspondent claimed to hear gunshots coming from inside the compound.[15]

To conclude the operation, engineers from Charlie Company, 41st Engineer Battalion, identified further targets and destroyed them with thermite grenades. The Sappers left on the last departing helicopter, with one survivor of the attack as a captive. In total, only two survivors were taken prisoner.[16] The total time of the raid, from the first TOW hitting the villa to the last soldier departing on the Black Hawks, was about seventeen minutes, according to UN spokesman Lieutenant Colonel David Haynes.

Scott Peterson, an American journalist, was an eyewitness to some of the events of that day.[17] He, accompanied by his driver Duguf, and translator Hassan, arrived on the scene at about minute fifteen. Peterson wrote later:

> The Americans disappeared … and there was a strange moment of silence, a solitude virtually unknown in this country, and one that immediately forced the lump in my throat to attention and filled my emotion with terror. The quiet roar of the flames was muffled by my crippled consciousness. Then – with the army snipers gone – Somalis began to rush at me from all sides.
>
> I could see that they were enraged by the concentration of the attack, so I turned and walked, then I ran to get back to the corner where I knew Hassan would be able to calm the crowd. I was running then I saw Hassan, but the Somalis were upon him too and we were engulfed by the mob. In the last moments they had watched their fathers, sons and grandfathers die in a fusillade of UN-sanctioned violence, so quickly and finally. In 17 minutes that single compound had been obliterated by 16 TOW missiles and 2020 rounds.
>
> The mob surrounded me, grabbing hold of my cameras and bag, and my mind raced uncontrollably, knowing instinctively that there would be no running away from this violence, from this seething group that grew larger every moment. It all happened in seconds: I saw Hassan fist fighting, trying to explain that I was innocent. I screamed 'Hassan, Hassan Hassan', until I was hoarse, and we were losing the battle.
>
> It was all I could do to parcel my cameras to buy time, but I was being clubbed, and a boy brandished an 18-inch blade toward my face and as I fended that off a machete smashed into my head. My arm was struck again and again and the crowd tightened around me. I was fighting and this was never my war but now I had gone too far … I had crossed the line that divides observer from killer and victim.
>
> Death in Somalia is inevitable – who can stop the sunrise, and I felt my last of dawn were giving way.
>
> Duguf was stuck in the mob and waved his 9mm Beretta, but it was hopeless. I knew that I couldn't run – even if I could, I would never have

> escaped. The cameras were gone and there was nothing left to ransom my life, my throat was exposed but allowing no sound anymore, and I knew that if I lived this would be as close to … as close to … the end. Pistol blasts but not shot at me, the bastard with the machete went down, then a Somali man hugged me his tears soaking through my T-shirt into my thin Kevlar flak jacket. I was sure that he was going to knife me, his arms locked at around me and hands behind, but he showed mercy – here was mercy, mercy, mercy – he disentangled me for a split second from the crowd and there was hope though the tenacious furies followed me, grabbing hold again, then this question pervaded my thinking cutting through the din of the attack. 'Where are you from?' Lying without thinking I blurted out 'I'm British!' Duguf got to me with his pistol and two Somalis – here was mercy again – dragged me away and bundled me into the car. Hassan was there unhurt. We raced back to the Sahafi Hotel bouncing along the deeply potholed sand alleys, the blood flowing from my head down my neck and into my flak jacket.
>
> 'Jesus Christ are you OK?' asked Dan Eldon, a young British/Kenyan photographer for Reuters bounding out of the hotel. Dan and a German AP [Associated Press] photographer, Hansi Kraus, helped me to my room … the others all wanted to go (to visit the scene). I gave a warning matter-of-factly 'Be careful out there – it's fucking dangerous today.'[18]

Peterson's warning was ignored and journalists from several nations stationed in Somalia, and alerted to the incident, travelled to the scene to collect data for their reports. Several went with SNA escorts who had insisted that the journalists see the carnage unhindered, so they could tell the world. However, when they reached the site, the party was at once confronted by the same enraged crowd. The main body of journalists were quickly whisked away by their escorts, who realised how volatile the situation was.

Five of the journalists were isolated and encircled by the crowd. Three of the five journalists were killed on the spot: they were shot, stabbed or bludgeoned to death. The fourth was able to make his escape despite suffering gunshot wounds. The fifth was Dan Eldon. He too was able to make a break for it and ran. A Black Hawk from the American Quick Reaction Force spotted him but was, allegedly, ordered not to intervene. This was possibly due to the rules of engagement, which prevented engagement unless they or other UN individuals were directly threatened.[19]

Eldon was caught, and murdered; later, US forces recovered his body. The savagely mutilated bodies of Hos Maina, Hansi Kraus and Anthony Macharia were dumped in the Bakaara Market. Their recovery was thwarted by armed SNA members. Incredibly and unforgivably, the UN declined to assist, and it was left to the combined efforts of Reuters and Associated Press to hire armed assistance to retrieve the bodies of their employees.[20]

The appalling murder of the journalists was deemed by the Pentagon as being of more import than the slaying of seventy unarmed civilians. It was clearly US defence policy to ignore the massacre as the Official History of American Operations in Somalia covered this major incident in just forty-seven words. These were:

> On 12 July, in a direct challenge to Aideed's [alternative spelling] leadership, the American QRF attacked a major Aideed compound with helicopter gunships. After the raid, a hostile crowd near the compound killed four western journalists covering the action, displaying their bodies for the world to see.[21]

This glib and a wholly inadequate summation of an avoidable and criminally culpable event reflects no credit upon the author of that text. The murder of unarmed civilians at a conference was, and is, a blot on the face of the US Army and it should have been acknowledged and faithfully recorded.

Historians have a duty to present the facts in their context, no matter how distasteful. Ignoring the facts, as this spurious 'official history' does, is, at best, designed to conceal and mislead. It is, by any yardstick, dishonest and corrupt. It reflects very badly on all the Americans who had a hand in this criminal endeavour and on those who concealed the criminality. After the withdrawal of the USA from Somalia, the conduct of American forces during the campaign was subject to the closest scrutiny by American analysts, staff college students and military historians. The criminal behaviour of the QRF on Black Monday and its consequences were either ignored or downplayed by many.

The Black Monday killings shocked international news organisations and led to the withdrawal of reporters from, among others, the *New York Times*, *Washington Post*, *Los Angeles Times*, ABC News and NBC News.[22]

The 'butcher's bill' for Bloody Monday was large but its size was disputed, and different sources gave differing figures. The Italian press suggested seventy dead.[23] The Irish press favoured eighty.[24] There were no UNOSOM casualties, but the Red Cross said that 54 Somalis were killed and 215 injured. The SNA disagreed and said that there were 273 casualties, 73 killed, including unnumbered women and children among the dead.

A reason for the wide discrepancy in the numbers killed is, in part, because the fearsome weaponry employed against the conferees did not just kill – it shredded, dismembered and destroyed many of the dead. The site was covered in body parts. Hands, feet, fingers, legs, arms and heads were thrown together in a ghastly melange. The body parts were mixed with remnants of clothing all drenched in blood, and sitting in puddles of blood. Not everyone was killed outright. Fifteen wounded lived for just a few more minutes before, as Hussein Sanjeeh alleges, they too were shot.

CNN obtained, from a Somali cameraman, a video tape he recorded immediately the last American soldier left the ruins of the house. The tape revealed the extent of the violence visited on the occupants in all its gruesome detail. The tape was judged to be too extreme to be displayed on TV, but it was the crucial evidence that damns the perpetrators. Howe viewed the tape and declared that it was 'suspect' as it was counter to his absurd claim that few people were killed.[25] The killing of one person would have been reprehensible, something Howe clearly did not understand.

Doctors Without Borders protested that one of their leading Somali administrators for the city of Merca, the capital city of the Lower Shebelle province, was one of those attending the meeting and who had been killed.[26] Some of the other notable figures killed were:

Sheikh Haji Mohamed Iman Aden, the most senior elder of the Habar Gidir[27]
Moallim Soyan, highly regarded poet and elder
Sheikh Hassan Abdi Naleye, Habar Gidir
Dr Abdirahman Hassan Elmi, lecturer at Somali National University
Dr Khalife Adawe Ali, former jurist and intellectual from the Hawadle clan[28]
Abshir Qahir Farah, Habar Gidir elder[29]
Osman Hassan Kulmiye, Hawadle elder.

These men were not hard-line guerrillas. Far from it; they were the potential leaders of a future peaceful Somalia. Counting the dead would have been difficult for American troops as they were in a hurry and not least because the stairs leading to first floor of the villa, where the meeting had been taking place, had been destroyed in the minutes preceding the ground raid.

Keith Richburg noted that the video recording of the attack showed women among the dead.[30] Multiple children and numerous women had been killed in the missile strike. Somali journalist Cabdulqaadir Aroma reported that fourteen women (two pregnant) and ten children had been killed.[31] Several days later, UNOSOM dropped leaflets over Mogadishu proclaiming: 'The SNA said women and children were killed, but that was pure propaganda.'[32]

Notwithstanding the body count, the Bloody Monday action generates the question 'Was this a war crime?' This author thinks that it most certainly was, and that the planners of the operation have a case to answer. The reality is that it was all over thirty years ago and the time for effective retribution is probably long past. The USA has had, since Vietnam, a poor track record in bringing its war criminals to book. Operations in Somalia added to that record.

Admiral Howe underscored his ineptness when he defended what he was pleased to describe as 'a very key terrorist planning cell'. He went on to state: 'Appeasement is the wrong strategy when terrorism continues. … There is a time when you must stand up and use strength. I hope we can minimise the use of force and that we'll use it responsibly.' He concluded this blustering statement about the deaths of people he had been negotiating with only the previous a day by confirming his personal culpability. 'We knew what we were hitting. It was well planned,' he averred proudly.[33]

It is evident that Montgomery may have been the planner, the facilitator and commander of the operation. However, his culpability is shared with the chain of command, which was fully aware of the proposed massacre. How far up that command chain did compliance go? Montgomery was, indisputably, directed from Washington. Was President Clinton privy to the proposed action? One hopes not, but the probability is that we will never know. As commander-in-chief, he, nevertheless, is responsible for all actions taken on his behalf.

Major General Thomas M. Montgomery (1941–), Deputy Commander of UNOSOM II. He was responsible for the planning and execution of the Bloody Monday operation.

What did this brutal attack on a group of predominantly elderly, unarmed civilian men and women achieve? Montgomery's aim is unclear but there was one product of this murderous operation and that was to generate hatred for the USA and all its works among the Somali public. At a stroke, the positive, generous and effective humanitarian aid of Operation RESTORE HOPE just six months earlier was squandered. For the USA, the operation was a serious self-inflicted wound, and it was to have significant consequences.

The killing of civilian non-combatants was regularly practised by both the French and Americans in Vietnam without penalty and, similarly in this case, there was to be no attribution of guilt – quite the reverse, as Major General Montgomery was later promoted to lieutenant general.

However, Anne Wright, seconded from the US State Department to fill a senior appointment in the Justice department of UNOCOM II, wrote a memo to Admiral Howe in which she warned 'against applying military methods traditionally found in declared war/combat areas without a UN declaration of war'. She went on to say:

> One could argue that in previous attacks the short prior notice of impending attack somehow gave persons in the attacked building option to choose between life and death. ... This is the first incident in which no option was given.[34]
>
> While the Security Council has given UNOSOM the authority to hold persons accountable for attacks against UNOSOM forces and to take all necessary measures against those responsible, UNOSOM should anticipate that some organizations and member states will characterize a deliberate

> attack meant to kill the occupants without giving all the building occupants a chance to surrender as nothing less than murder committed in the name of the United Nations.[35]

Anne Wright, to her credit, could not stomach the doubtful moral values of Howe and his ilk and she, along with nine other UN employees, resigned in protest. Many of those who remained expressed the view that the UN had forfeited its moral authority.

International reaction was almost completely negative. There was consensus among relief agencies, human rights organisations and journalists in Somalia, all of whom publicly decried the attack. For example, Human Rights Watch remarked that the attack 'to the casual observer looked like mass murder'. The president of Doctors Without Borders commented, 'For the first time in Somalia there has been a killing under the flag of humanitarianism.'[36] In the process, Major General Montgomery had done for UN viability in Somalia what Goering had done for Coventry.

The level of anger generated by the attack was so deep that even those Somalis opposed to Aidid declined to endorse the operation. Consequently, after Bloody Monday, UNOSOM could no longer rely on the support of politico-military groups that were directly opposed to Aidid.[37]

There was consensus that 'Bloody Monday became the turning point – the day that Somalis turned almost unanimously against the UN miss-steps'.[38] Many Somalis from all walks of life felt that the peacekeepers had crossed a significant line.[39] This line between peacekeeping and combat operations was termed the Mogadishu Line and it affected international foreign policy for years to come.[40] Mohamed Sahnoun, a former UN envoy to Somalia, and a man who had strived to affect positive change in the country, commented:

> it's incomprehensible.... This attack was excessive and unjust. You can't explain it to the Somali people or the international community. Now people are very, very angry. There is a total divorce between the UN and the Somali people. The Somali feel now that it is an occupation force with a hidden agenda to take over the country. They don't feel UN troops have come to protect the humanitarian assistance.

The UN's objectives and its veracity were persistently challenged following Bloody Monday. Not least because the leading Somali elders and moderates who had met with US Admiral Jonathan Howe to discuss a peaceful resolution, just three days prior, had been among those killed.

Abdiqasim Salad Hassan, who was later to head a Transitional National Government, had taken positive steps among his clan to seek a diplomatic resolution to the war with UNOSOM. He had met Admiral Howe before the attack but gave up his efforts following the raid. To the Habar Gidir, including the former moderates, and even other clans that had formerly opposed them, the attack marked a declaration of outright war from the United States and signified the point where a diplomatic solution to the 'Somalia problem' had become inconceivable.[41]

It was in Italy that the disgust at American behaviour was most stringent and most vehemently expressed. *Avvenire*, *la Republica* and *L'Osservatore* were unanimous in their pungent criticism of American activity in Somalia. The suggestion that Italian troops be withdrawn from the theatre enjoyed support. The Italians believed that the *raison d'être* of UNOSOM II had been superseded by an American-led campaign against Mohamed Farrah Aidid.[42]

The Italians were not alone in their concerns. There were deep rifts and dissension amongst other coalition nations contributing troops to UNOSOM II – in particular, Ireland, Kuwait, Saudi Arabia and Zimbabwe. Pakistan, Malaysia and Italy were focused on maintaining stability and ensuring the delivery of humanitarian aid. This created some friction within the UN command, as the continuing military operations against Aidid diverted resources from other aspects of the mission. Most of these 'resources' were in American hands.

In Kenya, *The Standard* published a headline that read, 'Who are the Warlords Now?' In Germany, the death of photographer Hansi Krauss at the hands of the mob, compounded by reports of unarmed Somali civilians being killed by US helicopters, appalled many citizens. The outrage led to strong emotions and the press focused on Germany's role in Somalia.[43] The Social Democratic Party resisted a plan by Chancellor Helmut Kohl to boost the UN in Somalia by sending 1,600 soldiers. The day following the raid, former British Prime Minister Edward Heath added his weight and experience to the debate by saying, 'The UN in Somalia was costing innocent lives and fuelling hatred for the West.'[44] He was absolutely right, and the stock of the UN in Somalia plummeted.

In the United States, public support for the mission began to wane as reports of the ongoing violence and lack of clear progress dominated the news. There was growing scepticism about the efficacy of the mission, particularly the singular focus on capturing Aidid, which many saw as a distraction from the broader goal of stabilising Somalia.

A week later there was further bloodshed when, on Sunday, 13 June, at 10.30 in the morning near a Pakistani position, 3,000 to 4,000 Somalis demonstrated against UNOSOM. The Pakistani troops opened fire with a machine gun from a secure emplacement on a rooftop. They gave no warning and at least twenty people were killed, including women and children, and around fifty were wounded.[45] A journalist representing the *Toronto Star* who was present at the protest said, 'I do not recall hearing a shot before the Pakistanis opened fire. They fired hundreds of rounds.'[46]

The situation was going from bad to worse and the standing of the UN, and especially the Americans and Pakistanis, was at rock bottom. These two component parts of UNOSOM II had, between them, destroyed any chance that the UN had of effecting social, domestic or political change in Somalia. With 20/20 hindsight, the UN presence in Somalia could, and should, have been terminated following this latest massacre. There were several public figures who shared this view.

Public opinion of the UN/US was negative and there were demonstrations outside the US Embassy in London. In the USA, Senator Robert Byrd distanced himself from his Democratic Party and called for the US troops in Somalia to come home. On 27 July 1993, Ohio Congressman Sherrod Brown introduced Resolution 227, urging the withdrawal of American forces from Somalia as soon as possible.

UNOSOM II threw fuel on the Bloody Monday fire by its crass response to criticism. It sought to justify the US actions and, in the process, lost further credibility. Among its more absurd assertions were:

- The house was a military facility.
- No innocent civilians had been killed.
- All the casualties were armed, adult males.[47]
- The photographs taken inside the villa proved that it was an SNA command centre.

- Admiral Johnathan Howe claimed that there was no evidence of non-combatant casualties from the raid.
- The attack had been conducted on a key terror cell.[48]
- Montgomery, and others, claimed that among those killed were several top financiers and military planners, including the overall planner of the 5 June attack on Pakistani soldiers.[49] He was not named.
- Montgomery acknowledged that some of the casualties were elders but stated that they were still considered militia combatants.[50]

Montgomery also had his back to the wall and his assertion that 'tactical radios' were found in the wreckage of the villa was rejected by critics. In an interview with the *New York Times*, Montgomery suggested that it seemed that Somali militias had the 'inalienable right of the Somali militia to kill and maim United Nations' soldiers. But it is treated as a human rights violation if there is any military response against those responsible.'[51]

The general was interviewed on PBS radio several months after the US withdrew from Somalia in 1994. An extract from the transcript of the interview is below.

Can you talk about the incident on July 12th at Abdi House and how it was conducted?
The Abdi House raid was my responsibility, and it was conducted by the Quick Reaction Force.... We had excellent intelligence about the Abdi house. We knew that every day at 9:30 the Militia leadership met there. Not all of them showed up; Aidid didn't come very often, but most of them showed up. There was one woman who worked there. We knew the day we launched the raid that she was not there, we knew there were no children. We knew that that was a Militia headquarters. We also knew that leadership was the leadership that was responsible for that mine that blew up the four MPs and orchestrating all the acts of violence against the US and UN Forces. And so we decided to take it out.

And again, I could not do anything like that without approval from higher headquarters.... We had a five-day window, it was about the 4th day before I launched, although we were set to go every day. It was a classic air mobile raid in which we engaged the building with TOW missiles and then we landed on the roof of the building next door, and on the street in front, and were in and out within 10 minutes, with Air Mobile Infantry troops.

> When the troops got in the building, there were either dead or wounded but there were others that took them under fire, so they had to fight their way in.
>
> **How many people died?**
> I don't know. … 20, 25 Somalis as I recall, were dead. So, it was large, but of course the Somalis made claims, after the fact, that women and children had been involved and there were like 70 or something – which is ridiculous. I mean I was overhead in the helicopter. … From a military standpoint, [it was] a very precise, and very decisive operation and the intent was to kill bad guys, to decapitate part of the command staff that were making the decisions about the attacks on the United States and the United Nations.
>
> Now at the same time, looking back on it, it also worked against us from the standpoint that the suddenness and the violence of it shocked a lot of UN civilian personnel, I think, and some of the humanitarian people that were not at the site. But I mean the fact that we did that had a tendency to make the Somalis and the faction – it really stirred them up a lot, too. And you may recall that a couple of reporters or photographers were subsequently killed by the Somalis on that side.
>
> **So, was July 12 a significant turning point in the whole Somalia US–UN operation?**
> Yes, it was clearly the most amount of force that we had used, but I wouldn't call it a turning point. From a military standpoint, I think it was a logical continuation. I mean we were being attacked nightly, there were ambushes, and we had already taken a significant number of casualties, and not just us, the United Nations troops as well.[52]

The consensus is that Montgomery, among others, conceived and executed a heinous war crime for which they should have been called to account. The sole product of Operation MICHIGAN was to generate in, most, Somalis an unbridled and very deep hatred for America and Americans. Montgomery *et al* were, in effect, the architects of the American defeat in Somalia.

Scott Peterson had been present immediately after the attack and the carnage clearly affected him, especially the loss of four journalist colleagues. Seven years after Bloody Monday, he wrote in the most vivid terms of his experience. He summarised by saying, 'CNN acquired a videotape of the attack from a Somali cameraman who must have entered the target house the moment the last American soldier pulled out.'

Chapter 10

Guerrilla War and the US Response

A good general not only sees the way to victory but he also knows when victory is not possible.

Polybius, *Histories*, 125 BC

Post Bloody Monday, the UN was engaged in a full-on, if low-key urban guerrilla war and Mogadishu was to be the setting for frequent street skirmishes. Aidid's militia launched ambushes, planted improvised explosive devices (IEDs), and engaged UN patrols in hit-and-run attacks. Aidid's forces were adept at exploiting the dense, chaotic environment of the city to evade capture. Its militia had shown a remarkable ability to regroup and strike back despite UN efforts to degrade their capabilities.

Guerrilla war, since 1945, had been largely fought in the jungles of Southeast Asia and the popular belief was that 'the jungle is neutral'.[1] However, in Somalia it was urban warfare, and the cards were heavily stacked in favour of the guerrillas. Foot patrols in the labyrinthine streets of Mogadishu were very vulnerable. The increasing dependence on US air-mounted operations was an inevitable result, as was the UN dependence on US participation.

For those opposing a guerrilla enemy there was constant and protracted frustration, because the enemy could not be brought to fight a set-piece battle. Captain 'Chick' Reindenlaugh served as a 'military advisor' at Xuân Lộc, east of Saigon, during the Vietnam War. He wrote home in 1966 and described his war in footballing terms. He wrote:

> Our weakness is rooted in our inability to garrison every village, hamlet or settlement … they attack where our forces are not stationed … imagine a football game in which one of the teams is conventionally uniformed and

> observes the rules of play. The opposing team however wears no uniform and, in fact, [has] been deliberately clothed to resemble spectators. This team plays to no rules, refuses to recognize the boundary markers or the Ref's whistle and when hard pressed by their own goal, the team's quarter back will hide the ball under his shirt and run into the spectator boxes and defy you to find him.[2]

Reindenlaugh summed up guerrilla warfare: it is not fair, there are no rules, there are no boundaries and there certainly is no referee. The sole aim of the guerrilla is to win by any means possible and this usually means a disregard for his casualties. The UN sought to fight this war along conventional lines, but Aidid was far too wily to allow that and, by mid-1993, he had taken the initiative.

The USA knew from its experience in Vietnam that a force cannot be defeated from the air alone. Nevertheless, having complete control of the air and setting lessons of history aside, the US employed area weaponry against its enemy. There was a downside to this tactic. An air strike is a blunt instrument and area ordnance invariably causes collateral damage, not least civilian casualties, and, accordingly, it was often heroically counter-productive.

US military commanders, who were leading the operations, found themselves in a difficult position. While they had the manpower and firepower to launch raids, Aidid's militia had the advantage of local knowledge and wide civilian support, making it impossible for UN forces to exercise even minimum control of Mogadishu. Colonel T.E. Lawrence CB DSO (Lawrence of Arabia) concluded:

> Guerrilla war must have a friendly population not actively friendly, but sympathetic to a point of not betraying rebel movements to the enemy. Rebellions can be made with a two percent striking force and a ninety-eight percent, passively sympathetic [population].[3]

In Somalia, these criteria were already handsomely exceeded. One of the most significant challenges for UNOSOM II, after Bloody Monday, was the increasing hostility of the civilian population. The propaganda, broadcast on Radio Mogadishu, portrayed UN forces as foreign occupiers, which, of course, they were. This aggressive messaging contributed to rising public animosity, and civilians occasionally joined militia members in attacking UN forces.

The SNA focused on the US troops. On 8 August, four US soldiers were killed when their vehicle drove over a mine, and two weeks later a further six more were wounded.[4] President Clinton responded by promising retaliation. The UN response the following day was to 'reduce non-essential land missions around Mogadishu'. This supine reaction played into Aidid's hands. Three days later, on 11 August, when a US helicopter was fired upon by a group of Somalis, they attracted effective return fire in reply and seven were killed. There were four more American casualties on 19 August.

After Black Monday, predictably, SNA attacks on UNOSOM II had accelerated and Howe and Bir felt the need to ask for further assistance from the USA. Specifically, they requested that the US Army's 1st Special Forces Operational Detachment – Delta (Delta Force) – be assigned to the Somalia theatre. Their shared belief was that success would be theirs if the Quick Reaction Force was supplemented by the Delta commandos and provided with an up-gunned intelligence effort.

The new organisation would be designated Task Force Ranger (TFR) and commanded by Major General William F. Garrison – a noted Special Forces warrior. His command was to include 75th Ranger Regiment, a specialist intelligence team associated with the CIA and the comprehensive air support of MH-60 Black Hawks and AH-6 Little Bird helicopters flown by 160 Special Operations Aviation Regiment pilots.

The Italians had been in deep disagreement with UNOSOM for some months about the leadership of the organisation and it disputed the US-led strategy in fighting Aidid. Bloody Monday was the final straw, and matters had come to a head on 13 August when Italy gave notice that it was withdrawing its troops and abandoning UNOSOM II and all its works.

> At 7 p.m. on Sept. 14, Army Major General Thomas M. Montgomery sat down in his battle-scarred headquarters in Mogadishu and transmitted a call for help. Montgomery, the American commander in Somalia, asked for tanks and armoured vehicles 'at the earliest feasible date.' Montgomery said in his classified message, 'I believe that US forces are at risk without it.'
>
> Montgomery faxed Hoar [Commander of CENTCOM] a written request in the second week of August for a battalion task force of 28 Abrams tanks and 28 Bradley Fighting Vehicles. That would have been a substantial increase in US firepower, and Hoar took no immediate position. But the

> four-star Marine, an experienced player in the defense bureaucracy, began 'working the proposal' in his staff and exploring it informally in Washington, according to a knowledgeable official.
>
> The armor proposal found high-ranking allies on the Joint Staff and an adversary in policy undersecretary Frank G. Wisner. Wisner, according to an official who knew his arguments, was 'very troubled' at the thought of 'increasing the amount of military punch out there' at a time when the Clinton administration was trying to renew its emphasis on a political solution.
>
> The text of Montgomery's message, which Aspin [Secretary of Defense] read, and which has not been disclosed before, made clear the general had pressing concerns for safety of his troops. Aspin and his top aides have been reluctant to acknowledge that, publicly describing Montgomery's aim as protection of logistical lines.[5]

In New York, the Italian decision had to be faced by the embattled Secretary-General who, on 18 August, tabled a requirement for 3,000 troops to make up the deficiency left by the departing Italians. General Powell, although distanced from operations in Somalia, was by the nature of his job an active participant. On 21 August, he discussed with Secretary of Defense Aspin the merits or otherwise of sending Special Forces to Somalia.

Leslie Aspin and President Clinton, 1993.

Although the US force strength in Somalia was less than 2,000 men, they did provide the cutting edge of UN operations. The outcome of the discussion was that Powell, despite appreciating the risks inherent in the type of operations that Special Forces conducted, reluctantly recommended that TFR be supplemented in Somalia. It was agreed, on 24 August, to send 400 Special Forces soldiers to Somalia, 'to quell unacceptable violence and to restore security'.[6] Powell's judgement was enough to persuade President Clinton and his close advisers. However, Aspin urged Powell that 'at the same time the visibility of the US effort should be reduced'.[7] Not unreasonably, this was interpreted to mean that the force level should be the minimum that was viable.

General Joseph Hoar USMC (1934–2022), commander of CENTCOM 1991–94.

General Joseph Hoar USMC was a key player, and he opposed the deployment of Special Forces. This was because he did not envisage a situation in which they might be engaged in productive operations. Later he gave evidence to a Senate Committee to this effect.[8]

On 22 August 1993, the unit deployed in Somalia under the command of Major General William F. Garrison, commander of the special multi-disciplinary Joint Special Operations Command (JSOC) at the time.[9] The force consisted of:

- B Company, 3rd Battalion, 75th Ranger Regiment under the command of Captain Michael D. Steele.
- C Squadron, 1st Special Forces Operational Detachment-Delta (1st SFOD-D) under the command of Lieutenant Colonel Gary L. Harrell.
- A deployment package of sixteen helicopters and personnel from the 1st Battalion, 160th Special Operations Aviation Regiment (160th SOAR), which included MH-60 Black Hawks and AH/MH-6 Little Birds.
- Navy SEALs from the Naval Special Warfare Development Group (DEVGRU).
- Air Force Pararescuemen and Combat Controllers from the 24th Special Tactics Squadron.

All major elements of TFR were in Somalia by 28 August. During August and September 1993, the task force conducted six missions into Mogadishu, all of which were tactical, but unproductive, successes. In one instance, the task force members mistakenly raided an unlisted UN facility and temporarily restrained some UN employees.

* * *

It is germane at this point to elaborate on the aircraft, the pilots and their organisation, 160th Special Operations Aviation Regiment (Airborne) – the 'Night Stalkers' – because the anti-guerrilla operations in Somalia were hugely dependent upon the American air power and upon 160th SOAR(A) in particular.

It was the aircraft of this organisation and the men who flew them that are central to this chronicle, and it is useful to consider the background of this elite force. It was created as a direct result of a military debacle in April 1980, when the Iranians had taken fifty-three Americans hostage and was detaining them in Tehran. President Carter resolved to free these people, and the means to do this was an engagement designated Operation EAGLE CLAW. The USA had the Special Forces capable to carry out the mission, but it lacked a dedicated squadron of aircraft able to insert the Special Forces and exfiltrate them and the hostages.

Despite the shortfall in aviation expertise, the operation went ahead. It was not a simple plan, and it was to be conducted over hostile territory. EAGLE CLAW required four C-130 Hercules transport aircraft to fly from Masirah Island, near Oman, into the bleak Iranian desert. Here they would land at a spot termed 'Desert One'. The C-130s carried the assault force and aviation fuel. Meanwhile, eight Sea Stallion USN helicopters from USS *Nimitz* would make their way to Desert One. The plan was that the Special Forces would vacate the Hercules and transfer to the Sea Stallions. The assault force would then fly towards Tehran, stage briefly at 'Desert Two', then move on, free the hostages and bring them back to Desert One. There was a marked degree of naïvety in this plan and, to succeed, it needed good fortune. There was none of that available.

The helicopters allocated to the operations were not adapted to low-level flight over desert, and the pilots were inexperienced in the use of the newly acquired night vision goggles (NVG). The helicopter incursion into Iranian airspace was conducted at night and at very low level to avoid radar detection. However, the aerial armada ran into a sandstorm and two of the aircraft were incapacitated by the airborne sand that blocked their fuel lines. They had no other option but abort the mission and retreat to *Nimitz*, accompanied by a third Sea Stallion with a hydraulic issue.

The assault force, now reduced to five Sea Stallions, was unable to continue, and as they refuelled from a C-130 one of the Marine pilots became confused by the 'brownout' caused by his rotors. In his disorientation, he flew into one of the fully fuelled Hercules. The impact was catastrophic. A lethal fireball consumed both the Hercules and the Sea Stallion. The eight men crewing the two aircraft were consumed in the flames. The four surviving helicopters were abandoned and the whole force fled in the C-130s. By any yardstick, it had been a complete debacle and national humiliation. It was a factor in President Carter's failure to win a second term.

A positive result of EAGLE CLAW was the realisation that, increasingly, the USA would, in future, be fighting guerrilla wars and that there was a need to realign, re-equip and retrain its forces to meet the eventuality. Task Force 158 was formed by amalgamating several helicopter units with varying degrees of expertise. The Vietnam War had been lost in 1973, but it had been the early catalyst for major changes in the way wars would be fought in the future. This was the advent of the heliborne air assault, and this needed not only commando type 'special' troops but also a commensurate need for the means of delivering and exfiltrating them anywhere in the world.

Very few of the pilots in 158 were qualified to fly with NVG and no one was qualified to fly Black Hawks whose cockpit instruments had been adapted to be compatible with NVGs. Pilot selection was rigorous, and their training very demanding. 'In separate locations Little Bird and Chinook pilots underwent the same transitions. Ultimately, all the elements linked up to fly coordinated training missions, at night in all kinds of weather, navigating over routes as long as 1,000 miles.'[10]

> Throughout the fall of 1980, Task Force 158 pilots flew thousands of hours honing desert environmental skills and close formation precision navigation under NVGs. Late that autumn, the TF commander asked the aircrews for volunteers to remain with the project, almost everyone stayed on board. The volunteers were briefed on Operation HONEY BADGER and TF 158 would be the air component of a second attempt to rescue the hostages in Iran. But, in January 1981, the hostages were released, and HONEY BEAR was cancelled. The volunteers were retained as a unit and 160th SOAR – 'The Night Stalkers' were born.[11]

The early days were testing and as the pilots flew to the limit of their and their aircrafts' capability, inevitably there were accidents. In October 1983, the

160th was put to the test during the American invasion of Grenada. Although the operation met its objectives by the application of disproportionate force, the Special Forces did not excel. Against a numerically weak, third-class, ill-equipped and poorly trained opposition, nine aircraft were lost, three in accidents – not all flown by pilots of 160th.

Pilots flying Delta and SEAL soldiers had to be almost as skilled, resourceful and physically fit as their passengers. Durant wrote in his book of the arduous physical, swimming, and small arms training that he and his fellows underwent. He commented:

> If you didn't have patience, determination and nerve, the 160th SOAR(A) was 'not for you'. You would be constantly honing your skills, improving, improvising, developing new techniques. You had to fly right and shoot straight, 24/7. You had to be cool under fire, take harsh criticism, and offer it constructively. The unit's motto 'Night Stalkers don't quit', and its motto 'Time on target plus or minus thirty seconds' had to seep into every aspect of your life. It was the ultimate team effort, but every member of the team had to have the skills of a quarter the grit of a linebacker and the brains of a coach.[12]

In October 1983, a paranoid President Ronald Reagan launched Operation URGENT FURY and invaded the Commonwealth country of Grenada. This was nothing less than a 'masterclass in military and political ineptitude'.[13] Militarily, everything that could go wrong, did. Politically, it was no better and the invasion was declared to be illegal by the United Nations.

In this operation, the USA pitted an armada of war ships and 7,300 highly trained soldiers against a force of several hundred unmotivated militia and Cuban labourers. The campaign was 'won' but the outcome was never in doubt, given the vast disparity in military power.

However, the USA loss of those nine helicopters become a contentious issue in the post-operation analysis. The conclusion was that, during the operation 'command and control' was inadequate and intelligence minimal. However, what was never in doubt was the courage and commitment of US soldiers, Marines and sailors. The invasion of Panama in 1989 went rather better and, by 1993, the Night Stalkers were at their very best.

* * *

In mid-1993, and engaged in a guerrilla war, Task Force Ranger mounted raids that were launched by day and night and used both helicopters and vehicles to reach their target. However, for the first time the US Rangers received rocket-propelled grenade (RPG) fire from the Somali militia they engaged. Although Aidid himself remained free, the cumulative result of these efforts was to severely hamper his movements and effectiveness. Significantly, his forces were also showing a greater willingness to engage TFR elements with heavy small arms and rocket fire.[14]

People on both sides continued to die and, on 5 September, in yet another well-planned ambush, seven Nigerian peacekeepers were killed and at least six more were wounded. This brought UNOSOM losses to forty-seven.[15] However, Somali losses, uncounted, were vastly greater. On 9 September, the situation worsened, and Keith Richburg filed a lengthy report. The extract below provides the bones of the story.

> The clash, one of the largest since a US-led international military force was sent to Somalia in December, left one Pakistani soldier dead and two US soldiers and two Pakistanis wounded, a UN spokesman said. Although there was no firm figure on the number of Somalis killed and wounded, the United Nations' account indicated that 20mm cannon fire from two US Cobra helicopters inflicted casualties among militiamen and their civilian backers. Somali sources reported seeing scores of bodies in the street.
>
> The violence today began in the late afternoon, on a notoriously dangerous stretch of 21 October Road, an Aidid guerrilla stronghold and scene of most of the recent attacks against UN troops. Pakistani troops, responsible for policing the southern half of Mogadishu, moved out of their base at an old stadium in three tanks and four armored personnel carriers, together with an American bulldozer, in an attempt to remove road barricades erected by Somalis five days ago.
>
> The unit came under intense fire shortly after leaving its base. Somali gunmen hit one tank and set it ablaze with an anti-tank round, and the two remaining Pakistani tanks fired at guerrilla positions. It was the first time tanks had been used in battle in the capital since June 17, when UN troops attacked Aidid's headquarters compound and chased the warlord into hiding. Today was also the first time the Somalis have succeeded in destroying a tank with their anti-tank weapons.
>
> In the initial phase of the battle, two American soldiers working with the bulldozer crew were hit by gunfire. They were reported to be in stable condition.

> 'The Somalis attempted to commandeer the bulldozer, but two US Cobra helicopters fired TOW antitank missiles and destroyed it,' said US Army Major David Stockwell, the UN military spokesman.
>
> After about an hour of fighting, the UN troops ran out of ammunition and were forced to return to their base. The helicopters were in direct communication with the troops on the ground, Stockwell said, but it was not certain how the decision was made to open fire on the attackers, even though women and children were among the combatants. 'This was not a matter done lightly,' Stockwell said. 'This was a last resort in order to save our troops.'
>
> Stockwell went on to say that the two US Cobra helicopters opened fire with their 20mm guns when women and children joined heavily armed militiamen throwing grenades and firing weapons at the UN troops. He said another group of women and children began gathering at a roadblock, threatening UN troops and throwing grenades, and that the Cobras fired down the center of the road to disperse them but did not fire into the people.
>
> Stockwell, in that first report of the incident, said the helicopters decided to open fire on the women and children because, 'From their bird's eye view, it was apparent that the soldiers' lives were in danger. This was a last-ditch, last-resort effort,' Stockwell said. 'It's entirely possible that women and children could have been hit and killed.'
>
> Noting that Aidid has in the past used women and children as human shields for his guerrillas to ambush UN troops, Stockwell said that in this case, the women and children 'became combatants, armed or not.'
>
> Women and children were behind a wall throwing grenades and firing weapons alongside armed militiamen, Stockwell said. All the women and children likely hit by the US fire were among the group behind the wall and were armed combatants. 'They were engaging with arms and grenades.' The gravity of the Pakistani troops' situation can only be judged by those present. Their rescue from a very hostile armed crowd required an immediate and firm solution. The UN/US had aircraft at their disposal and their use was, at the time, considered to be the only viable option.

War, in any of its forms, is a cruel, brutal business. In this case, which was determined to be a matter of life or death for the Pakistani soldiers, it was reasonable to apply whatever force was required to save them. From a public relations/political standpoint, the use of overwhelming aerial firepower was problematic. However, from a military point of view it was an effective solution to a dire situation. Keith Richburg concluded his graphic report by harking back to earlier incidents that served to emphasise how confusing the Somali situation had become.

> The incident resembles several other recent cases where Aidid's militiamen have used women and children as cover during engagements with UN forces. On June 4, when two dozen Pakistani soldiers were killed in an ambush, women and children first closed in on Pakistanis at a feeding center, while hidden gunmen opened fire from nearby rooftops.
>
> On June 13, Pakistani troops drew widespread international outrage when they opened fire on women and children who were besieging their stronghold, although UN officials said there were gunmen in the crowd who had fired first.[16]

There were reports of great loss of life among Somalis on 9 September and a conveniently round figure of 200 was floated as the number of Somali dead. Although that figure was never verified, the loss of any life on either side was to be deplored. However, the unpalatable fact was that this conflict was accelerating in pace, the violence was growing more intense, and to a degree that a UN peacekeeping force had been obliged to fire on civilians. General Colin Powell, commenting later on his preparation for Operation DESERT STORM, observed:

> Air strikes are so tempting, so swift, so seemingly surgical. We might be able to win a war by air although so far, no one had. 'The trouble with air power', I had warned the president, 'is that you leave the initiative in the hands of the enemy. He gets to decide when he has had enough.'[17]

It was blindingly obvious that the mission to capture Aidid had failed and that UN forces were bogged down in a protracted and probably unwinnable conflict. The UN was now on a downward spiral and observers were at a loss to see how it could possibly achieve any of its aims when its forces were fighting for their lives.

The situation was not just Somalis versus the UN because it was reported by Agence France-Presse (AFP) that on 10 September there were firefights between the Habar Gidir and Hawadle clans in the south of the capital.

Chapter 11

Tanks and Rocket-Propelled Grenades

Admiral Howe and Lieutenant General Bir were confident that, given effective intelligence, the US Army's 1st Special Forces Operational Detachment-Delta (Delta Force), when teamed with the Quick Reaction Force, would lead to the capture of Aidid. The forces they assembled and designated Task Force Ranger. To complete the team a small CIA intelligence team, already in station, were co-opted. The organisation was led by Major General William Garrison, who had commanded Joint Special Operations Command (JSOC) since 1992.

To add to the mix, the Italian Minister of Defence condemned the UN actions in Somalia, on 9 September, by denouncing them as the destruction of Mogadishu. He averred that (translation) 'Firing on the crowd is the very antithesis of the humanitarian mission.'[1] He was quite correct, but the humanitarian mission had been unviable for some time. The UN's residual humanitarian mission was thwarted by Aidid's SNA, which controlled large portions of the city and often blocked or diverted aid shipments. The UN's inability to secure the city was a major failure.

The UN's original goals were to alleviate famine and restore stability. The famine had been curtailed but stability in Somalia was now no more than a UN pipe dream. The killing of people going about their business in a peaceful manner on Bloody Monday assured all members of the UN force the enmity of the entire Habar Gidir clan and, as a direct result, thereafter other clans showed increasing sympathy for Aidid's aims.

There was no discernible change in UN tactics as its soldiers continued to pursue the SNA and, on 14 September, enjoyed some success when they arrested two colonels in General Aidid's militia. The following day, the UN Security Council unanimously passed yet another resolution. This was Resolution 865, and it promulgated a policy of ending UNOSOM operations, in Somalia, by March 1995. It directed the Secretary-General to 'advance the process of national reconciliation and political rule and take the necessary steps toward the restoration of the police, judicial and penal systems'.[2] To those soldiers deep into a vicious guerrilla war, these well-meaning resolutions, passed by people thousands of miles away from the abject misery of Somalia and its people, merely added to their scepticism.

A week later, on 21 September, US soldiers captured four SNA personnel in Mogadishu. These included Osman Hassan Ali ('Osman Ato'), General Aidid's chief financier. Osman Ato was suspected of having orchestrated the massacre of the twenty-four Pakistani peacekeepers on 5 June and was held in administrative detention under UN Security Council resolution 837. This authorised soldiers 'to use force to capture those involved in the massacre of 5 June'.[3] Ato was captured by US Rangers at a location near Digfer Hospital. Lieutenant Colonel William Boykin, responsible for the operation, recounted, 'There was a man in Mogadishu named Osman Ato. He went on CNN, and he laughed at us, and he said, "They'll never get me because Allah will protect me."' The arrest was later portrayed in the 2001 film *Black Hawk Down*.[4]

Despite this minor success, Montgomery was still concerned at his deficiency in armoured vehicles in that he had 'only had eight tanks in Mogadishu. ... They were old American tanks that had been given to the Pakistanis, and of those only four were operational.'[5] His request for armoured support was considered by Aspin, the Secretary of Defense, who consulted Powell, the Chairman of the JCS.

The request was rejected.

The reason for the rejection was entirely political and calculated to avoid causing a stir in Congress and to avoid 'mission creep'.[6] Powell asked Aspin to reconsider because he understood that Montgomery was concerned about the safety of his men. Nevertheless, Aspin stuck to his decision, notwithstanding his being made aware that US light infantry troops, equipped with Humvees and trucks, had inadequate defences against mine warfare and, specifically, rocket-propelled grenades. RPGs were more usually employed against armour, but there could be no doubt how very vulnerable helicopters and relatively soft skinned vehicles were to this weapon.

* * *

The term 'rocket-propelled grenade' is from the Russian acronym РПГ (Ручной Противотанковый Гранатомёт, *Ruchnoy Protivotankovy*

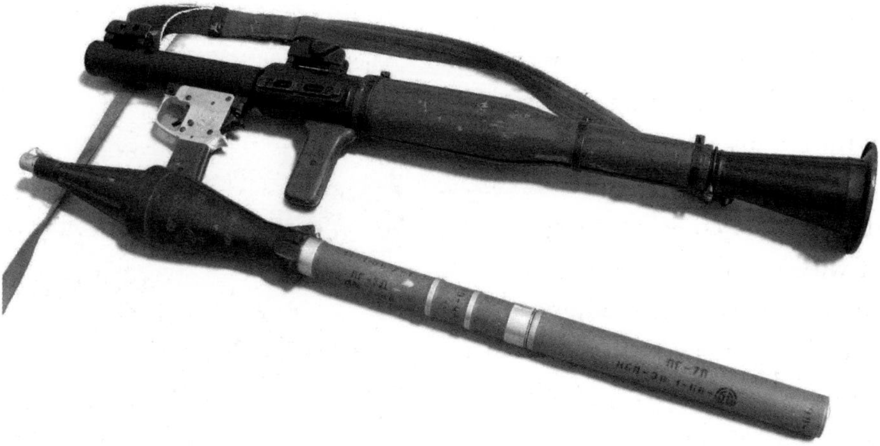

The RPG has two components. These are the launcher, pictured at the top, and the warhead below. The long tail of the warhead slides inside the launcher mechanism.

Granatomyot), meaning 'hand-held anti-tank grenade launcher', the name given to early Russian designs.[7]

A rocket-propelled grenade weighs about 15lb (6.8kg) and is a weapon carried by an individual soldier. It fires a high-explosive, anti-tank (HEAT) warhead discharged from the shoulder. It is an ideal weapon with which to engage vehicles, including tanks. Helicopters that are stationary at the 'hover' are particularly vulnerable. An RPG is most effective when engaging targets within 218 yards (200m).

The grenade is fitted with fins that stabilise it in flight. Some early model RPGs were single use, but reloadable variants were available in 1993.

The antecedents to the RPG can be traced back to the turn of the twentieth century when the value of the 'shaped charge' was first recognised. The charge is constructed with a conical hollow and this serves to concentrate the energy of the weapon on the impact point.[8]

The only countermeasure that can be taken against RPGs is to identify the individual armed with the bulky weapon, one difficult to conceal, and to eliminate him before he can bring the weapon to bear.

* * *

The increasingly widespread scepticism about the UN's activities in Somalia was manifested by the French humanitarian organisation Médecins Sans Frontières, which voted with its feet. On 27 September, it abandoned Somalia to its fate. The highly respected medical organisation voiced stringent criticism of the UN for favouring military action at the expense of humanitarian work.[9]

Major General William F. Garrison (1944–), the planner and leader of Operation GOTHIC SERPENT.

The turmoil in Somalia had created thousands of homeless refugees, many of whom fled across the border into Kenya. 'Africa Rights', a humanitarian and human rights organisation, observed that many of the refugees were ill-treated in Kenya and accused the Kenyan Government of failing to prevent the high level of violations suffered by Somali refugees in Kenya, especially women, 'thousands of whom have been raped'. Africa Rights also condemned the attitude of the UNHCR.

It was against this unremittingly bleak background that Major General William Garrison planned and implemented his operations to capture Aidid that culminated in Operation GOTHIC SERPENT.

The UN and US forces either deployed or available to support the operation were comprehensive. However, in the event it was a predominantly US Army operation, and only 160 personnel were in the initial assault. Nevertheless, readily available was a vast force, thousands strong. It was composed of:

US Ranger Task Force

- C Squadron, 1st Special Forces Operational Detachment-Delta (1st SFOD-D) – also known as Delta Force[10]
- Bravo Company, 3rd Ranger Battalion, 75th Ranger Regiment
- 1st Battalion, 160th Special Operations Aviation Regiment (Airborne) (the Night Stalkers) with MH-6, and AH-6 Little Birds and MH-60 Black Hawks.
- Combat Controllers and Pararescuemen from 24th Special Tactics Squadron[11]
- US Navy SEALs – Naval Special Warfare Development Group
- CVN-72 USS *Abraham Lincoln* and Carrier Air Wing 11[12]

- Amphibious Squadron 5 USS *New Orleans*, *Denver*, *Comstock* and *Cayuga*
- BLT 1/9 Battalion Landing Team 1st Battalion/9th Marines/13th Marine Expeditionary Unit
- USS *New Orleans* LPH-11 Amphibious Group

US 10th Mountain Division

- 2nd Battalion, 25th Aviation Regiment
- 1st Battalion, 22nd Infantry Regiment
- 2nd Battalion, 14th Infantry Regiment
- 3rd platoon, C Company, 1st Battalion, 87th Infantry Regiment
- 41st Engineer Battalion

Pakistan Army

- 15th Battalion, Frontier Force Regiment[13]
- 7th Battalion, Frontier Force
- 19th Lancers
- 10th Battalion, Baloch Regiment
- 977 Military Police Company

Malayan Army

- 19th Battalion, Royal Malay
- 11th Regiment, Grup Gerak Khas.

Chapter 12

The Plan

Every great operation of war is unique ... there is no surer road to disaster than to imitate the plans of bygone heroes and fit them to novel situations.

W.S. Churchill, *Marlborough*, 1933–38

Wherever in the world a military officer plans an operation, he applies his hard-earned military common sense to the matter. In the British Army, it is termed 'appreciating the situation'. This is a rather overblown description of a simple mental process in which the multiple factors that might have an effect on the operation are weighed, judged and given an appropriate degree of priority. These factors could be reduced to writing but often aren't, and the appreciation is 'done on the hoof', so to speak.

The officer would first select his aim.

It should be singular, achievable and readily understood by his soldiers. Everything thereafter flows from this selected aim. The planner must now consider his own force – its numbers, morale, equipment, armament. These details will not detain him, and he will move on to give thought to the terrain, the weather, the light, timings, his transport, casualty evacuation, logistic issues – food, water, ammunition, medical support, maps, location and strength of units in support, and many others, factors germane to his situation. There are no rules; he can ignore anything if he thinks it is irrelevant.

At this stage, he turns a metaphorical page and assesses his enemy. What intelligence on them is available? How reliable is this intelligence? He must know his enemy's perceived aim, where they are, how many of them, how they are organised and how they are armed. What are key points in the ground they hold, how strong is their morale, how competent their leadership? Is there a local population? If there is, are they likely to participate and, if so, who will they support?

This side of the equation is no more than a series of well-informed estimates. Nevertheless, although a general may not have all the answers, he should have posed all the questions and made his judgement on the best information available.

Napoleon said, 'A battle sometimes decides everything and sometimes the most trifling thing decides the fate of the battle.'[1] He was correct, and in Somalia, a forthcoming battle would indeed decide everything.

* * *

General Garrison had conducted his 'appreciation' weeks before. Since then, his Task Force Ranger had conducted operations, all with the intention of capturing Aidid, although by now repetitive failure had caused the aim to be extended to the capture of his close adherents. CWO 3 Michael Durant, who flew a Black Hawk, observed:

> The Mission profile wasn't new. We'd practiced it more times than I could count and had already executed it six times inside the city, three at night and three in daylight. We hadn't encountered much resistance, just some inaccurate small-arms fire and a few Rocket Propelled Grenade rounds, but no aircraft had been damaged, and no ground troops seriously injured. It was like a well-rehearsed ballet of zipping helos and lightning infantry. First, Little Bird gunships would take out any heavy weapons at the target. Next, Wolcott's assault flight would take in the Delta operators to make the snatch. Just behind them, I would bring in my Rangers as the blocking force, and then the entire Task Force would withdraw with its shocked and blindfolded prisoners. The only factors that differed with each of these missions were the target details: Who, Where and When.[2]

Notwithstanding Durant's summation of the TFR missions, they had not gone well from the very first. When the TFR assaulted a suspect building and, therein, arrested a group of men – who turned out to be UNOSOM II employees, albeit engaged in nefarious black-market activity – the US press seized on the story and heaped derision on Garrison and his men.

The six operations had an inevitable 'sameness' about them, something that had been noted by the opposition. The Somalia National Alliance was aware that the TFR was either inserted from the air and evacuated on the ground or inserted and extracted on the ground. The transport variants had little discernible benefit. Significantly, and hitherto, all assaults had been aimed at targets *outside* the city centre and had been conducted with such speed that there had been no negative response by the local population. As Durant indicated, a significant plus from these unsatisfactory operations was that all the TFR participants were well rehearsed in their role and could respond very quickly, when given the nod.

The guerrilla activity of the SNA in Mogadishu was directed by Colonel Sharif Hassan Giumale, who was designated Deputy Commander of the SNA High Commission on Defence. He was a seasoned soldier and, after training at a Russian military academy, had continued his military education in Italy. He had seen active service during the Ogaden War with Ethiopia and during the recent civil war. As a commander of guerrilla soldiers, he took his lead from those who had conducted successful operations – not least the Vietnamese. China was another source of tactical wisdom. Among the SNA ranks were mujahideen who had served during the Russian–Afghan war; their valuable experience was turned to advantage by Hassan.[3]

The SNA had organised South Mogadishu into eighteen military sectors. Each of these had its own command structure and was equipped with radio communications. The SNA 'soldiers' lived in Mogadishu and knew its layout backwards – it was their home, and many had been born in the city. There was in place a polished mobilisation plan that, when implemented, would allow the assembly of large numbers of SNA militants anywhere in Mogadishu, within half an hour.

The commander, Colonel Sharif Hassan Giumale, had of course analysed all the TFR raids, and for the future, he sought to employ the tactics that had been successful elsewhere in the world. He noted the way that the Farabundo Martí National Liberation Front (FLMN) in El Salvador had developed the use of small arms against aircraft and particularly helicopters. The colonel was only too aware that the US forces depended on speed to obviate any interference by the population. He concluded that he had to counter that, either by slowing the Americans down or speeding up the assembly of his forces. Military appreciations really are just the application of common sense, and although Sharif Hassan Giumale was not a Somali manifestation of Clausewitz, he was nevertheless a capable and resolute adversary.

The Americans had overwhelming force at their disposal and one of their greatest assets was their command of the air. They were able to commit a plethora of helicopters to roam constantly over Mogadishu. However, a slow-moving or hovering helicopter provided a juicy target for RPGs, of which Colonel Sharif Hassan Giumale had an ample supply. It was evident that an RPG strike on a helicopter would bring it down and that the Americans would then make every effort to rescue any survivors from that crashed aircraft.

At 0200 hrs on 25 September – a week before the Battle of Mogadishu – the SNA used an RPG to shoot down a Black Hawk (call sign Courage Five-Three) while it was on patrol above Mogadishu.[4] The pilots were able to fly their burning aircraft away from Aidid's territory and make a crash-landing. The pilot and co-pilot survived, but three crewmembers were killed. A minor battle ensued as Pakistani peacekeepers fought their way to the helicopter. The event was a propaganda victory for the SNA.[5] The UNOSOM II spokesman in Mogadishu, US Army Major David Stockwell, referred to the downing as 'a very lucky shot'.[6]

> The loss of a helicopter had not been unanticipated [*sic*] by Major General William F. Garrison, commander of the task force. Ten days earlier, on the coast south of Mogadishu, Delta commandos had rehearsed a scenario in which a Black Hawk was downed, the pilot and co-pilot were killed, and the four injured men in back needed to be rescued. By [what turned out to be an] eerie coincidence, the helicopter used in that exercise was *Super Six-One.*[7]

The SNA had a plan to implement if, and when, it managed to shoot down another helicopter. The American route to the crash site would be ringed by barricades of burning tyres, with ambushes laid and ready to counter any US/UNOSOM ground forays.[8]

It is a characteristic of the US Armed Forces that its members, given constant assurance of their very high quality and with unlimited logistic support, assume that they have tactical and moral superiority over any enemy. This is a by-product of the systematic indoctrination of Americans from childhood. Not least of the effects of this system is the production of widespread, ingrained arrogance. In this case, the Somali commander had seen ample evidence of the arrogance of his adversary and intended to exploit, first, the American underestimation of the forces that opposed them and, second, the lethal effect of an RPG.

In about 500 BC, Sun Tzu was a Chinese general, military strategist and philosopher. He is credited as the author of *The Art of War* and over the last 2,500 years, the book has influenced military men who care to read it. General Garrison is probably one of those who did *not* read it, because Sun Tzu advised:

> Do not repeat the tactics by which have gained you one victory, but let your methods be regulated by the infinite variety of circumstances.[9]

To be fair to Garrison, the circumstances in which he would have to commit his troops were limited and he could only react to a reported enemy gathering. Curiously, this gave Aidid the unconscious initiative. Hitherto, TFR had not operated in the city centre of Mogadishu.

For the activity of TFR to be successful, it was completely dependent on the quality of the intelligence it received. However, what passed for 'intelligence' in Somalia was invariably little more than rumour or speculation. The CIA-led intelligence gathering had proved to be ineffective.

A measure of the intelligence on offer was that, on one occasion, a local agent reported that Aidid was a passenger in a three-car convoy. The surveillance aircraft with their sophisticated equipment did not confirm the existence of any such convoy and the TFR, straining at the leash, was stood down.

On 14 September, the assault force was launched, merely on the basis that a Ranger *thought* he had seen Aidid in a car outside the Italian Embassy – perhaps he was just passing by? Consequently, the fast ropers attacked the home of a General Ahmed Jilao and took thirty-eight baffled Somalis prisoner. General Jilao was violently anti-Aidid and a firm supporter of UNOSOM II. It was all very embarrassing and abject apologies followed. Robert Gosende, a US official, contacted his masters in Washington and, later, explained:

> We understand that some damages to the premises took place. … General Jilao has received apologies from all concerned. We don't know if the person mistaken for General Aidid was General Jilao. It would be hard to confuse him with Aidid. Jilao is approximately ten inches taller than Aidid. Aidid is very dark. Jilao has a much lighter complexion Aidid is slim and has sharp Semitic-like features. Jilao is overweight and has a round face. We are very concerned that this episode might find its way into the press.[10]

Of course, the debacle was reported in the press, to the embarrassment of all concerned, not the least of whom was Garrison, for whom inaccurate intelligence was worse than no intelligence at all. Garrison vented his frustration in a signal he sent to his commander, General Joseph Hoar:

> As a result of this, we have experienced some weariness between the local (spy ring) and the Task Force. Generally, the local (spy ring) appears to believe that a second-hand report from an individual who is not a member of the team should be sufficient to constitute current intelligence. I do not. Furthermore, when a local (spy ring) is reporting something that is totally different to what our helicopters are seeing (which we watch back here at the JOC) I naturally weigh the launch decision toward what we actually see versus what is being reported. Events such as last night, with Team 2 stating that Aidid had just left the compound in a three-vehicle convoy. I knew for a fact that that no vehicles left the compound. This tends to lower our confidence level even more.[11]

This lack of confidence would cause Garrison to be more cautious in future. He would require a fortuitous set of confirmed circumstances before he would implement any further operation. Over recent weeks, there had been any number of false alarms and usually, after broiling in the sun waiting for code word IRENE, the operation would be called off, to the frustration and irritation of all.

The high probability was that there would be many more aborted missions in the future. Nevertheless, Garrison's troops were kept continuously at very short notice, and they were primed and ready to go into action on receipt of the code word. The likelihood was that their objective, when firmly identified, would be somewhere in Mogadishu.

Mogadishu, the unlovely capital of Somalia, was composed of a labyrinth of narrow, dirty streets filled with rubbish and burned-out vehicles. In places there were the remains of burned vehicle tyres. Remnants of electricity and telephone wire hung from telegraph poles. The city was unremittingly bleak, it epitomised the Third World and exuded poverty in all its forms.

The buildings bore testament to the ongoing civil strife with their display of bullet marks, broken windows and general disrepair. It was evident that anything of any value had been stripped from abandoned buildings, all fitments such as doors and windows looted and sold. In an earlier time, there had been statues depicting the unloved Siad Barre, but the statuary had long since been reduced to scrap metal and now the plinths stood as mute witnesses to what had once been, briefly, a relatively stable state.

> At night campfires glowed from the third and fourth storey windows of the old Polytechnic Institute. Every open space was clotted with the makeshift villages of the disinherited, round stick huts covered with layers of rags and shacks made of scavenged scraps of wood and patches of rusted tin. From above they looked like an advanced stage of some festering urban rot.[12]

The population of this place was largely of clan Habar Gidir and most, if not all, of these supported Aidid's Somalia National Alliance. Nevertheless, and regardless of their clan, there was almost unanimous hatred of the United States of America – an emotion entirely generated by the brutal and ruthless conduct of American forces earlier in the year when, on Black Monday, they had killed uncounted numbers of Somalis.

Unattractive though it was, Mogadishu was where the SNA conducted its business. At 1350 hrs on the afternoon of 3 October 1993, it was reported by a Somali agent who worked for the CIA that senior members of the Habar Gidir and SNA were to meet in a building near the Olympic Hotel in the Bakaara Market district of Mogadishu, the very centre of the city. It was known as the 'Black Sea area' for no perceivable reason.

The meeting would commence at about 1500 hrs and among the attendees were two men closely connected to Aidid. They were Omar Salad Elmi and Mohamed Hassan Awale, and were of particular interest. The TFR wanted to join the party, and so this was not an opportunity to be missed.

Omar Salad Elmi – one of the two targets. Photo of Abdi Qeybdiid Hasan Awale on page 75.

Immediately before the operation there was the usual briefing and, at that, one participant remarked to General Garrison that he 'had some exfil issues'. Asked to explain, the officer replied, 'Okay, air exfiltration is not an option, so we're forced to use the ground convoy. But I think we might wrap it up long before the vehicles are in position.' Lieutenant Colonel Danny McKnight, who would be commanding that convoy, assured the room that he and his vehicles would be in place and on time when required. The consensus was that a rooftop exfiltration was simply not practical and an extraction by road, although unattractive, was the only viable option.[13]

A priority was to establish in which the building this meeting was to take place. That critical function rested on the shoulders of the CIA agent. This man was instructed to drive to the Olympic Hotel, park and, feigning a problem with the vehicle, raise the bonnet. This pause would give the surveillance aircraft sufficient time to identify the agent and his vehicle. However, obviously beset by perfectly reasonable anxiety, the agent hastened his actions, and the necessary identification could not be made in the short time frame he had provided.

The agent was equipped with a small radio strapped to his leg and through this device, he was promptly ordered to repeat the process. However, this time he was to drive straight to the objective. The agent entered Hawlwadig Road, drove north and stopped outside a building next to the hotel. Unfortunately, he had lost his nerve and was well short of the anticipated meeting place. The agent was being watched from above and by Garrison, on a screen, in his headquarters some 3 miles away.

The agent's failure was quickly appreciated and seen to be potentially disastrous. In Garrison's headquarters there was a hasty rethink and the agent was told to have a third attempt. This time he got it right and drove further up the street, went past the hotel and stopped about a block north of the hostelry. This was a building that Salad had been seen entering earlier

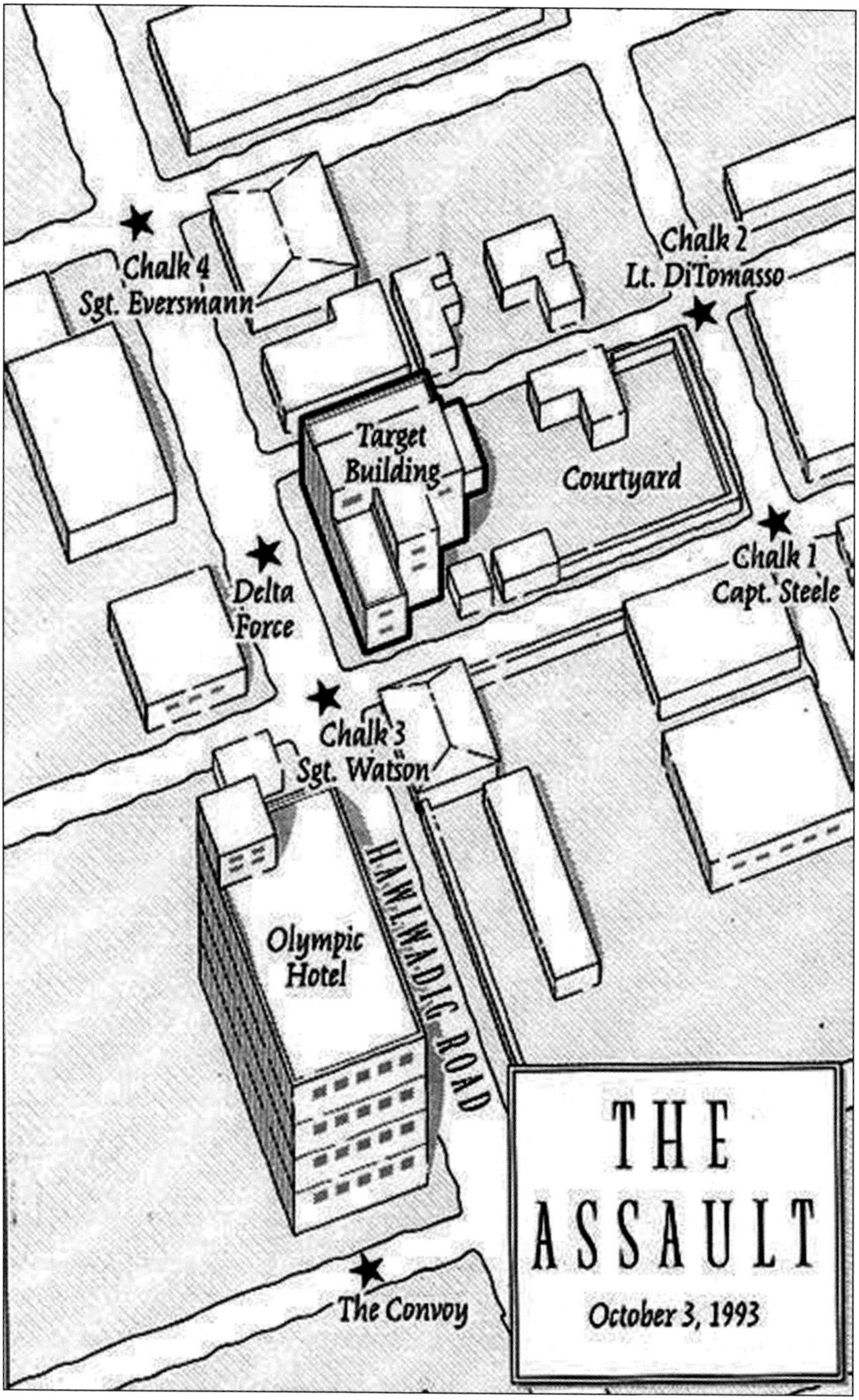
Chalk 4
Sgt. Eversmann
Chalk 2
Lt. DiTomasso
Target
Building
Courtyard
Delta
Force
Chalk 1
Capt. Steele
Chalk 3
Sgt. Watson
HAWLWADIG ROAD
Olympic
Hotel
The Convoy
THE
ASSAULT
October 3, 1993

(*Bowden*)

in the day. Given that Omar Salad Elmi had been spotted at this address, the agent's activity had been confirmatory in nature.

It now seemed that Garrison 'had all his ducks in a row' and so he advised Montgomery that he was about to initiate his operation but first needed confirmation that there were no UN staff or NGOs anywhere in the immediate area. He did not want to replicate earlier blunders. Montgomery included among his responsibilities command of the US 10th Mountain Division's Quick Reaction Force; he directed the commanding officer of the 2nd Battalion, 14th Infantry Regiment, a component of that division, to place one company, about 100 men, on 'standby'.

General Garrison considered how best he might exploit this latest, attractive situation. Although time was very short, his force was nevertheless ready to go. The operation, now called GOTHIC SERPENT, would take place in the centre of the city of Mogadishu – a teeming metropolis firmly controlled by the SNA.

This was the military equivalent of poking a ferocious tiger with a sharp stick. Garrison was a capable officer, fully aware of the potential for disaster, and in a memo to his boss, General Hoar, he had observed, 'There is no place in Mogadishu we cannot go and be successful in a fight. There are plenty of places we can go and be stupid.'[14] Garrison's plan was to be carried out in three phases – on receipt of the code word IRENE.

- **First phase:** Deliver cordon parties at four points around the target building and insert the Delta team to snatch the two Aidid lieutenants.
- **Second phase:** Concurrently – initiate the road convoy *en route* to the target building.
- **Third Phase:** Evacuate all participants and prisoners by road.

All very simple, but for success it depended upon each of the component parts of the American force achieving their aim swiftly and in sequence. The critical features of all Special Force operations are shock, speed and unhindered violence. The enemy must be denied the opportunity to think and the time and opportunity to react.

It was presumed that the energy and speed of the assault would negate any SNA response. Accordingly, a response was not expected nor planned for.

Bravo Company, 3rd Battalion, 75th Ranger Regiment supplemented by Delta Force soldiers were the assault force on 3 October 1993.

About an hour after Garrison was alerted, members of the Habar Gidir and the two senior SNA leaders came together at a house in central Mogadishu.

An hour and a half after the CIA warning, at 1532 hrs on 3 October, GOTHIC SERPENT was launched.

Boeing AH-6 Little Birds.

Chapter 13

Assault

GOTHIC SERPENT would involve four AH-6 Little Birds, formidable aircraft despite their size, and unusually, for this mission the two-seater helicopters were armed with rockets. A variant of this aircraft was the MH-6, which was specifically designed around the requirements of US Special Forces; they had 'benches mounted on both sides for delivering the spearhead of the assault force'.[1] There were four of these allocated to the Delta snatch squad.

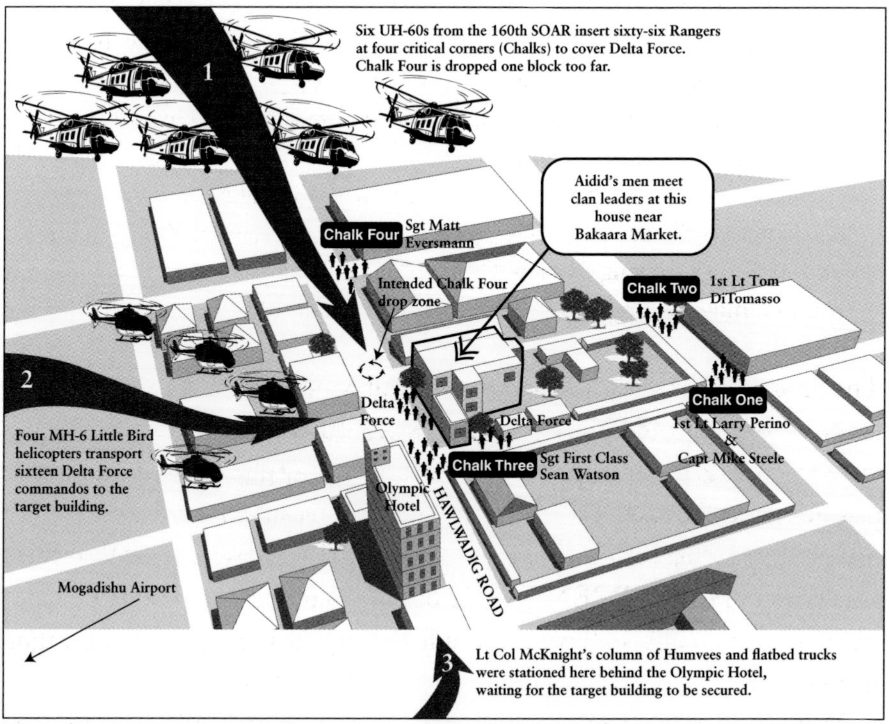

(*Diagram based on an original by Akhil Kadidal*)

Eight troop-carrying Black Hawks bore the bulk of the force. Two of them carried Delta and their ground command team and four were allocated to Bravo Company 3rd/75th Ranger Battalion. One transported the Combat Search and Rescue team. The eighth Black Hawk was allocated to two lieutenant colonels. One, Tom Matthews, was the air commander and responsible for coordinating the missions of his 160th Special Operations Aviation regiment (SOAR). The other was Gary Harrell, who was the ground commander.

The Black Hawk helicopter was a state-of-the-art aircraft and CW3 Michael Durant, who flew one, commented:

> The Black Hawks in Somalia were that latest Sikorsky model; twin engines MH-60L with myriad Special mission equipment. Under the right conditions, they were capable of 193 knots and a service ceiling in excess of 20,000 feet [6,096m]. But with our load of eighteen Rangers and four crewmen, the best we could do was about 160 knots. The Black Hawk became the work horse of army aviation, with the capability to haul 9,000lb of external payload on the cargo hook or the equivalent amount of cargo inside. It could be set up for a wide variety of missions and, in Somalia, we were configured to carry the maximum number of troops.
>
> We could also be called upon to fly our Black Hawks in an attack helicopter profile using them as a gun platform … we [had] 19-shot 2.75-inch rocket pod, a wing-mounted 30mm M-230 chain gun and two 7.62mm window-mounted mini-guns all fixed forward.[2]

The ground convoy was a separate and vital component of the force. It was made up of nine wide-bodied Humvees and three 5-ton trucks. The latter were to provide the transport for the evacuation of the as yet unnumbered prisoners and the assault force. Three OH-58 surveillance helicopters were patrolling overhead and above them flew a P3 Orion spy plane. With these assets, GOTHIC SERPENT would be recorded in graphic detail on video and Garrison and his staff would be able to view the passage of the operation in real time.

William Garrison was a capable and experienced officer. He was admired and respected by his soldiers, who relished his easy manner and evident empathy. Garrison was a 'soldier's officer'. There is no higher accolade.

As the convoy sat restlessly waiting for IRENE, General Garrison wandered down the line showing his face and speaking, albeit briefly, with as many of his soldiers as possible. To a soldier, any soldier, a kind and encouraging word from a senior officer, especially at a tension-packed time such as this, was to be treasured. His interface with his men that afternoon was important to them, and it was a measure of his leadership style.

It was the intention that the troops being carried in the Black Hawks should fast-rope down. The Black Hawk was of a size that it could not squeeze into the narrow streets of Mogadishu, and on that basis, some other means had to be employed to deliver the soldiers to the ground.

* * *

Fast-roping is a technique used for evacuating a helicopter by descending a thick rope. The soldier is equipped with thick gloves with which to grasp the rope. He then slides down the rope, checking his progress by adjusting

MH-6M from the 160th Special Operations Aviation Regiment (Airborne) inserts a team of Army Rangers atop a building using the Fast-Rope Insertion/Extraction System (FRIES). (*PFC Gabriel Segura US Army*)

his grip on the rope. He can also gain greater control by gripping the rope with his feet.

Using this technique, several soldiers can leave the aircraft in quick succession providing that they leave a gap of about 10 feet (3m) between them. Fast-roping is quicker than abseiling/rappelling although it is hazardous, and the greater the soldier's burden, the greater the difficulty to control the rate of descent.

The British were the first to use fast-roping during the Falklands War in 1983. The system was introduced after consultation with British rope manufacturer Marlow Ropes. The original rope was made of thick nylon that could be used in a manner similar to a fireman's pole. The employment of fast-roping, now used around the world, has led to the development of custom-made rope. This is usually plaited to produce a rough surface. The special ropes used today are braided (plaited), producing a pattern on the outer circumference that is not smooth and so is easier to grip.[3]

Fast ropers need to use heat-resistant gloves because the friction with the rope produces powerful heat that would make grasping the rope impossible. These very heavy gloves are designed for the sole purpose of protecting the hands and they severely limit normal dexterity. They are discarded after the descent. Just as rope technology has advanced, so too has the design of roping gloves and specialised gloves have been developed for this purpose.

* * *

The code word IRENE was issued at 1532 hrs and it initiated the deployment of 19 aircraft, 12 vehicles and 160 men. The morale of the men was sky-high; they knew they were well trained and had been assured that, being Americans, they were, incomparably, the best and toughest soldiers on the planet.

They aspired to achieve higher standards than other members of the US Army. To a man, they had lean, well-muscled bodies and each had the Ranger's characteristic crew cut, with the sides and back of the head close shaved. They had a tribal ritual in which they greeted a fellow Ranger with the salutation 'Hoo-ah'. Many of them had ambitions to move up the Special Forces' ladder and win selection for Delta. The 'D boys' were the *crème de la crème* and only the exceptional could hope to join their exclusive ranks.

In the meantime, there was the prospect of a firefight very soon, and they were all busting to get to it. The pouches on their load-carrying equipment were stuffed with ammunition, grenades, chocolate, and all the other impedimenta that might just come in handy in the immediate future.

This was going to be only a brief skirmish, lasting an hour or less, and so there was no evident requirement for bayonets or night vision goggles. But there was a need for their water bottles (canteens to an American). This latter piece of equipment held a litre of water. Bowden reported that some soldiers went into action without their water bottle. In a temperate climate this would be foolish, but in a hot climate it is beyond moronic. Water bottle or not, every man still had about 50lb (22.6kg) of equipment – and his personal weapon to carry.

It was 1533 hrs when the helicopters lifted off from the down-at-heel airport and rose into the enchanting scene of the bluest of blue skies from which a shimmering and very hot sun beat down on the beautiful desert

The Black Hawk designated *Super Six-Four*. Piloted by Chief Warrant Officer 3 Michael Durant, over Mogadishu on 3 October 1993.

coastline that fringed the Indian Ocean. The aerial armada followed the coastline and only moments ahead lay Mogadishu and its port. Distance softened the reality of the city's desolation, and it was only the mosques, which had survived the continuing urban civil war and accompanying blight, that rose to greet the incoming force. The flight time was only three minutes.

Each of the four 'chalks'[4] occupied a Black Hawk, and the thirteen men, all in desert fatigues, were crowded into the space alongside the two crew chiefs. The aircraft had been stripped of its seats and the Rangers sat on ammunition boxes or Kevlar mats. It was uncomfortable, but the flight was very short and, at 1542 hrs, the storming of central Mogadishu got under way. The Ranger insertion was being made from a greater height than usual because the helicopters had to be above the roofline of adjacent three-storey houses. This would test the roping gloves to the limit and any pause in descent would be painful, to say the least.

* * *

Below the incoming assault force, the people of Mogadishu realised that something was 'up'. The aerial activity was not unusual, but on 3 October, it seemed to be rather more intense. When the assault commenced there was an immediate response. Colonel Ali Aden's radio came to life and the voice of his commander, Sharif Hassan Giumale, issued his orders to Aden. The 41-year-old was to activate his militia and 'reinforce the western sector'. Giumale added, 'Don't let reinforcements reach the enemy pocket.'[5]

Aden and about forty of his men mounted two elderly trucks and drove off towards the sound of gunfire about a mile away. A group of Aden's militias remained behind with instructions to prepare ambush positions along the likely route that US ground forces would take from the airport and the university.

* * *

Ranger Chalk Four was transported by Black Hawk *Super Six-Seven*, and piloted by CW3 Jeff Niklaus and CW2 Sam Shamp. The chalk was erroneously put down a block north of their intended point. Sergeant

Eversmann realised the mistake and decided to decline the pilot's offer to move them, saying it would take too long and leave the helicopter too exposed. Eversmann's intentions were to move to the planned position once he had consolidated his chalk on the ground, but he was thwarted when the fast-roping of Chalk Four did not go smoothly.

PFC Todd Blackburn, 3rd Battalion, 75th Ranger Regiment – the first US casualty in GOTHIC SERPENT.

Private First Class Todd Blackburn became the first GOTHIC SERPENT casualty. Blackburn had not yet passed through Ranger School but he was nevertheless still a very capable young soldier. It was evident to Eversmann when he got to the ground that Blackburn, when reaching out for the rope, had missed. He had fallen about 70 feet (21m) to the dusty surface of Hawlwadig Road.

Staff Sergeant Matt Eversmann, commander of Chalk Four.

Eversmann's men deployed to cover their designated arcs but Eversmann, the last to exit the aircraft, knelt by Blackburn's side, who was being attended by PFC Mark Good, a medic. However, even to Eversmann's medically untrained eye, it was clear that his comrade was very severely injured. He was making a gurgling sound and bleeding from the mouth. Eversmann, Blackburn and Good were in the middle of the road and the sergeant suddenly realised that they were under fire. With Good's help, the injured man was dragged to the edge of the road to rudimentary cover. His evacuation was now a priority.[6] The intensity of the incoming fire made any move impossible, and Matt Eversmann would have to start his battle from where he was.

Eversmann found to his dismay that his radio operator, PFC Jason Moore, was unable to join the company radio net because, in his descent, he had accidently allowed the wire to his microphone switch to rub on the rope, and the friction had severed it. After a brief but frustrating delay, Eversmann did establish contact with Lieutenant Perino. Two Delta medics, Sergeants First Class (SFC) Kurt Schmid and Bart Bullock, hurried to the scene and, 'The more experienced men quickly began to assist Good; Schmid inserted a tube down Blackburn's throat to help him breathe. Bullock put a needle in the kid's arm and hooked up an IV.'[7]

The two medics were very concerned about Blackburn's condition, and they were unequivocal in their opinions that the injured man had to be evacuated at once. In the meantime, the incoming fire grew in intensity. The small group of people had swelled into a crowd and that crowd was growing at an alarming rate. Gunmen were mixed in with unarmed men, women and children.

* * *

A young Somali, Ali Hassan Mohamed, was a student studying English and Business but, on the afternoon of 3 October, he was managing his father's sweet and snack shop. It was from the shop doorway that he witnessed American soldiers descending from their helicopter. In the distance, Ali could see a group of soldiers drag another from the middle of Hawlwadig Road; this was obviously Eversmann, Good and Blackburn.

Then a helicopter came roaring down the street, at rooftop height, and from it came a sustained burst of automatic fire that raised a cloud of dust as its rounds pulverised the walls.

Ali's younger brother, 15-year-old Abdullahi Hassan Mohamed, was standing outside by the gate to the property. The burst of fire engulfed Abdullahi and he died instantly. He was an uncommitted spectator, little more than a child. At that point, Ali too was only a spectator, but the death of his brother changed that.

Ali ran away from the scene of his brother's death no longer a spectator but a young man intent on exacting revenge on these foreign invaders. 'People were scrambling everywhere, racing around dead people and dead animals. Some who were running went toward the fight, others ran away from it.'[8]

Confusion was the common factor, and this was exacerbated by the roar of the aircraft and the incessant crack of small arms fire. The citizens of Mogadishu had no idea why this massively lethal incursion was taking place. Aidid sent his militia men on to the streets with megaphones through which they encouraged Somalis to 'come out and defend your homes'.[9] Many, including Ali, needed no encouragement and there was a general thirst for American blood. Ali, like most male Somalis, owned a gun, an AK-47. He retrieved the weapon from the house of a friend and then joined up with a group of his contemporaries.

Untrained but enthusiastic, they positioned themselves in the rear of the hotel and, from behind a wall, they would discharge bursts of unaimed fire in the general direction of the American soldiers. Inevitably, they drew attention to themselves. Adan Warsawe, one of the group, stepped out from behind cover. He paid for his indiscretion with his life when a Ranger fired a single well-aimed round. Warsawe's life ebbed away in the dusty street from the hideous exit wound in his back.

* * *

The convoy was wending its way towards the pick-up point, but it took a wrong turn. The timing of the operation required the convoy to arrive just after Delta had taken the prisoners, but now the convoy was running, vital minutes, late. Sergeant Jeff Struecker, who was in the leading Humvee, assured Sergeant Bob Gallagher over the radio that they were on their way.

The composition of the convoy was four Humvees followed by three trucks and then the last five Humvees. This was a unit that could not be turned and a wrong turn called for the quick calculation of a new route. Struecker was intent on getting back on track when, at 1558 hrs, an RPG hit and destroyed one of the three 5-ton trucks – an ominous precursor of what was to follow.

The convoy was planned to be available to receive the prisoners just as soon as the Delta team had secured them. This was an element in the overarching need for speed. However, the convoy had to cope with hostile Somali citizens and the SNA militia who were already building barricades along Mogadishu's streets with anything available, including rocks, wreckage, rubbish and burning tyres. The convoy arrived at the Olympic Hotel, close to the target building, about ten minutes late. It was now ready to load up the captives.

General Garrison was watching the progress of his soldiers, on a screen, in his headquarters about 3 miles away. He realised that even this brief delay had caused his operation to lose some of its impetus.

* * *

When the convoy finally hove into view, Eversmann made several attempts to get a Humvee to Blackburn, but they came to naught. Two members of Eversmann's chalk, Sergeants Casey Joyce and Jeff McLaughlin, were called to assist. A foldable stretcher was produced, Blackburn was moved very gently onto it and the four men, Joyce, McLaughlin, Bullock and Schmid, lifted the injured man and set off for the distant convoy. Good ran alongside holding up the IV bag. The party moved as quickly as possible but, at intervals, had to lay their burden down to return fire. Schmid was in no doubt, and he said, 'We've got to get those Humvees to come to us … We keep picking him up and putting him down like this and we're going to kill him.'[10] Casey Joyce, to his great credit, responded by leaving the group and sprinting towards the distant Humvees, intent on bringing one to Blackburn's side.

At 1542 hrs, and just previously, the Delta element had landed in their first two Little Birds just south of the target on a narrow alley. Their rotors kicked up an all-enveloping dust, sand and rubbish storm so thick that visibility was only a few feet. It was an unexpected hazard. The third Little Bird managed to land on Hawlwadig Road right outside the target. The team in the fourth Little Bird, led by SFC Norman Hooten, were unable to see the ground through the dust and dropped a rope – they then discovered that 'they were only a foot off the ground'.[11]

Hooten and his men had just joined a flourishing firefight, but the very poor small arms skill of the SNA only resulted in a great deal of ineffective shooting in the general direction of the American invaders. In comparison, the TFR were all skilled marksmen, and their return fire was lethally effective. The Somali body count started to rise.

The Delta operatives, led by SFC Matt Rierson, moved very quickly, dispensing flashbang (percussion) grenades along the way. They passed through a courtyard, pushed open a gate and gained access to the house. SFC Paul Howe and three men entered the target building from the southern courtyard to find that Rierson had wasted no time and already had twenty-four Somali men prone on the floor. Among the captives were the two prime objects of the operation. The two men of particular interest had every cause to be surprised at their being targeted, because the SNA view was that it was only Aidid who was at risk. It was now 1602 hrs.

SFC Paul Howe and his team had been the last to arrive and, after surveying the scene, Howe asked if the upper floor had been cleared. On being told it had not, he led his team up the stairs and they cleared the rooms, one by one, in the approved manner – all were empty. Then, through one of the windows, a burst of machine-gun fire peppered the ceiling and wall. It was 'friendly fire', but just as lethal for all that. Clearly, this was the work of someone who had seen movement in the room but had not identified his target as comrades.

The incident served to reinforce Howe's distain for non-Delta members of the US Army. It is a characteristic of most, if not all, armies for those who consider themselves to be part of an 'elite' to hold in low regard those who do not share their distinction; this is usually the rest of their particular army. The Rangers were one such elite, but not nearly as elite as Delta, and there was a huge professional gap between Rangers and Delta. Not all of the aspiring Delta candidates was assured of success and only about 10 per cent of Ranger applicants were accepted for Delta training.

Howe's team moved quickly to clear the building's flat roof. There they were once again fired upon, and they identified the weapon being used against them as American. They took cover behind a decorative perimeter wall. It was only after Howe had contacted Captain Scott Miller, his commanding officer and the Delta commander, that the 'friendly' fire ceased.[12]

* * *

After the operation, this friendly fire incident was investigated, and it was thought that the fire had come from a member of Chalk Two, commanded by Lieutenant DiTomasso and including Staff Sergeant Steven Lycopolus. Lycopolus admitted that one of his team was responsible but refused to name him when asked to do so by Captain Steele, his commanding officer. Steele said, 'Then you will have to accept the responsibility.'

Lycopolus agreed and, on the face of it, his conduct was a demonstration of loyalty to his subordinates and firm leadership. However, Bowden pointed out that the staff sergeant was unpopular, and the friendly fire incident was coupled with his later apparent failure to arm a grenade before he threw it. The grenade was, allegedly, the direct cause of several US casualties when the SNA threw an armed grenade in return.

Lycopolus was vehement in his defence and believed he was treated unfairly. He said:

> I threw six grenades in all, the first five exploded, so obviously, with all the stress and excitement I was remembering to pull the pin and remove the safety strap correctly. I would have done exactly the same with the last one as I did with the first five.

Notwithstanding his protests, the combination of the two events sufficiently damaged Lycopolus's reputation that his service with the Rangers was terminated.[13]

* * *

In the JOC, Garrison was able to watch events as they unfolded. The injury to Blackburn was unexpected, as had been the loss of the truck. But in neither case had the operation been disrupted. In any plan, first contact with the enemy invariably calls for adjustments – but well-trained and resourceful soldiers can cope. The target house had been stormed and the prisoners restrained, ready to be loaded onto the convoy. So far, everything was going well, and success was close by.

* * *

Sergeant Dominick Pilla – the first US fatality.

At 1615 hrs, the prisoners had been loaded into their transport for about five minutes, and the evacuation convoy was ready to go, but there was a delay. Communications were confused between the ground convoy and the assault team. The two elements each waited orders to move out. Delay was the enemy of any special forces' operation, and in this case, it was because of an avoidable communication glitch. The Delta Force was waiting for the ground commander to dispatch the convoy while the convoy was waiting for Delta to give the 'go'.[14] Operational impetus was now lost and there would be a price to pay.

Meanwhile, Joyce had brought a Humvee down to Blackburn, who was laid in the vehicle by way of the rear hatch. Two medics came with him and that vehicle, with two others, Struecker leading, set off at once. Struecker knew his way and decided that he would follow National Street, which led directly to the K4 roundabout (called a traffic circle in the USA).

The local situation was deteriorating minute by minute. Barricades were springing up everywhere. In all three vehicles, the occupants were dispensing automatic fire as their passage was contested by the crowd, which would be more accurately described as a mob – but a very hostile and dangerous mob.

Sergeant Dominick Pilla, a very popular man and something of a unit character, was manning the machine gun mounted on Struecker's Humvee. The three vehicles were making good progress despite the opposition. However, as they made the turn onto National Street, Pilla was shot in the head and died instantly. He was the first US fatality.[15]

* * *

The buses carrying Colonel Aden and his militia careered down Armed Forces Street before turning into an alley short of Hawlwadig Road. Dismounting, the platoon splintered into half a dozen squads of six or seven men each – plus the one woman among them. Most militia were poor marksmen, Aden knew that, and he had tried to distribute at least one true sharpshooter in each squad.

Darting through alleyways, sheltering in doorways and beneath trees as they eyed the helicopters overhead, the squads crept closer until they were within range of the Americans and their vehicles around the three-story building. In addition to the militia, scores of other Somalis sprinted through the streets in a confused melee. Everyone in south Mogadishu who could put their hands on a weapon seemed to press towards the battle. Aden shouted at several to stay back, but they ignored him.

As the firing intensified, he felt growing confidence. This claustrophobic battleground, in Aidid's stronghold, was where Aden had hoped to fight. Other militia platoons, he knew, would be rushing from the north, south and east. The Americans were not supermen. In these dusty streets, where combat was reduced to rifle against rifle, they could die as easily as any Somali.[16]

* * *

The small crowd had swelled into a mob and was now hundreds strong, but with perhaps thousands more making their way to the Black Sea. This was in response to Colonel Sharif Hassan Giumale's order, by radio, to his officers across the city to assemble at the Black Sea.[17] Concurrently, they were well advanced in their setting of ambushes along likely reinforcement routes from the UNOSOM bases. Within ten minutes, the roads surrounding the Olympic Hotel were covered with militia and nearly sealed.[18]

Captain Steele, the Rangers' commanding officer, was very conscious of being under fire directed on his position. He decided that the most likely source was from a single gunman who was about a block west and on the roof of the Olympic Hotel. Steele called for Corporal Jamie Smith, who was recognised as being an exceptional marksman. Smith and Steele both focused on the man on the roof and fired. Although they did not see the man fall, there was no further hostility from that particular roof.[19]

Sergeants Mike Goodale and Aaron Williamson were taking cover in an alley from behind a wrecked car. The alley was typical of so many in the city.

It was unsurfaced and in profile, it sloped up on both sides to the bordering buildings. The bare earth had an orange hue and so dust rising from the alleys coated everything and everyone.

A Somali, only about 100 yards (90m) away, appeared behind a wall and he fired a long burst from his Kalashnikov. Goodale decided, in First World War parlance, to 'find a better 'ole'. The new position was not better, and so Goodale promptly returned from whence he had come. The Somali opened up again and this time he was on target. One of his rounds took off the end of one of Williamson's fingers.

Williamson was in great pain, but he was also furious. He levelled his rifle and waited for the gunman to reappear. A trained soldier would not have fired from the same place more than once, but this assailant was not trained and, when he stuck his head out again, it was into Williamson's sights. He squeezed his trigger and the man's head dissolved in a red mist of blood, brain and bone.

Moments later, a man in a loose shirt ran into the alley, and as he did so his open shirt revealed an AK-47. This attracted the close attention of several Rangers, and the shirt was riddled with their combined fire. Goodale had qualms about the man's death, because he had not been overtly hostile. Goodale was not alone and across central Mogadishu there were other young men who were killing for the first time and trying to balance the need for self-defence with the normal, civilised revulsion at the taking of life. Specialist Shawn Nelson was Chalk Two's M60 gunner. This weapon is a machine gun.

> It fires the standard NATO 7.62mm round and is used as a general support crew-served weapon. It has a removable barrel which can be easily changed to prevent overheating. The weapon has an integral, folding bipod and can also be mounted on a folding. It can fire 100 rounds a minute and its effective range is out to 1,200 yards [1,100m].[20]

Nelson had been engaging targets even before he started his rope descent. One was a man armed with an AK shooting up at his helicopter. Nelson fired a burst, and the individual died on the spot.

Just after landing, Nelson was able to see an elderly man with 'bushy white hair' seeking to get into position to fire on Chalk Four. The gunman was unaware that he was being watched and, in his ignorance, moved to within 50 yards (45m) of Nelson. The man started to change the magazine on his weapon when Nelson fired a dozen 'plastic coated, titanium rounds' into him. He should had been killed instantly, but he was not.

Incredibly and courageously, the man turned his AK towards Nelson and discharged several ill-aimed rounds in Nelson's general direction. The M60 delivered a further dozen rounds, but the gunman, who was clearly hit again, still managed to crawl behind a tree. He was moving, and it was only when Nelson fired his third burst that he finally succumbed.[21] The elderly, anonymous man had epitomised the obdurate and selfless attitude of many Somalis towards their American foe, and the selfless manner in which they were prepared to give their lives.

A little later, Nelson, behind his gun and taking cover from an abandoned car, saw a bizarre sight as an armed man rode into sight astride a cow. The 'cowboy' was accompanied by a group of about eight comrades, only some of whom had visible weapons. Nelson and his fellow Rangers opened fire. The man on the cow fell to the ground and his comrades, those who had not been shot, ran for cover. At that point, a Black Hawk flew onto the scene and opened fire with its heavy-duty weaponry. The cow, which hitherto had probably been an unwilling participant in this battle, was literally shot to pieces. Blood and flesh were strewn across the street.[22] It was a grim sight, but the Rangers took comfort that overhead they had constant, massive support.

The persistent issue for TFR was its interface with the mob. Nelson was faced by a group of about fifteen people. He wanted only to engage those with arms, but the gunmen took cover behind unarmed citizens, only emerging briefly to fire a couple of rounds. There were two options. One was to only shoot when there was a clearly identified target and there was no risk to others. The second option was to recognise that the civilians providing cover were an integral part of the enemy's tactics and treat them accordingly. Eventually, all the Rangers, albeit unwillingly, adopted option two.

A further example of that same moral dilemma affected Sergeant Chuck Elliot, who was manning an M-16 machine gun. Looking over the sights, he saw an armed man creeping up the alley towards him. The man was preceded by an unarmed woman. The sergeant shouted to his officer, Lieutenant Perino, who did not equivocate, and he told Elliot to shoot.

He did, and both Somalis crumpled under the burst of fire.

This was now an increasingly common situation. Elsewhere, Specialist Shawn Nelson 'saw a Somali gunman lying prone on the street between two kneeling women. The shooter had the weapon between the woman's legs and there were four children sitting on him.' To get at the gunman he would have to kill six unarmed civilians. Nelson opted to throw a flash bang, and it frightened the group, which fortunately scattered – the gunman left his weapon behind.[23] Elsewhere, the Rangers' superior weapon handling was killing dozens of enthusiastic, naïve and unskilled gunmen.

Chapter 14

Super Six-One

The whole operation was scheduled to take an hour but forty minutes after the initial, fast-roping incursion, GOTHIC SERPENT took a turn for the worse. Teenager Abdiaziz Ali Aden was frightened by the noise, a combination of engines, explosions and small arms fire.

> He could see a line of Somali men in handcuffs being loaded onto big trucks. On the street were dead people and a donkey dead on its side, its water cart still attached and upended. It terrified him. As he started back toward his house, one of the Black Hawks flew over him at rooftop level. It made a rackety blast, and wash from its rotors swept over the dirt alley like a violent storm. Through this dust Aden saw a Somali militia man with an RPG tube step into the alley and drop to one knee.
>
> The militiaman waited until the helicopter had passed overhead. Then he leaned the tube up and fired at the aircraft from behind. Aden saw a great flash from the back end of the tube and then saw the grenade climb and explode into the rear of the helicopter cracking its tail.[1]

The aircraft was Black Hawk *Super Six-One*, flown By CW3 Clifton Wolcott. The helicopter carried two crew chiefs, Sergeant Ray Dowdy and Staff Sergeant Charlie Warren, and two Delta snipers who were seeking to identify and eliminate RPG operators. Crucially, they had both missed this one, whose fire upon them was devastating.

The grenade incapacitated the rear rotor, and the Black Hawk spun out of control. The radio burst into life and Durant heard the voice of Cliff Wolcott. He and Donovan Briley, his co-pilot, were close friends and were flying *Super Six-One*. Wolcott said calmly, '*Super Six-One* is going down.'[2]

Wolcott was unable to correct the attitude of his aircraft, which clipped the house of Abdiaziz Ali Aden, removed part of the roof, hit a stone wall and then crashed very heavily, on its side in an alley, off Freedom Road about

300 yards (274m) east of the target building.[3] CW3 Mike Durant in *Super Six-Four* commented:

> In those seconds everything changed. The radios, which up to now had hissed the occasional code words or updates, went crazy. Sure, we'd all prepared for the possibility of a bird going down, but the timing and location were about as bad as they could be ... air elements were being summoned for support. It was now constant chatter back and forth, the voices still steady but ominously urgent. ... We had a bird down and the survivors were surrounded.[4]

Durant had decanted his eighteen Rangers and keyed his radio to report, '*Super Six-Four* is out.' He took up his holding pattern, in which he would make long circles about 2 miles from the city centre. The plan was that he would maintain this pattern until the road convoy made its victorious passage from the city.

At 1622 hrs, Wolcott and his co-pilot, CW Donovan Briley, were dead, killed by the massive impact. Staff Sergeants Ray Dowdy and Charlie Warren were seriously wounded. However, the two snipers, Staff Sergeants Daniel Busch and Jim Smith, survived the crash and prepared to defend themselves against the hostile crowds now racing to the crash site.

General Garrison was witness to the loss of *Super Six-One* as his surveillance aircraft was transmitting pictures of the scene. It was not quite a disaster, more an unfortunate, albeit manageable, situation for which there was a contingency plan in place. Nevertheless, Garrison realised that the assembly of such an enormous mob at such short notice, and now the effective use of RPGs, was a combination he had not planned for.

The initiative in this battle had shifted in favour of the SNA militia. The TFR was on the defensive, but there were survivors of the crash to be rescued and, if possible, the dead to be recovered. By happy chance, an MH-6 Little Bird *Star 41* flown by CW3 Karl Maier, was close at hand. In a demonstration of the most extraordinary airmanship, Maier flew the aircraft as close to the crash site as possible while firing a weapon at the mob from his seat.[5]

As soon as *Star 41* landed in a cloud of orange dust, the co-pilot, CW3 Keith Jones, jumped out and helped the two wounded crewmen and two

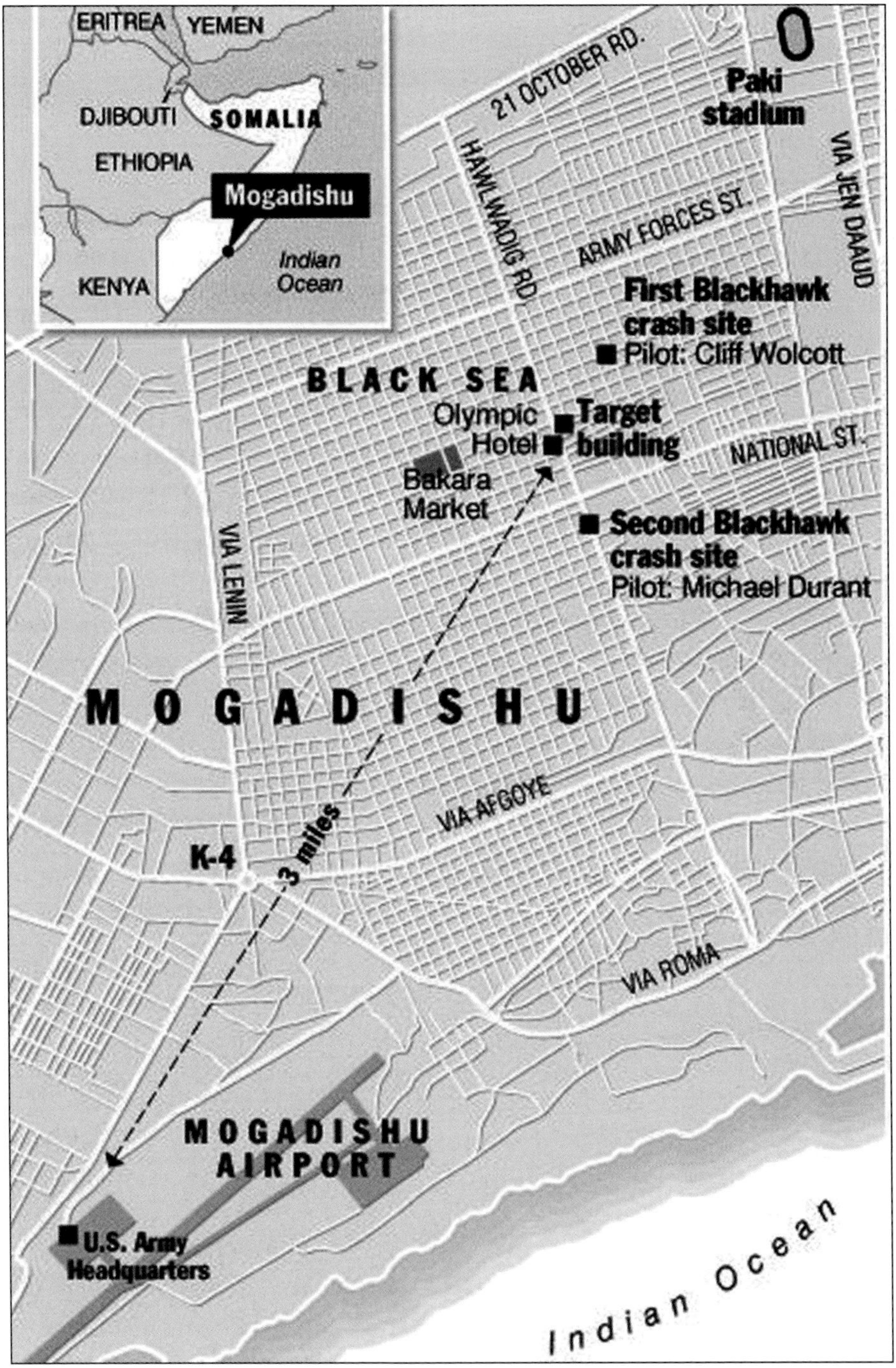

The scene of the Battle of Mogadishu. (*Bowden*)

Delta snipers into the helicopter. One of the snipers, Daniel Busch, had engaged and killed several gunmen in the brief period since the crash but, in the process, had himself been mortally wounded. Maier took off and raced Busch to medical assistance, but to no avail and he succumbed to his wounds.

There were contingency plans in place to deal with the loss of an aircraft. A specialist Combat Search and Rescue team commanded by Captain Bill Coultrup was circling above in Black Hawk *Super Six-Eight*, piloted by CW3 Dan Jollota and Major Herb Rodriguez. It was now no longer necessary to deploy the CSAR because *Star 41* had already rescued the survivors. Nevertheless, the fifteen-man team fast-roped into the crash site, but as the last two reached the bottom of the rope, an RPG hit Black Hawk *Super Six-Eight*. The aircraft was severely damaged, still flyable, but no longer operationally effective. The rotor blades were chewed up, and the helicopter's body was ragged with shrapnel holes, but it started limping back to the airport, trailing black smoke.[6] The seriously damaged aircraft made its way, safely, the few miles back to its airport base.

At the *Super Six-One* crash site the CSAR team found both the pilots dead and two wounded inside the wrecked helicopter. Under intense fire, the team moved the wounded men to a nearby collection point, where they built a makeshift shelter using Kevlar armour plates salvaged from *Super Six-One*'s wreckage.[7] It became evident to Captain Bill Coultrup that the two dead aviators could not be extricated from the battered remains of *Super Six-One* without cutting equipment. The survivors having left on *Star 41*, the CSAR team now had no specific mission. It had to focus on its own survival, having just joined a very serious gunfight.

At this point, TFR had suffered three fatalities; Busch would make it four. On the other hand, Somali deaths were uncounted but were probably well over 100. Hundreds more were wounded and the medical services in Mogadishu, limited at any time, were now totally overwhelmed.

Chapter 15

Super Six-Four

In the skies above Mogadishu, Black Hawk *Super Six-Four* took over the role of *Super Six-One*. This aircraft was flown by CW3 Michael Durant and co-pilot CW2 Ray Frank. Radio traffic was intense, and a significant change in the original plan was the new directions just given to the convoy commander.

Durant had seen the Little Bird lift off the crash site with the survivors and he just hoped that Cliff and Donovan were among them. As expected, he had previously heard the order to *Super Six-Eight* to deliver the Combat Search and Rescue. Durant was directed to join *Super Six-Two* in orbiting above the crash site. He acknowledged the order, and then the radio told of the damage to *Super Six-Eight*, which had now limped from the scene.

From his viewpoint, Durant could see that the neat boxlike cordon surrounding the target building had broken down. The Rangers were inextricably mixed with SNA gunmen and their unarmed shields. It was clear that GOTHIC SERPENT was failing, and that damage limitation was now the order of the day.

For the ninety or so US soldiers consolidating near the downed helicopter, Freedom Road and the adjoining alley had become a killing zone. AK-47 bullets flew overhead with a loud pop, punctuated by the red streak and ominous swoosh of rocket-propelled grenades. Within an hour, ten of the thirteen men with Lieutenant Larry Perino (second-in-command of Bravo Company, 3rd Battalion, 75th Ranger Regiment) would be wounded. Delta and the search-and-rescue team suffered comparable casualties. So many Somalis swarmed through the neighbourhood that helicopter gunners overhead ignored those with rifles to concentrate on the more lethal rocket-propelled grenade gunners.[1] Durant and Frank did as they were ordered, circled the crash site and prepared to engage any target on the ground that offered itself.

CW3 Michael Durant of 160th Special Operations Aviation Regiment at the controls of his Black Hawk. CW3 Dan Jollota is in the background.

Their aircraft and its repetitive circuit was noted by Yusuf Dahir Mo'alim, commander of a seven-man SNA rocket-propelled grenade team that was slowly moving up towards the first crash site. One of the men in Mo'alim's squad knelt on the road, aimed at *Super Six-Four*'s tail rotor and fired.[2] Durant later recorded:

> Something slammed into my helicopter.
>
> We didn't know what it was or where it had impacted, but the helo bucked hard, like a small sports car going over a large speed bump. We'd been passing by the Olympic Hotel for the *third time* [author's emphasis], doing fifty knots at about seventy-five feet, when an RPG round rocketed into the tail section. But that was thirty-five feet behind me, the aircraft was eighteen thousand pounds of metal muscle, and it wasn't coming apart. At least not yet.
>
> I looked quickly around the cockpit, while Ray did the same, both of us testing the controls and checking gauges. Everything was 'in the green': no flight control problems, engine malfunctions, or weird noises. No one in my bird said a word and then …

> '*Super Six-Four*, you're hit bad.' It was Matthews up in the C2 bird. 'You'd better put it on the ground.' From his position high over the battle, he had seen the rocket impact just below my tail, raking pieces away in pinwheels as it detonated.
>
> 'No shit,' I thought as I rolled out of the turn. Just ahead, maybe a mile off, was what appeared to be a clear area, certainly large enough to land a Black Hawk. But the aircraft still seemed to be flying normally, and I was facing the decision to crash it in the middle of a fire fight or fly just two miles to the safety of the airfield. I didn't hesitate or discuss it with anyone. It was my decision to make. We'd go for the field.[3]

Durant was a man brimming with self-confidence and he described himself in his book as:

> Having been in the Army for twelve years, I had become just about all that I could be. I was still young, yet far from green, a thirty-two-year-old battle-tested helo pilot. Cocky, maybe, but my reflexes and instincts were at their peak, a man who could meld with a multi-ton [weighing more than 1 ton] machine and bend it to his will.[4]

Durant had every cause to be 'cocky'. He was a highly trained, multi-skilled and very tough Special Forces soldier. Although he was a versatile and expert pilot, that was not in itself sufficient to win selection to fly Delta soldiers on covert operations. He had undergone the most vigorous preparation for his role in 160th SOAR (A). He had been exposed to the mentally demanding and physically stressing 'escape and evasion' training. Of necessity, he was skilled in the use of small arms and was at the peak of physical fitness.

In the weeks to follow he would need to draw on all his training, experience and resolve, because life was about to become very difficult for CW3 Durant.

He continued:

> Still, I kept my eye on that midway point. It looked sort of like a city park, which it had been, long ago when the place was prosperous. Now, as we closed on it, I could see that it was covered with tin shacks and huts. But none of that mattered, because within a few seconds the world went completely to hell.
>
> The RPG had smashed into the rear gearbox, a fixture the size of a watermelon and full of oil and gears, where the drive shaft came in to have

> its speed and direction ratios altered for the tail rotor. The bottom of that box had been blown off, the drive shaft bent and twisted. I heard a rapidly accelerating whine, an unearthly, building scream, and then the tail rotor assembly completely disintegrated into vapor with an ear-splitting BANG.
>
> The nose of the helicopter immediately started to spin to the right. The tail rotor on a Black Hawk is designed to counter the torque created by the main rotor system and the pedals control the pitch of the tail rotor. As we passed through the first ninety degrees of rotation, I instinctively countered with left pedal, and I knew we'd lost it. I'll never forget looking down to make sure I was pushing the pedal and seeing my boot jammed all the way to the floor. My body was reacting properly, but my helo was not. I keyed the mike.
>
> '*Six-Four* has lost the tail rotor. We're going in hard.'
>
> I looked at Ray and said, 'I guess we better pull 'em off.' I was referring to the engines because the only way to counter the spin was to shut them down and eliminate the torque. But, just as the Black Hawk manual describes such an emergency, if you don't kill the engines right away the centrifugal force will make it physically impossible to reach for the power control levers.
>
> I always thought that sounded a little extreme. It wasn't.
>
> *Super Six-Four* started to spin so fast that the sky and ground became nothing but two blurred stripes of blue and brown in front of my eyes. It was like riding a merry-go-round and looking straight out to the side of your horse, while the teenage operator hauls it up to fifty revs per minute. I was hurled against my harness, my hands desperately yanking and twisting the controls and I looked over to Ray to see him fighting the force with every muscle, his gloved hands quaking as he tried to reach up for the power levers.
>
> I knew I was going to die, and I must have clenched the mike key as I screamed his name, shooting a paralyzing chill through everyone on the net.
>
> 'Raaaayyy.'[5]

And then the rubber and steel met the road. All 16,000lb of it.

With the benefit of 20/20 hindsight, it is possible to conclude that Durant was the architect of his own misfortune. Williamson (see pages 131–2) had waited for a Somali gunman to reappear in the same place and, when the gunman obliged, Williamson was able to kill him. Durant had flown the same pattern three times as he circled above the crash site.[6] It is improbable that he was the victim of anything but an observant Somali leader whose team was armed with RPGs. To fly the same pattern three times was sufficiently repetitious to invite a spirited and effective response.

The wreckage of *Super Six-Four* on about 5 October 1993. (*US Army Archive*)

All the RPG hits on US helicopters struck the rear of the aircraft; the RPG gunners were aware that the most vulnerable part of any helicopter is the rear rotor. Their training had been sufficiently effective that TFR, having lost three helicopters, was now beset by a mob of thousands and was at risk of complete annihilation. For TFR, everything depended on the road convoy. For the SNA every sinew would be strained to halt and eliminate that convoy.

Meanwhile, Durant lay in the wreckage of his helicopter, where there was a powerful scent of aviation fuel. The air was filled with dust, stirred up by the impact. The windshield was shattered, 'pierced by a slab of corrugated metal that had stopped only inches from his face'. He was aware that he was seriously wounded and that his back was badly damaged. Two of the vertebrae had 'smacked together on impact displacing the disc between them and pulverizing each other'.[7]

Durant was in the agonising pain that only a back injury can produce. His right leg was numb and when he tried to move it, he realised that his femur was broken. He looked across at Ray Frank, who was trying to get out of the wreck. They exchanged a few words and then Frank grunted,

'Left tibia broken, I think.' He added, 'I'm moving, Mike.' So saying, Frank moved out of the helicopter. Durant never saw his friend and comrade again.

Bill Cleveland's voice was audible, but Tommy Field was ominously silent. Durant was able to reach his MP-5 submachine gun and had no doubt that he was going to have to use it in the very near future.

Bill Cleveland was moaning and making unintelligible noises, but they soon ceased.[8] Durant was now alone in the wreck, in which the heated metal continued to whimper.

He did not know it, but he was the sole survivor. He was badly injured but having determined to go down fighting, cradled his MP-5 submachine gun and waited for a target. The watchers in the sky above could see that the convoy would not get to *Super Six-Four* in the short term and certainly not before the mob now racing towards the crash site.

To protect any survivors of the crash, and only two minutes after impact, at 1642 hrs, two Delta Force snipers, Sergeant First Class Randy Shughart and Master Sergeant Gary Gordon who, hitherto, had been providing covering fire from the air, volunteered to be inserted into the crash site. These two Delta soldiers had been circling overhead shooting at SNA gunmen racing towards the site and they knew that it would not be long before the site was overrun. Urgent, positive action was needed. They made three requests to be inserted into the crash site. Colonels Matthews and Harrell finally acquiesced and they were duly inserted about 100 yards (90m) from the wreck.

It was evident to all concerned that this was akin to jumping into a fire, because, once in, there was no way that the two men and any survivors could be extracted. The mob was close to hand and getting closer. The two Delta soldiers realised that this was about as hazardous as it gets but, to their undying credit, they insisted.

Durant did not know either, but recognised friendly faces when they suddenly appeared at his side.

> Randy was carrying a high-tech sniper rifle and Gary had a CAR-15 – the short-barreled version of the M-16 assault rifle. Their load-bearing harnesses were slung with ammunition and grenades. They were the kind of professionals who could pick off a rabbit from a roller coaster with a BB gun. To me they were Batman and Robin, only much better, and they just walked up to my aircraft like they were out for a stroll in the park.[9]

Durant was lifted from what remained of his seat and then the two men extracted Tommy Field and Bill Cleveland. Durant participated in the ensuing firefight despite being immobile. But when a target presented itself, he fired upon it – apparently with modest success. The two snipers engaged the closing mob and eliminated many, but they faced the usual fusillade of ill-directed fire. However, the weight of fire was bound, eventually, to hit a target, and Gary Gordon was heard to exclaim, 'Damn, I'm hit.'[10] He died soon after. Durant recorded that 'Shughart, came back around the cockpit, striding toward me and showing little more than professional concern in his expression.'

> 'They're throwing grenades in here,' I told him, but he didn't seem too worried about that. He was focused on our critical shortage of ammo and he looked at my now useless MP-5.
>
> 'Are there any weapons in the aircraft?' he asked.
>
> 'My crew chiefs keep their M-167s between the seats.'
>
> He went off to the helicopter, climbed in and started digging around. Moments later he returned carrying the longer M-16s and a CAR-15, the short barreled submachine gun I had seen in Gary's hands.
>
> 'What channel is the fire net on?'
>
> It was odd. He didn't have to shout. There was gunfire echoing from the far side of the aircraft but in hesitant ones and twos.
>
> 'Channel Bravo,' I replied.
>
> He worked the radio and suddenly I wondered if we'd been communicating with anyone out there. We had to be. I assumed that Randy and Gary had at least been talking on their own internal radio net … Randy made a call on the fire support net which gave him a direct line to the Little Bird guns and fire support officer. A Little Bird was flying high over our position.
>
> 'A reaction force is *en route*,' came the return call from one of the helicopters. The voice sounded familiar. I was sure it was one of the Little Bird pilots named Chris. … We gotta hang in there just a little while more. Randy probably knew right then that 'a little while more' would not be soon enough. He squinted at the radio and stuffed it into his combat harness, hefted his weapon, and moved off around the nose of the aircraft. He left without saying another word. I would never see him again.[11]

Duran saw a Somali trying to access the site by climbing over a wall. He aimed the CAR-15, squeezed the trigger and was surprised when the weapon

Master Sergeant Gary Gordon and Sergeant First Class Randy Shughart, the two Delta soldiers who gave their lives in the defence of the survivors of *Super Six-Four*. They were each posthumously awarded the Medal of Honor. Although their citations were similar, that of Gordon is at Annexure D on page 225.

loosed a burst at the climber, who vanished behind the wall and did not reappear. Durant observed, 'I can't say for certain, but I think I killed that man.' He fired on every fleeting figure he saw and emptied the weapon's magazine. There were 6,000 rounds of 7.62mm ammunition just a few feet away but with his injuries, he could not reach them.

By 1740 hrs, Randy Shughart's weapon was silent and the probability was that he, too, had now been killed. The resistance had lasted just short of an hour and in that period the two Delta snipers had killed twenty-five of their enemy.[12] However, and notwithstanding the extraordinary and selfless bravery of Gordon and Shughart, the outcome was entirely predictable.

Durant expected to be killed and, when the mob reached him, its hatred for Americans in general seemed to be entirely focused on him. Those of the mob who could reach Durant all wanted to hit, club or kick him and this they did with relish. They stripped his shirt, his shoes and his dog tags. At one point he was clubbed with a weapon that he realised was the severed arm of one of his comrades. This grisly detail he kept to himself until he wrote his book, some ten years later.[13]

Chapter 16

The Lost Convoy

The vehicles had been sitting idle for far too long, an estimated twenty minutes, but even half that time would be crucial.[1] As a result, the impetus and urgency of the operation had been completely lost whilst the SNA had gained valuable time to marshal its forces. It was at 1622 hrs that *Super Six-One* was shot down. The prisoners were loaded into vehicles and someone needed to give the order to 'go' and, at 1626 hrs, that order was finally given. Lieutenant Colonel Danny McKnight led the way. Driving his leading vehicle was Staff Sergeant Dan Schilling USAF.

The convoy was composed of three Humvees, followed by two flatbed trucks with three more Humvees bringing up the rear. The trucks were marked with fluorescent orange panels as an aid for the airborne surveillance circling above. A late change in the plan had been the Delta assault force being ordered to make its way, on foot, to the site of *Super Six-One*'s crash.

The radio transcripts that follow are part of those found by Bowden during his meticulous research of military archives. At 1626 hrs, McKnight radioed the Ground Force commander, Lieutenant Colonel Gary Harrell, who was watching proceedings from his vantage point high above in the C2 Black Hawk. McKnight said:

> 'This uniform Six-Four I am ready for exfil I am loaded with everything. I can get here and am ready to move to the crash site. Over.' [This was the first crash site.]
>
> 'Roger, go ahead and move. The streets are fairly clear. There have been reports of sniper fire from the north of the crash site.'
>
> 'Roger. We'll take right out of here and we'll head down to the crash site to the east. Over.'[2]

Colonel McKnight had been given specific guidance when he set out with his convoy on his short journey to the crash site. 'Go two blocks north and three blocks east,' he was told. This all sounded simple enough. The convoy

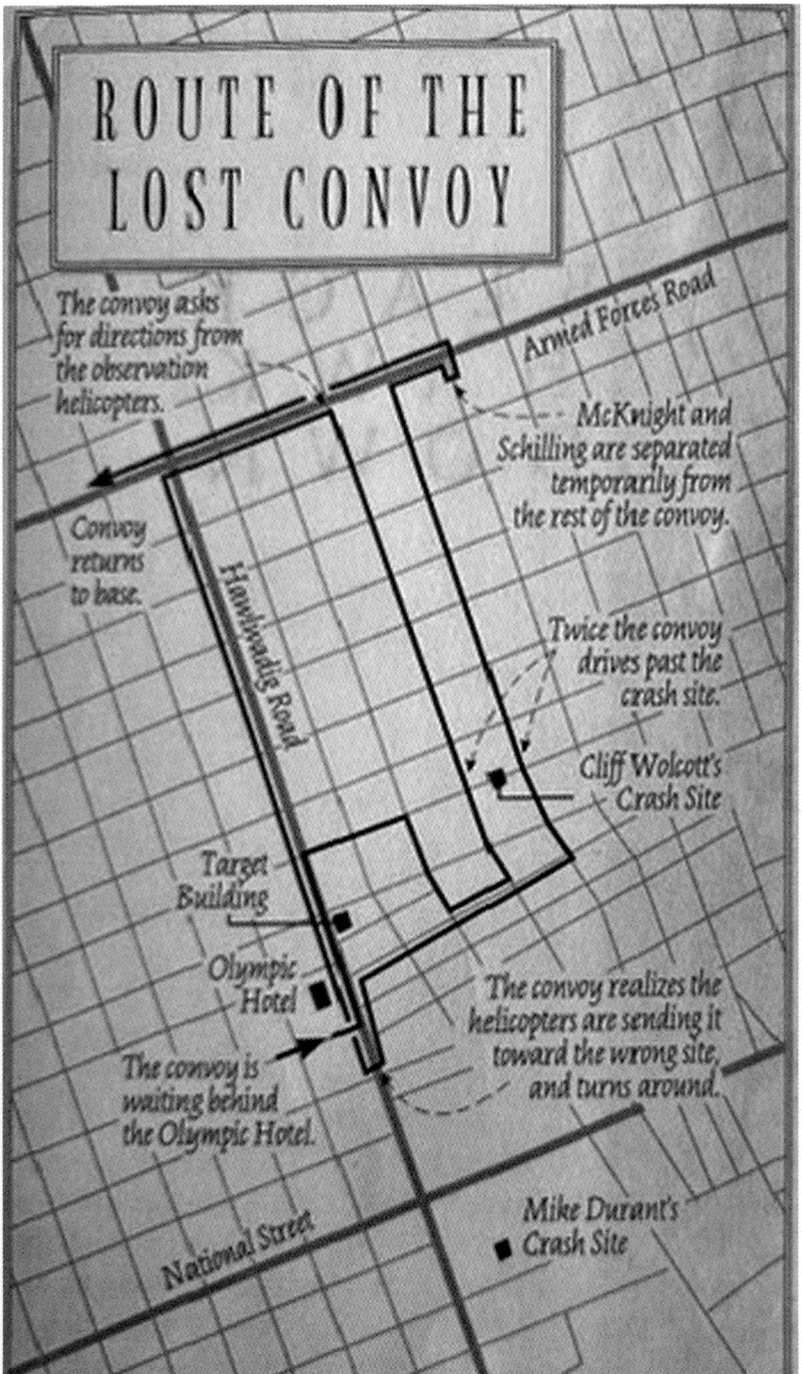
ROUTE OF THE LOST CONVOY
The convoy asks for directions from the observation helicopters.
Armed Forces Road
McKnight and Schilling are separated temporarily from the rest of the convoy.
Convoy returns to base.
Hawlwadig Road
Twice the convoy drives past the crash site.
Cliff Wolcott's Crash Site
Target Building
Olympic Hotel
The convoy realizes the helicopters are sending it toward the wrong site, and turns around.
The convoy is waiting behind the Olympic Hotel.
Mike Durant's Crash Site
National Street

(*Bowden*)

moved forwards and immediately came under sporadic and ineffective small arms fire. It was a foretaste of what was yet to come.

On the way and as they passed the Olympic Hotel, McKnight scooped up Sergeant Eversmann's Chalk Four as it was making its way to the wreck of *Super Six-One*, in accordance with Captain Steele's order. Eversmann was concerned about McLaughlin, Joyce and the two medics he had sent to accompany the injured Blackburn, but they were already passengers in a Humvee. The remainder of Chalk Four all found a space on a vehicle. Eversmann could see the crash site just before he got aboard a Humvee. He was unaware that that was the immediate destination of the convoy and assumed that the convoy's aim was to get the prisoners back to secure detention.

The mission seemed to be simple enough. McKnight had been told how to get to the site of the *Super Six–One* crash but the labyrinthine streets of central Mogadishu were confusing, and they were difficult to identify. It was only nine minutes later, at 1635 hrs, that McKnight realised he was lost. He was unable to find either the wreck site or the CSAR team that had been inserted to rescue survivors.

Then, at 1640 hrs, there was the second helicopter crash: Mike Durant's Black Hawk, *Super Six-Four*, crashed about a mile south-west of the target building. It became an additional and immediate focus for the mob. Hostile crowds of Somalis began moving towards the wreck.

Far from the streets being 'fairly quiet', the convoy was now attracting increasing enemy small arms fire, and several soldiers had been wounded. Among the surveillance measure in place was a USN Orion spy plane. This sophisticated aircraft contained the highest-grade cameras, and from 1,000 feet (305m), they had an overview of the entire operation. Inexplicably, it was not permitted to communicate directly with Colonel Danny McKnight in the convoy below them. The Orion could see the preferred route for the convoy but was obliged to pass the information to Garrison's headquarters (JOC), who would then relay the advice to Harrell in his command helicopter and, from there, the information was sent on to McKnight.

The problem generated by this convoluted system was that by the time McKnight got the message, his convoy had passed the desired turning. Reacting to the message 'turn right', the lead Humvee, having driven past the preferred road, would take the next right. Little wonder that confusion and indecision were passengers on this convoy. The peregrinations of the convoy are shown on the map on page 148.

Lieutenant Colonel McKnight was leading his convoy in a southerly direction when he received a transmission from Lieutenant Colonel Gary Harrell:

> 'Danny, we just had another Hawk go down to RPG fires south of the Olympic Hotel. We need you to get everybody in that first crash site. Need QRF to give us some help. Over.'
>
> 'This is Uniform. Understand aircraft down south of Olympic Hotel. Recon and see what we can do after that.'
>
> 'We are going to try to get QRF to give us some help. Try to get everyone off the crash site [*Super Six-One*] and let's get out of here down to the other Hawk and secure it. Over.'[3]

McKnight had just been given an unrealistic task. He was completely lost and disoriented, he had a number of wounded soldiers and prisoners, and he had yet to find the first crash site, let alone the second. In the happy event that he did find either crash site, there would be no room on his vehicles for more passengers.

The drivers of the convoy were not briefed. They knew nothing of the two downed Black Hawks and presumed that the convoy was on its way back to the American base. Ignorant of the bigger picture, they were obliged to follow the lead vehicle wherever it went – for good or ill. If McKnight's Humvee was disabled or he was killed, the probability was that the entire leaderless, ill-informed convoy and its passengers would be lost. 'Sergeant Matt Rierson and his Delta team were on the second truck with the prisoners. Rierson knew that it was standard operating procedure [SOP] for every vehicle in a convoy to know its destination.'[4] Rierson did not know, and, as a man used to being fully briefed, he was frustrated and angry. Meanwhile and along its length, the convoy was under constant fire.

The omens were not good.

The passage of the convoy was spasmodic. The drivers realised that they were at their most vulnerable as they crossed an intersection and could expect to receive enhanced hostile fire during the crossing. However, having crossed, some then stopped.

> The running Somalis could keep pace with the vehicles because the trucks and Humvees stacked up at every intersection. Each driver waited until the vehicle in front had completely cleared the crossfire before sprinting through it himself. To get stuck in the open was suicidal. Every time the convoy stalled, it gave the bands of shooters time to reach the next street and set up an ambush for each vehicle as it gunned through. The convoy was getting riddled. Harrell and Matthews could see roadblocks and places where Somalis had massed to ambush. So, they steered the convoy away from these places.[5]

Private Maddox, driving one of the trucks, was shooting out of his window when he saw a woman in a purple dress, carrying a child – and a pistol. The woman raised the pistol and Specialist Eric Spalding shot her five times before she fell. Spalding hoped that he had not hit the child, but he thought that the probability was that he had. He was at a loss to understand why a mother would expose her child like that. Spalding, like many others this day, had been faced with a dreadful dilemma.

The convoy made its way past the original target house, at which point the third vehicle was hit by an RPG with devastating effect. The grenade pierced the steel skin of the vehicle and exploded within it. Three men were literally blown out of the Humvee by the blast. Delta Master Sergeant Tim Martin was blown in half. Rodriguez suffered severe wounds to his legs and McLaughlin had been hit in the arm and hand. Carlson, still in the Humvee, was also wounded in several places in the arm – and what's more, his boots were on fire! This was the result of a drum of .50 calibre ammunition being hit; the packaging was burning and Carlson was fully aware of comrades urging him to kick the drum out of the Humvee.

The convoy halted; it had no other option. Help came to assist the wounded while dismounted Rangers formed a defensive cordon and engaged any visible enemy. There were several courageous acts during this little microcosm of a greater battle. Specialist Aaron Hand and Sergeant Casey Joyce were at once involved in a firefight all of their own. Apparently, they were unaware of their extreme vulnerability as both knelt in the open and engaged SNA gunmen. It took the intervention of SEAL John Gay to get Hand to disengage and remount a vehicle. The noise was intense and shouted advice or commands were not heard.

Joyce was continuing to fire aimed rounds when the muzzle of a gun appeared in a widow directly above his head. He was hit by a burst of fire at very short range and fell forward onto his face, mortally wounded. The window was then the recipient of sustained fire from all those able to bring a weapon to bear. Sergeant Jim Telscher seized Joyce and got him onto a Humvee, where a Delta medic did what he could. Nevertheless, it was clear that Joyce was close to death.

Private Ed Kallman was the driver of the penultimate Humvee and, in an interview with Mark Bowden, he described seeing:

> a line of trees on the sidewalk begin to explode one after the other, as if someone had placed charges in each and was detonating them at about five-second intervals. Either that, or someone with a big gun was systematically taking out trees, each about two stories [storeys], perhaps thinking that they might be hiding snipers.[6]

The convoy restarted, turned east and, high above them, Colonels Matthews and Harrell could see the entire scene. They could see a group of armed Somalis were keeping pace with the convoy by running along parallel streets. The convoy's pause at every intersection played into Somali hands. It made yet another left turn so that it was now heading in a northerly direction. This manoeuvre meant that they were travelling up an unnamed road, only one block west of their destination. It was so close, and two blocks further north and a right turn was all that was needed. It was at this stage that Colonel McKnight was wounded in the arm and neck. The incoming fire was ceaseless.

At the back of the line of vehicles, Sergeant Lorenzo Ruiz had taken over a .50 machine gun from Private Clay Othic, who had just been wounded. Ruiz suddenly sagged onto the men below him. The gun above was unmanned and the incoming fire went unanswered. That is, until Specialist Dave Ritchie climbed up to fill the hazardous position, albeit with difficulty as Ruiz's body was blocking the turret. Sergeant John Burns attended to Ruiz and found the entry wound under his right arm. Its gravity was clear as the injured man started to cough blood. He went into shock; it was evident that the wound was life-threatening.

Soldiers operating a machine gun from a Humvee turret were extremely vulnerable. Their vehicle was a large juicy target, but they provided a live target and drew rather more than their share of fire.

One such was Corporal Jim Cavaco, who was operating a 40mm grenade launcher to great effect. He was firing his munitions through the windows of a building that gave cover to enemy gunmen. Specialist Eric Spalding, in the second truck, admired his friend's expertise, but it could not last, and Cavaco was killed instantly when he was shot in the head. The convoy halted and Spalding helped to recover his friend's body and put it in the back of his truck.

* * *

Unknown to the injured and lonely Durant, his situation was parlous in the extreme, because a large and very hostile mob, which had already killed his two very gallant protectors, was now only too anxious to kill him too, despite Durant being a helpless prisoner. He anticipated that the physical assaults he had already suffered would surely continue until his death. The SNA were not signatories to the Geneva Convention and the USA only complied to its protocols when it was convenient. The outlook was very bleak.

Those monitoring events on the ground, by way of the cameras in the sky, could see how the developing battle was going to focus on the two crash sites.

* * *

American battle technology was probably the best in the world, but its command-and-control systems were not of commensurate quality. When invading Grenada ten years earlier, massive superiority had been successful but, in part, negated by inept command arrangements.[7]

It was evident, in Mogadishu, that in these unexpected circumstances, the command-and-control communication arrangements were not only inadequate but had become a further obstacle. The Orion surveillance aircraft could see the big picture but was not permitted to communicate directly with the beleaguered McKnight. The Orion's reading of the situation, and in particular its grasp of the location of the multitude of barricades, could only be passed to the convoy by the unnecessarily convoluted and ineffective system already described. This tortuous and heroically inefficient communication process had apparently been designed by someone; he remains nameless, perhaps as well. A product of the communications deficiency was that all the ingredients for mayhem were now firmly in place.

Gunfire raked the convoy at every intersection. Somalis sprinted across the street, spraying bullets. Three rounds spattered against the armoured glass of McKnight's Humvee. Somali Adan Warsawe was an interested spectator who saw a rocket-propelled grenade detonate against the cab of a truck right in front of him. The explosion decapitated the American driver.

One of the captives who was demonstrably terrified by this onslaught by his fellow Muslims was reciting text from the Koran. The fusillade was unabated but suddenly the recitation from the Koran ceased. The praying Somali had been shot dead and he would be joined in death, ere long, by two further captives. Four US soldiers were killed during the convoy's peregrinations. The SNA gunmen fired upon the convoy from both sides of the street; rounds that did not find an American target had every chance of hitting a fellow Somali on the other side of the street.

Kallman's Humvee was hit by an RPG, but the vehicle was not penetrated although Kallman was thrown from his seat and momentarily stunned. He woke with his ears ringing and saw the convoy ahead turn left – he raced to catch up, followed by the last Humvee.

The fighting was constant, and at short range, typical of urban warfare. Sergeant Mike Pringle, a Humvee turret gunner, in the first Humvee was manning a .50 calibre machine gun, and he was not short of targets. It was when the column stopped, for whatever reason, that it was at its most vulnerable.

At one pause, Pringle fired upon a group of armed Somalis, one of whom was 'a tall skinny man wearing a bright yellow shirt and carrying an AK-47'. The man 'came apart as the big rounds tore through him. Deep red blotches appeared on the yellow shirt. First an arm came off. Then the man's head and chest exploded. The rest of the Somalis scattered.'[8] Staff Sergeant Dan Schilling, in that same vehicle, had also been engaged and had shot two men, both at very short range – 10 yards or less.

The convoy continued, albeit slowly, up the tarmacadamed Armed Forces Road (AFR) for about nine blocks and unknowingly passed west of their designated destination. The wreck of *Super Six-One* was just a block away.

Private Joe Harosky was driving the lead Humvee with McKnight. The colonel, now wounded, seemed to be dazed, perhaps it was shock, but for the moment he was not his usual commanding persona and Schilling, alongside in the cab, was now, in effect, in command. He did at least know the aim of the mission. Advice from the sky called for a right turn but Schilling could see that the alley was too narrow and there was every chance that a flatbed would get stuck. Schilling ignored the advice. Later it emerged that some of the passengers had seen the crash site but were unaware that that was their objective said nothing. The radio burst into life:

> 'Uniform Six-Four, you got everybody out of the crash site? Over.'

McKnight was not himself but had recovered sufficiently to respond. He replied, saying:

> 'We have no positive contact with them yet. We took a lot of rounds as we were clearing the area. Quite a few are wounded including me [McKnight]. Over.'
>
> 'Roger. Want you to try to go to the first crash site and consolidate on that. Once we get everybody out of there, we'll go to the second crash site and try to do an exfil. Over.'

It is clear from these transmissions that, despite being lost and wounded, McKnight was not completely incapacitated and was even in an optimistic frame of mind. However, his next transmission was telling:

> 'Roger. Understand. Can you give me some? We just need a direction and distance from where I am at. Over.'

McKnight's request for directions did not receive a reply but he was asked to say how many of Chalk Four he had picked up. He did not say and after a lengthy pause, McKnight radioed and said:

> 'Romeo Six-Four, this is Uniform Six-Four. From the crash site where am I now? How far over?'
>
> 'Standby. Have good visuals on you now. Danny are you still on that hardball [tarmacadamed] road?'
>
> 'I'm on the exfil road. Down toward National.'

Notwithstanding McKnight's statement of his current position, Harrell clearly did not understand and presumed, incorrectly, that McKnight and his vehicles were in Hawlwadig Road, not far from the original target house and the start point of the convoy. This misunderstanding now added further confusion, as Harrell replied:

> 'Turn east. Go about three blocks east and two blocks north, they're popping smoke. Over.'
>
> 'Understand. From my location I have to go east further about three blocks and then head north. Over.'
>
> 'Roger. That's from the hardball road the Olympic Hotel is on.'
>
> 'I'm at the hardball road east of the Olympic Hotel. Do I just need to turn around and head north?'
>
> 'Negative. They are about three blocks east and one block north of Building One [the target building].'

At this distance, it is difficult to understand why the location of the convoy was not readily understood by the spectators in the sky. The trucks were clearly marked and a block of vehicles moving through the centre of a city with little other vehicular traffic should have been evident. But it was not, and it reveals that the spectators in the JOC, and above in the air, were just as confused. They did not appreciate just how dire was the convoy's situation. The communication arrangements had by now become a major obstacle. The Orion surveillance aircraft could see the big picture but was not able to help the beleaguered McKnight. Aboard the aircraft, there was a combination of frustration, concern and irritation. It was at this this point that Schilling took it upon himself to use the radio and:

> using a frequency he knew helicopter pilots used to talk among themselves he bypassed the CV2 Black Hawk and contacted the observation helicopter flying orbits higher up. Coordinating communications between air and ground was Schilling's speciality. He asked them to vector him to the crash site. The choppers were eager to oblige. They told him to steer west on Armed Forces Road and then hang another left. McKnight gave permission for Schilling to direct them, and the convoy was moving again.[9]

The convoy turned left off Armed Forces Road assailed by gunfire at every intersection. Schilling led for seven blocks and was nonplussed to see ahead of him the wreckage of the truck demolished by an RPG earlier. He realised that they had driven in a circle. To further complicate the situation, the directions being given by the aerial spectators were to the second crash site – McKnight's instructions were to go to the first site.

Garrison had directed the formation and despatch of a rescue convoy, from the airfield, to pick up his men at the first crash site. The Somali opposition had anticipated the appearance of the small relief force and it ran into coordinated and effective ambushes. The relief force managed to advance only about 1,000 yards (915m) and on the way, two of its Humvees were destroyed and three men were hit.[10] The American force, sensibly, withdrew.

Another attempt to make an incursion into central Mogadishu was by the Quick Reaction Force, drawn from 10th Mountain Division. This too was ambushed, this time on Via Lenin. Scott Peterson alleged that, in the breakout attempt, about 100 US soldiers fired nearly 60,000 rounds of ammunition and used hundreds of grenades in 30 minutes before being forced to withdraw to the airfield.[11] That level of ammunition expenditure seems unlikely, despite the intensity of the combat.

Back in the city centre, the convoy edged forwards while Somalis surrounded it, spraying bullets as they ran close by. Three rounds spattered against the armoured glass of McKnight's Humvee and the fusillade was unabated. Meanwhile, men were dead and dying. In the second-to-last Humvee, Sergeant Lorenzo Ruiz was in extremis. He had been wounded at the same time as McKnight and had been hit while operating the .50 machine gun. Sergeant Burns realised that the only chance Ruiz had was to get him into the hands of a doctor and very soon. He could not speak to the convoy commander on the radio and so, courageously, he advanced up the length of the convoy on foot. He had got to the head of the convoy, when a Delta operator said to him, 'You've been hit.' Burns denied that he was injured because he had felt nothing. The Delta soldier would not take 'no' as an answer. Reaching inside his jacket, he felt Burns's right shoulder. That gentle touch got Burns's full attention as he experienced a violent, sharp pain.

Burns could not speak to McKnight and so he made the case to Sergeant Bob Gallagher that a single Humvee should be detached to get Ruiz to hospital. Burns's care for his wounded comrade was, and is, to be admired but it was a lost cause, and Gallagher knew that the convoy could not bear the loss of another vehicle and its onboard firepower.

The confusion on the ground was shared by those several hundred feet above, illustrated by a further flurry of radio traffic.

> 'Danny, I think you've gone too far west trying to look for the second crash. You seem to have gone about four blocks west and five blocks south. Over.'
>
> 'Romeo Six-Four [Harrell], this is Uniform Six-Four [McKnight].Give me a right turn, right turn. Right turn!'
>
> 'Uniform Six-Four, this is Romeo Six-Four. You need to go about four blocks south turn east. There is green smoke marking the site south. Keep coming south.'

At this point, a new voice came up on the radio and, against normal wireless procedure, he did not identify his call sign.

> 'Stop giving directions. I think you are talking to the wrong convoy.'
>
> 'This is Uniform Six-Four, you've got me back in front of the Olympic Hotel.'
>
> 'Uniform Six-Four, this is Romeo Six-Four. You need to turn east.'[12]

GOTHIC SERPENT was clearly in shreds and Harrell was considering the merits of releasing his prisoners, the capture of whom had been the object of the exercise. The merit of such a measure would be to free up space on the vehicles for the embattled, friendly forces at the crash site. Harrell concluded that the prisoners were going to have to take their chances alongside their captors but only in the short term. He issued orders to the Delta units:

> 'As soon as we get you linked up with the Uniform element throw all precious cargo. We're going to try and get a force down to the second crash site.'

Harrell had no idea what a dreadful state McKnight's command was in. Some of the Humvees were running on the rims of their wheels; all were damaged, carrying wounded or dead passengers and running with blood. The unremitting stress of the sustained enemy fire was affecting some of the Rangers quite badly. The probability of McKnight getting to either crash site was very low, getting to both, most unlikely. There existed the very real possibility that the entire convoy could be wiped out. The radio traffic took on a frenetic quality:

> 'Uniform Six-Four, this is Romeo Six-Four. Next right. Next right. Next right. Ally-way. Ally-way!'
>
> 'They missed the turn.'
>
> 'Take the next available, Uniform.'
>
> 'Be advised they are coming under heavy fire.'
>
> 'Uniform Six-Four this is Romeo Six-Four.'
>
> 'God damn it, stop it. Stop!'
>
> 'Right turn. Right turn. You're taking fire. Hurry up!'[13]

At this stage, most of the American participants in this mayhem had no idea where they were or how they were going to get out – if at all. They could only deal with their immediate situation and fight for survival.

* * *

At 1703 hrs, General Garrison had despatched a Quick Reaction Force relief convoy manned by a company from 10th Mountain Division. Their aim was to reach a crash site but they never got anywhere near, as Aidid had anticipated such a manoeuvre. He had prepared ambushes along the obvious route and the relief convoy found itself in a similar situation to those comrades it was trying to extricate. It was now another group of US troops surrounded by an armed and hostile mob.

* * *

Specialist Eric Spalding, in the first truck, was engaging targets when he was shot in the right leg. Moments later, he was shot in the other leg. Both bullets had cut neat holes in the door of the truck and sunlight, looking like two laser beams, fell on his wounds, which were spurting blood. At this point, his driver, Private Maddox, was hit by an enemy round to the back of his head. By the happiest chance, Maddox was not killed because his helmet absorbed the force. The helmet was knocked sideways and dislodged Maddox's glasses. He was concussed and rendered temporarily blind. Although the severe impact on his head briefly stunned him, Maddox still had his hands on the wheel of the truck. The vehicle was moving, but out of control. Spalding, seriously wounded, was unable to assist but he was able to shout instructions to the blind Maddox.

'Turn Left! Turn left! Now! Now!'

'Speed up.'

'Slow down.'[14]

The truck's movements were markedly less than normal, but the vehicles behind had no choice but to follow on. Then, during its gyrations, the truck ran down a Somali citizen who, for some inexplicable reason, was walking on crutches through this raging battle. Maddox, of course, could not see the individual. Nevertheless, when Spalding told him what the bump had been, Maddox stopped the truck. Fortuitously, one of the Delta soldiers riding in the back of the truck dismounted and came to see what was causing the hold-up. Sergeant Mike Foreman peered into the cab, now liberally marked in Spalding's blood, and took charge of the situation. Spalding and Maddox squeezed up and Foreman took the wheel. Spalding, with both legs propped on the dashboard, continued to engage any target that offered itself.[15]

Private Richard Kowalewski, with a name some found difficult to pronounce, was, accordingly, called 'Alphabet' by his comrades. He was a popular member of his team and was driving the second truck, which was already carrying several wounded men. Private Clay Othic, who had been shot in the arm some time earlier, dismounted from his Humvee, selflessly making room for others. Unfortunately, his wound made it difficult for him to pull himself aboard his desired transport, the second truck. Eventually, and with help from Specialist Aaron Hand, Othic managed to get into the cab of the truck next to Kowalewski.

The truck was a large, slow-moving target and the driver an obvious and specific target of choice to the SNA gunmen. Kowalewski was shot in the shoulder but insisted that he could still drive while Othic tried to apply a field dressing to the wound. Then an RPG struck the cab. The missile severed Kowalewski's left arm and lodged in his trunk.

Incredibly, the grenade did not explode when it pierced the young soldier's body. The tip protruded from his right side, and the rear fins of the awesome ordnance could be seen sticking out from his left side in the space normally filled by his arm. This grievous wound had not killed its victim, who, although clearly mortally wounded, was hanging on to life.

The driverless truck collided with the back of the preceding truckload of prisoners – the one with Spalding, Foreman and Maddox in the cab. The collision had the effect of forcing the prisoner's truck into an adjacent wall. Mark Bowden wrote fluently, as ever, about the immediate aftermath.

> Othic had been knocked cold. He awakened to Specialist Hand shaking him, yelling that he had to get out. 'It's on fire.' Hand shouted. The cab was black with smoke and Othic could see the rocket fuse glowing from what looked like *inside* Alphabet [author's emphasis]. The grenade lodged in his chest was unexploded, but something had caused the blast. It might have been a flash bang mounted on Kowalewski's vest, or a rocket propellant from the grenade.
>
> Hand jumped out of his door, Othic reached over to grab Kowalewski to pull him out, but the driver's bloody clothes lifted damply from off his pierced torso. Othic stumbled out to the street and noticed that his and Hand's helmets had been blown off. Hand's rifle was shattered. Death had buzzed past close enough to kill Kowalewski and knock their helmets off but left them virtually unscathed. Hand couldn't hear from his left ear but that was it. Both men found their helmets down the street – they had evidently been blown right out of the window.
>
> Hand also found the lower portion of Kowalewski's arm. Just the left hand and a bit of wrist. He picked it up and ran back to the Humvee where the D-Boys [Delta Force boys] had placed Kowalewski and put it in the mortally wounded man's pants pocket.[16]

That part of the convoy behind Kowalewski's truck had been obliged to halt while the survivors collected themselves. McKnight, driven by Private

Joe Harosky, with Schilling in the cab of the leading Humvee, was unaware of the drama enacted behind him. He pressed on up and turned right onto Armed Forces Road and he was now out of sight of his other vehicles, isolated and particularly vulnerable.

The belated advice from aerial observers had been for McKnight to turn right and when he made the turn onto AFR they did not warn him that he had, in effect, lost his convoy. Neither did they comment that he had just passed the first crash site for a second time while searching for that desired right turn.

McKnight, no doubt guided by Schilling, had only gone about 40 yards on AFR. They were crossing an intersection when an RPG gunner, in the street (really no more than an alley) on the right, confronted them. He was going to have an unopposed shot at the Humvee because the turret gunner, Sergeant Mike Pringle, was not manning his gun but searching for more ammunition in the back of the vehicle. Harosky had to take a decision, and he promptly turned right and drove at the enemy, who released his missile at very close range.

It missed.

Schilling ordered Harosky to back out of the alley as Pringle reloaded the machine gun. The fate of the RPG gunner is unrecorded, and the probability is that he was either killed or wounded. Had he been accurate with his grenade, and killed the occupants of the Humvee, the impact on the remaining participants in GOTHIC SERPENT might well have been disastrous. Battles can, and do, swing on the simple actions of one man or a very small group.

As the Humvee backed out back onto AFR, Schilling was disconcerted to discover that they were alone. He sensibly directed the retracing of their steps, and they found the convoy just where they had left it only a few minutes before.

McKnight now seemed to have recovered. He dismounted to speak to Sergeant Bob Gallagher, who was visibly angered and frustrated by the thick blanket of confusion that had covered the convoy since it left the target house, not quite half an hour earlier. They had been speaking, only for moments, when Gallagher was shot in the arm. The impact knocked him over. The wound was spurting copious quantities of blood, but Schilling managed to stem the flow with a field dressing and got the injured man back to his vehicle.

McKnight did a rapid 'appreciation' of his parlous position. The convoy vehicles and its passengers were in very bad order. Many of the tyres were holed and the Humvees and trucks were running on their rims. Mechanical problems were surfacing from these ill-used vehicles. 'The second Humvee in line was almost disabled. It was dragging an axel and was being pushed by the five-ton truck behind it.'[17]

The bodywork was, in every case, pockmarked with bullet holes or the effects of shrapnel from RPGs; windows and windscreens were cracked and broken. About 50 per cent of his soldiers were either dead or wounded. McKnight had serious doubts about the possibility of reaching the crash site and in the unlikely event that they got there, there was no room on his vehicles for more passengers. He radioed Harrell and said, in a reasonable manner:

> 'Romeo Six-Four, this is Uniform Six-Four. We've got a lot of vehicles that will be almost impossible to move. Quite a few casualties. Getting to the crash site will be awfully tough. Are pinned down.'

This was a considerable understatement of the situation, and it is to McKnight's credit that he kept his cool in a desperate situation. It cut no ice with Harrell, whose immediate response was:

> 'Uniform Six-Four. This is Romeo Six-Four. Danny, I really need to get you back to that crash site. I know you turned left on Armed Forces [Road]. What's your status?'

Clearly, Harrell had not appreciated either his countryman's tactical situation or his vulnerability. The convoy was no longer an asset; it was now a burden and would remain so until its remnants returned to the American base. The time was 1654 hrs, just twenty-six minutes since it set out on its ill-fated odyssey. McKnight decided that enough was enough and he radioed Harrell, saying, 'This is Uniform Six-Four. I have numerous casualties, vehicles that are halfway running. Gotta get these casualties out of here ASAP.'[18]

Even as McKnight made that transmission he was under fire and, regardless of their wounds, many of the Rangers and Delta soldiers were still engaging enemy targets. However, the expenditure of ammunition had been prodigious and now it was starting to run short.

The decision to return to base was taken and passed down the line, to unanimous approval. Nevertheless, it meant a journey of almost 3 miles through the bitterly hostile streets in which ambushes were already prepared and manned.

Via Lenin was a four-lane road that led directly to the K4 traffic circle (roundabout) and back to the airport base. McKnight turned onto the highway but not before yet another human tragedy had played out.

A little Somali boy, probably no older than 5, carrying an AK-47, was discharging the weapon wildly from the hip because he was far too small to shoot from the shoulder. Nevertheless, a round from an AK-47 is lethal, no matter how it is fired or who fires it. Someone responded to the hail of fire from the weapon and shot the child dead. It was not an incident of which anyone would want to take ownership.[19]

The SEAL John Gay's Humvee was in a dreadful condition. It was covered in bullet holes and running on three wheel rims. Smoke was issuing from the bonnet but it provided cover of a sort to eight wounded Rangers and the body of Sergeant Casey Joyce, who had succumbed to his wounds. Gay's Humvee was now leading the convoy, but the journey home would be contested. Across the road, the SNA had spread a large barrier composed of all the available rubbish, added petrol and set it alight. This formidable obstacle was now burning furiously, and Gay had two options. One was to stop and dismantle the barrier. That would take time and, under fire, it was an unattractive option. The alternative was to charge the barrier and hope to force a passage through. He decided on the charge.

The Humvee was revved up and Gay's already badly damaged vehicle sustained further damage, but it succeeded in smashing a path through the flaming barricade. The rest of the convoy followed. Gay's immediate and bold initiative saved the convoy from a period of immobility that might have led to the possible annihilation of the convoy.

At his airfield headquarters, William Garrison was fully aware of events unfolding only just down the road. His master plan had anticipated that the operation would be done and dusted within an hour. Two hours had now elapsed, his plan had long since been abandoned and the name of the game now was 'survival'. The troops were in penny packets. Some were in the convoy heading back to base, others were making their way to the two crash sites. The number of casualties was mounting and each one of these was a priority for evacuation.

Aidid had marshalled thousands of very angry citizens, all of whom were intent on killing every American possible. At 1734 hrs, the Quick Reaction Force and the 'Lost Convoy' were returning to base. Both convoys, having sustained heavy casualties, linked up. They both abandoned efforts to break through to Durant. Meanwhile, the remainder of the ground force of Rangers, D-Boys and SEALs were converging around the first crash site, sustaining even more casualties. Ranger marksman Corporal Jamie Smith was in a small group with Lieutenant Perino. They were heavily engaged and occupying a small tin hut that was tacked onto a stone wall. It gave cover from sight but not from fire. They were very close to the wreckage of *Super Six-One* and Lieutenant DiTomasso and the CSAR who had roped in.

Perino and his men were under concentrated fire and, to eliminate one of the sources of this fire, Smith moved into a position from which he could launch a 203 grenade to dislodge an assailant hiding behind a tree. He was kneeling when he was shot in the thigh. The wound was very serious, and his femoral artery was damaged. Realising the gravity of Smith's wound, Medic Sergeant First Class Kurt Schmid asked for an emergency evacuation of his patient. It was impossible to get a helicopter into this very active battlefield and Schmid worked urgently to try to stop the flow of blood from Smith's leg, but without success. He was unable to reach the severed blood vessel and, despite his heroic efforts on his behalf, Corporal Jamie Smith died. His death became a point of contention long after the battle (see page 200).

In Perino's Chalk One, eight of the eleven Rangers were casualties. The young officer radioed to Captain Steele, his commander, and told him that he was unable to move on as he could not now carry his wounded. Steele was unconvinced and said, 'You've got to push on.' Neither officer realised that the remnants of Chalk One were within 50 yards of DiTomasso.[20]

The battle continued to produce ugly situations, which Bowden recorded after interviewing the participants. When considered together they demonstrate the uniquely unpleasant atmosphere of the Battle of Mogadishu.

An elderly man with long white hair and a beard appeared on the street carrying an AK-47, which he was discharging wildly in all directions. It was late in the afternoon, and he was drunk but more likely under the malign influence of khat. Nevertheless, he was a danger to life and limb and was duly shot. The Americans did not just face Somali men; the woman shared their hatred and resolve.

> A woman kept running out into the ally, screaming and pointing towards the house at the southeast corner of the intersection where many of the wounded had been moved. She was unarmed and drew no fire. But every time she stepped back behind cover a wicked torrent of fire would be unleashed where she had pointed. After she had done this twice, one of the D-boys behind the tail of *Super Six-One* said, 'If that bitch comes back, I'm going to shoot her.'
>
> She did and the D-boy shot her down.[21]
>
> A woman in a blue turban, a powerful woman with thick arms and legs came sprinting across the road carrying a heavy basket in both arms. She was wearing a bright blue-and-white dress that billowed behind her. Every Ranger at the intersection blasted her, Twombly, Nelson, Yurek and Stebbins all opened up. Howe fired on her from further up the hill. At first, she stumbled but kept on going. Then as more rounds hit her, she fell. RPGs spilled out of her basket onto the street. The shooting stopped. She had been hit by many rounds and lay in a heap in the dirt for a long moment breathing heavily. Then the woman pulled herself up on all fours, grabbed a RPG round and crawled. This time the massive Ranger volley literally tore her apart. A 203 round blew off one of her legs. She fell in a bloody lump for a few minutes, then moved again. Another massive burst of rounds rained on her and her body came further apart.[22]

This anonymous woman, not a soldier, but shot to pieces in her home city, was another striking example of the implacable will of Somalis. She was a courageous person by any yardstick, and merited respect. She didn't get it, and Bowden noted, 'It was appalling but some of the Rangers laughed.'

Courage takes different forms, and Technical Sergeant Tim Wilkinson, a USAF medic, was tending to wounded comrades when he was needed to cross the lethal intersection to the Delta command post to tend to Private Adalberto Rodriguez. He gathered his medical kit and contemplated the short but lethal journey he had to make. The intersection was regularly swept by Somali fire, and the probability was that he would be shot and killed. However, he took a deep breath and launched himself across the road. A torrent of fire was directed on him but to his amazement, and to that of witnesses, he was not hit.

Rodriguez was badly wounded. An enemy round had entered his buttock and travelled through his body by way of his pelvis. It had blown away one of his testicles as it exited. Rodriguez was bleeding heavily, and Wilkinson applied a field dressing to stem the flow of blood from the yawning exit wound. Rodriguez was helped into rubber pneumatic pants that, when inflated, would apply pressure on the wound. It worked. The bleeding stopped and, having given morphine, Wilkinson fitted up an IV to replace lost fluids. However, the available supply was insufficient for Rodriguez's needs.

Wilkinson knew he had a supply on the other side of the road, but he would have to go and fetch it. Once again, he faced the nightmare sprint, but he did not hesitate. He ran, the Somalis fired every weapon that they could bring to bear but without success, and Wilkinson made it safely to cover.

In a magnificent demonstration of cold courage, Wilkinson made the hazardous journey for a third time, to the admiration of all who witnessed it. He was decorated for bravery. His citation, for these three acts of courage, reads:

> Technical Sergeant Timothy Wilkinson, a para-rescue man, was awarded the Air Force Cross for repeatedly exposing himself to intense small arms fire and grenade explosions from three directions. He provided lifesaving medical treatment to the wounded while extracting the casualties from *Super-61*. He became the first enlisted Airman to receive the award since 1975.[23]

McKnight's battered convoy reached safety at 1745 hrs. Half of his men were wounded, and all the vehicles were swimming in blood. The medics were ready for them. The Army Field Hospital at the US Embassy stood by but the decision was that all casualties would be assessed by Major Rob Marsh, the Delta Force doctor, who had been recruited to the job by General Garrison several years earlier.

Marsh was assisted by two surgeons, a nurse anesthetist and two physician assistant nurses. They were supported by a USAF mobile surgical facility. It was a strong team and needed to be. Triage would be conducted just outside the medical tent. The critically wounded but with survivable injuries went straight into the tent, the less injured went to a holding area. Those men who were 'expectant' of death were taken to a separate place away from the other wounded. Beyond human help, the object was to allow them to die in peace. The dead were put into an ambulance, where they joined Sergeant Dominick Pilla.[24]

The reaction of the unwounded men as they dismounted, or were helped to dismount, was wide-ranging. There was anger, remorse, grief, sorrow, relief, satisfaction and pride. These survivors, of course still carrying their weapons, roamed around in the triage area either lost in thought or venting their rage. Some of those who were unwounded wanted to go straight back; others most certainly did not want a repeat of the last hour and a half.

Chapter 17

The Siege

In the city, the crash site of *Super Six-Four* had been overrun, and Durant, in excruciating pain, had been extracted from the wreckage and placed in bleak, pitiless imprisonment. He did not expect to survive. Elsewhere the condition of some of the wounded was extreme and gave rise to innumerable requests for helicopter evacuation, none of which could be provided.

The ninety-nine Ranger and Delta soldiers were concentrated around the remains of *Super Six-One*, but they were unevenly distributed, and one party was, in several cases, unaware of the presence of another group, perhaps on the other side of a wall. They were surrounded by 350 militiamen supported by a multitude of civilian volunteers.

It was hot, and the last two hours had been spent in arduous, stressing combat. Mouths were dry, and the folly of *not* carrying a water bottle became painfully obvious. Ammunition was running short, and IV fluids were needed to treat the multiple wounded. There was an urgent need for resupply. The US Army archive contains the following radio traffic between the overflying C2 helicopter and the now besieged men:

> 'Need resupply IV bags, ammo and water. Obviously we need them as fast as they can. Our boys are running out of bullets.'
>
> 'Romeo Six-Four [Harrell] this is Adam Six- Four [Garrison]. You want us to put resupply on a helo?'
>
> 'If you can. Put resupply on a helo. Try to take it out to the northern crash site. They're running out of ammo, IV bottles and water. Over.'

This exchange is revealing. That General Garrison should enquire as to the need for resupply and then ask if that resupply should be delivered by air throws some doubt on his judgement. Resupply should have been one of his most urgent considerations and he, by now, was fully aware that resupply by road was impossible.

The African night was not far off, and Captain Steele asked of his men, those he could reach, if anyone had brought with them their night observation device. The answer was completely negative. There was a further issue that would affect the conduct in what was now, in effect, a siege. That was that conventional army discipline had broken down. Captain Steele, the commander of the Ranger element, had some Delta soldiers with his group. They did not recognise Steele's authority.

Captain Miller, the Delta commander, was in radio contact with all his men and twice a Delta soldier in Steele's group invited the Ranger officer to talk to Miller on the Delta radio net. Steele declined. To compound the difficulties now being faced by the besieged soldiers they had two commanders who, although being in close proximity, were not talking to each other.

In Garrison's headquarters, the resupply operation was viewed with apprehension. It would call for a Black Hawk to fly into the small siege area, hover long enough to unload and hopefully avoid any RPG fire. There was every likelihood of the aircraft being shot down and the crew killed.

CWOs Stan Wood and Gary Fuller, who were piloting *Super Six-Six*, were given the unenviable resupply task. With their aircraft filled with all the necessities, and in the darkness of early evening, they flew over the city centre, looking for the infrared strobe lights that had been set out to guide them in.

The Somali opposition, seeing the strobe lights, was able to anticipate what would come next and as *Super Six-Six* hovered over the selected LZ just south of the crash site, it was greeted by machine-gun fire from several points. However, the rotors of the helicopter created a dust storm, which inadvertently provided some cover from the view of the enemy – but not cover from fire.

In *Super Six-Six*, Delta Sergeant First Class Alex Szigedi and a comrade had the task of pushing the resupply out of the aircraft. It was a most hazardous job in the face of a torrent of fire. The Black Hawk was absorbing countless bullet strikes and holes were now all over the helicopter. As the mixed load was pushed out, the aircraft was only hovering for about half a minute, but it must have seemed like an age as small arms fire swept around it. Szigedi, who had survived the peregrinations of the convoy unwounded, was now wounded, but survived.

The Black Hawk was badly damaged and leaking vital oil. The transmission system had been hit but, curiously, when the aircraft was a sitting duck for an RPG gunner, none brought such a weapon to bear and *Super Six-Six* was able to lift off and limp home. As it turned away, the recipients of its cargo rushed out and swept up the lifesaving bounty. This resupply mission was accomplished by a group of very brave men, and it was their courage that allowed the ninety-nine to fight on.

The command situation on the ground was confused, the disposition of the troops was 'untidy' in that they were split up in packets and spread across two blocks centred on the wreckage of *Super Six-One*. This was where the CSAR team had roped in for their, as it happens, unnecessary, rescue mission. Chalk Two of the Rangers, led by Lieutenant DiTomasso, were alongside them having taken advantage of a breach in a wall made by the crashing aircraft. These thirty-three men had deployed into adjacent and accessible buildings and courtyards but in total, there were ninety-nine Americans holed up in the middle of a very hostile city.

Despite constant air support, they could go nowhere, and it looked as if a long night lay ahead – and one to be shared with their enemies. The Rangers and Delta operators had spread themselves over a two-block area and were in contact with hostiles who were sometimes only a door away.[1] There were now many wounded to shield and treat and for that purpose the Americans grouped their wounded in four houses facing Freedom Road. Incarcerated alongside the American wounded were about twenty Somali civilians, including several children.

Colonel Sharif Hassan Giumale commanded most of the Somali forces on the ground in central Mogadishu. At 1840 hrs, Aidid sent him precise instructions to counter any forthcoming American ground reinforcements. His mission was to take and destroy the Americans, now surrounded – none were to escape. Giumale deployed about 360 of his armed SNA around the crash site and in addition had the support of hundreds of armed but ill-disciplined volunteers who were not, specifically, associated with the SNA.[2]

Giumale decided to reduce to rubble the four houses giving sanctuary to the Americans. To do this he would employ the six 60mm mortars he had in his arsenal. These were formidable weapons, which only hardened defences could resist. Then, the colonel was alerted to the presence of Somali citizens being held in his target area and realised that any casualties among them caused by SNA mortars would be highly counter-productive.

It was pure chance that these civilians had been caught up in the fighting, but their presence limited the options open to Giumale. Later, the SNA would allege that these civilians had been used as human shields, a claim hotly and reasonably denied by the Americans.[3]

Private George Siegler was responsible for guarding a group of the civilians – three adults and four children. They were all predictably distressed and one of the women, who was heavily pregnant, cried and indicated to Siegler that she was thirsty. The young soldier shared his canteen with her. It was a rare few seconds of compassion in a day filled only with anger, hate and death.

As night fell, the armed volunteers melted away and left the hard-core SNA to contain the invaders. The shooting level was reduced, but it was far more effective. The exposure of any sort of fleeting target attracted a fusillade, but curiously, the SNA did not assault the *ad hoc* Ranger and Delta defences. This was, perhaps, a missed opportunity because there was, in prospect, the inevitability of massive American response – a matter Garrison was now addressing.

The SNA might well have considered the merits of an all-out assault, but the constant presence of two AH-6 Little Birds was a significant deterrent as the aircraft repeatedly strafed presumed SNA positions. On this basis, the SNA massing in the open, under the Little Birds' sights, was a non-starter.

Monitoring the various radio nets provided a big picture but it was also misleading and disconcerting. The single item of information the besieged wanted was the ETA of the rescue mission, if indeed there was one. 'It's half an hour away,' was one report, followed soon after by, 'It's an hour away.' There were several such reports and eventually, 'They're on their way' became a joke.

In Washington, news of the situation spread quickly and the National Security Advisor, Tony Lake, was brought up to speed. However, in the context of world affairs, a minor, military clash on the far side of the world was relatively 'small potatoes'. President Clinton was far more concerned about fast-moving events in Moscow, where President Boris Yeltsin was resisting a *coup d'état*. The President did not make mention of Mogadishu in his press conference that morning just before he flew off to San Francisco for a speaking tour.[4]

Chapter 18

The Relief Convoy

Lieutenant Colonel Lawrence Casper, the commander of the US Quick Reaction Force, had responded to the developing debacle. He mounted a relief force that made a brief intervention, but it only got as far as the K4 roundabout. At this point, his force met overwhelming opposition from 'rifles and rockets' and in the face of this heavy fire he was obliged to withdraw.[1]

It was now evident to General Garrison that the rescue of his men, surrounded at the first crash site, was now well beyond the limited resources of his Special Forces, and that he would need assistance from other UNOSOM II nations.

The planning of GOTHIC SERPENT had, quite correctly, involved the smallest practical number of individuals. On this basis none of the UN contingents were aware of the operation and nor were other American formations 'who did not need to know'. In late afternoon on 3 October, Garrison had to start the salvation of his surrounded troops from scratch, and time was not on his side. It was early evening when he appointed Lieutenant Colonel Bill David, a battalion commander from 10 Mountain Division, to build and lead a rescue convoy.

There was a need for armoured vehicles, and these could only be furnished by the Malaysians and Pakistanis. The Malaysians had Condor APCs that could hold six men. The Pakistanis could provide four American-built M-48 tanks, but were unenthused at committing them to an urban battlefield. Like all tank soldiers, they would try to avoid situations in which their enemy could approach on foot. Mogadishu, with its narrow streets, would severely limit the ability of the tanks to manoeuvre and they were vulnerable to RPGs from close range.

Colonel David was going to use all his powers of persuasion to cobble together a viable relief convoy. Many of the survivors of the earlier 'Lost

Malaysian, German-built Condor armoured personnel carriers.

Convoy' had washed, eaten, changed clothes, cleaned their weapons and were anxious to get back in the fight. They were supplemented by two companies from 10 Mountain Division: in all, David assembled 500 men.

For the Mountain Division soldiers, long treated with distain by Rangers, Delta and SEALs, it was sweet to be tasked to rescue those who judged themselves to be so vastly superior in all the military skills.

David asked the Malaysians for the use of their armoured personnel carriers and then, with an extraordinary quality of insouciance, asked them to vacate their APCs and hand them over to American soldiers.

Predictably, this idea did not fly.

However, a compromise was reached. It was agreed that Malaysian soldiers would drive the APCs and provide the gunner in each vehicle. American infantry replaced Malaysian.

David had the men, the armour, the APCs, Humvees and several M-939 5-ton flatbed trucks – a total of around 100 sets of assorted wheels and some tracks. Now he had to determine their order on the road. The convoy would be 2 miles long and vulnerable along its entire length – it would be a tasty target for the SNA, although Black Hawk and Cobra gunships would be providing lethal top cover all the way. The Little Birds remained in the closest support of the surrounded men grouped at crash site one.

At 2130 hrs, the men of the rescue force left their airport base and drove to New Port, further north, where the Malaysians and Pakistanis were based. Here they met up with their armoured component. It took a further hour and a half to get everyone mounted and the vehicles arranged in the desired sequence. David had placed the tanks at the head of the column and following on would be groups of four APCs interspersed with trucks and Humvees.[2]

The master plan was that this vast convoy would split in National Street. One half would head south for the site of *Super Six-Four* and the other half to *Super Six-One* and the besieged group. The reason for going to *Super Six-Four* was because there was an outside possibility of there being survivors.

At 2300 hrs, and just as the vast cavalcade was to start, the Pakistanis threw a spanner in the works. The Pakistani commander, probably a major, now objected to leading the column. There were hasty negotiations, and the compromise was that the tanks would lead as far as K4 and then fall back in the column. This was a hammer blow to David's plan because the function of the tanks was to breach the many barricades, already erected, along the obvious route. The Pakistani's argument was that the Somalis sowed mines in their barricades and his tanks would be at risk. Armoured warfare is always risky, and armoured soldiers are expected to recognise this when they enlist. It's not like working in a bank!

To add to David's problems the Malaysians then announced that their APCs could only function on the main roads. They asserted, correctly, the narrow secondary streets, which gave little or no room for manoeuvre, placed them at undue risk too.

David dismounted, engines were turned off and the commander talked to Captain Drew Meyerowich, the commander of the leading rifle company, already mounted in the APCs. Meyerowich was told that he would take over the lead of the column when the tanks fell back at K4. Time had been lost, and it was now 2323 hrs.

The convoy lurched into movement and, under a bright moon, the sound of the engines and the tank tracks carried as far as the beleaguered

Captain Steele. He had noted, while waiting for relief, that inexplicably, Somali gunmen wandered in the street just up from his Ranger position. The Somalis seeming unaware of their danger, the Delta soldiers allowed them to come just so far and then ruthlessly shot them down.

The northern part of the rescue column came up to its first barricade in Hawlwadig Road. The leading APC stopped, and the driver refused to breach the obstacle. Despite Meyerowich cajoling and pleading, the driver was adamant and American soldiers dismantled the obstacle by hand. More time was lost.

Thereafter, as the column wove its ponderous way through the labyrinthine streets of Mogadishu the two leading vehicles, driven by Malaysians but presumably under the direction of an American officer, took a wrong turning. This was a replay of the earlier 'Lost Convoy's' peregrinations.

It was a dreadful mistake because they ran into the fire of a heavy machine gun and an RPG gunner. Both APCs were destroyed. One of the Malaysian drivers was killed and several of the American passengers were wounded.[3] The Pakistani tanks attracted heavy fire, and they promptly responded with their 105mm main armament.[4]

The brief halt had allowed the Somalis to focus their small arms fire and Colonel Bill David realised that he had to keep moving, despite the succession of ambushes laid for him. At National Street, close to the Olympic Hotel, as planned, the convoy split. The rate of incoming fire was now sufficiently intense that the Malaysian drivers refused to go on. There was no alternative but to take on the attackers and, despite numerous casualties, the troops dismounted to engage the Somali fighters. The Humvees discharged their 40mm grenades in support and this battle within a battle was eventually won. But it all took time, and it was not until 0155 hrs that the convoy reached its two destinations.

The 2-mile journey had taken three painful hours. Steele heard the vehicles before he saw them, his soldiers called out 'Ranger, Ranger' and drew the response 'Tenth Mountain Division'. Steele identified himself and went to find the commander.

The rescue column had come equipped to cut 'Elvis' Wolcott out of his twisted steel tomb. His Black Hawk was a mass of buckled metal, and it would not give up Wolcott's body without a fight. The heavy-duty metal saws now being employed were thwarted by the layer of Kevlar that lined the remains of the cockpit. The creed was that the dead and wounded would always be recovered but, in this case, it was proving to be particularly difficult.

It was taking far too long, and the delay gave the SNA an opportunity to position its forces to oppose the withdrawal of the column that would be bearing all the dead and wounded. That withdrawal was dependent upon the wreck of *Super Six-One* surrendering the body of its pilot, but the protracted delay in cutting him free posed a risk to the living. The recovery of one of the dead may not have been questioned publicly, but doubtless, some wondered if they should give their lives for this purpose.

The wounded were stoic to a man. Sergeant Mike Goodale had been shot in the backside. It was painful and when he limped out to board an APC, he was told to sit. He protested, saying, 'Look, I got shot in the ass.' The unsympathetic reply was, 'Then lean on something.' Private Carlos Rodriguez, who had been fitted with inflated rubber pants to alleviate the damage to his leg, had a positive attitude. When it was suggested that he would be moved on a stretcher, he said, 'I'm OK, I can stand on one leg. Just help me over to the vehicle. I've still got my weapon.'

The insides of the APCs were like ovens. They reeked of urine, blood and sweat. If this was safety, it did not have much going for it. Meanwhile, the entire column was stationery and there was mounting frustration and irritation among the men, who were only too anxious to start the return journey.

In the sky far above, the senior officers were similarly frustrated. Lieutenant Colonel Gary Harrell keyed his radio: 'Scotty [Miller]. Give me an update. Please.'

Miller was watching the struggle to free Wolcott's body and in the meantime, about 300 American soldiers were isolated in the middle of a hostile – very hostile – city. Miller replied cryptically:

> 'Roger. They're trying to pull it apart. So far, no luck.'
>
> 'Roger, you've only got about an hour's worth of darkness left.'[5]

The wounded, who had ached for relief, now found the waiting in the APCs added to their misery and most had no idea why they were slowly stewing in their own sweat. General Garrison shared their frustration. When he was told that the wreck of *Super Six-One* was being pulled to pieces, he radioed and, in typically forthright tones, he said:

> 'OK, are they going to be able to get the body out of there? I need an honest, no shit, for real assessment from the platoon leader or the senior man present. Over.'[6]

Miller replied, saying it would take twenty more minutes to extract the remains of Cliff Wolcott. Garrison accepted that all involved were doing their level best and told Miller to continue the task.

The sky started to lighten; there was a pink glow on the distant horizon and darkness, which had been such a good friend, was preparing to leave. Daylight would play into the hands of the SNA. To the 300 men waiting to get out of town, the twenty minutes seemed to take longer. Then, at last, Wolcott's body was finally cut from the wreck, and the moment generated a critical radio transmission from Harrell observing the scene from far above. He radioed his commander, Garrison:

> 'Adam Six-Four [Garrison]. This is Romeo Six-Four [Harrell]. They are starting to at this time. Over. Placing charges and getting ready to move.'[7]

The original invaders had been in continuous action for fourteen hours. They were all very tired, hungry and thirsty. They prepared to mount a vehicle for the long-awaited journey back to base, a shower and a cold beer. Rather like a child being told that Christmas was cancelled, it would be true to say that the Rangers, Delta and SEAL soldiers were somewhat discommoded to discover that all the APCs and trucks were full and there was no room for them.

The Malaysian drivers did not linger; and if their vehicle was full, or full enough, they left the scene at speed, leaving dozens of men behind. This unfortunate group would have to run through the city and along the same streets that the Somalis had defended so vigorously the day before. If ever the arduous training of US Special Forces needed to be justified, the events of the next half an hour would suffice.

Unknown to the Americans, Aidid had viewed the death toll among his countrymen and women with great concern. He had as his prisoner Michael

Durant, the pilot and sole survivor of *Super Six-Four*. Aidid saw Durant as a valuable negotiating asset. He realised that if he killed more Americans, it would trigger an overwhelming American response and cause further, vast Somali casualties. Shrewdly, Aidid instructed Colonel Sharif Hassan Giumale to open a corridor for the Americans to use.[8] His orders were to be disobeyed in places by some who probably did not get the message.

The men abandoned by the convoy were going to have to run, in full kit, for about 2 miles in the face of armed opposition. They could not afford to take any casualties because carrying a wounded man or men would reduce progress to a crawl and invite yet more casualties.

The possibility of running alongside the APCs disappeared as the Malaysian drivers had other, more urgent plans. This state of affairs reflects badly on the American officers safely aboard the vehicles. They clearly either did not check that everyone was loaded or they effectively ceded command of the massive convoy to private soldier drivers, uncommitted to the mission. This was a scenario that could, so easily, have ended in a debacle and a bloodbath.

The evacuation of the *Super Six-One* location was led by Captain Steele accompanied by nine of his Rangers and, just behind, were the Delta and SEALs. The CSAR team who had been inserted unnecessarily now ran for their lives. At each of the many intersections, the runners opened fire at any likely target.

Just before they reached the Olympic Hotel, Sergeant Randy Ramaglia could see the end of the convoy some way ahead. Even at a distance, he could see small arms fire hitting the armoured vehicles. This was the route home and he and his comrades were going to have to run through that same location. It was at this point that Ramaglia was shot in the back. He lost the use of his left arm, but his legs still worked, and he kept on running.

This running retreat had no cohesion, no plan, no command arrangements. It was every man for himself and 'All semblance of an ordered retreat was gone. Everybody was just scrambling.'[9] It was as well that Aidid was 'pulling his punches'. However, Stephen Biddle, writing in 2021 and long after the event, commented that, despite Aidid's orders, the American troops 'faced fierce shooting until they withdrew'.[10] He went on to say:

> It was the UN, not the SNA, that disengaged to end the fighting. The relief column that ultimately extracted TF Ranger had to fight its way into and out of the Bakaara Market. SNA fighters were resisting fiercely until UN forces crossed out of Aidid's zone of control and withdrew to their bases.[11]

Biddle's view is challenged. The lack of casualties during the 'run out' does not support the assertion of 'fierce shooting' or that the SNA were 'resisting fiercely'.

Delta Sergeant Paul Howe was as cool as ever. At one point in this mad race, he kicked open a door and several of the runners joined him to catch their breath and reload. Howe checked on each man. On Captain Miller's command, they all rejoined 'the race'.

As each man ran, he was aware of the helicopters overhead and the roar of their guns giving invaluable support. Bowden's summation of the situation cannot be bettered, and he wrote:

> They ran through the oily smell of the city and of their own bodies, the taste of dust in their dry mouths, with the crisp brown bloodstains on their fatigues and the fresh memory of friends dead or unspeakably mangled, with the whole nightmare now grown unbearably long with disbelief that the mighty and terrible army of the United States of America had plunged into this mess and stranded them there and now left them to run through the same deadly gauntlet to get out. *How could this happen* [Bowden's emphasis]?[12]

Bowden's incredulity was shared by many Americans, both military and civilian, who found it difficult to accept that the 'best army in the world' had been defeated by a disorganised, largely civilian mob. The wounded Ramaglia started to feel the effects of his wound, felt unstable and realised he was not going to go much further. It was with a mixture of relief and unabated joy that, as he approached the Hawlwadig Road and National Street intersection, he saw a line of vehicles and men in desert fatigues. He was safe, but it had been 'a close-run thing', as Wellington might have remarked.[13]

Above, AH-1 Cobras and Little Birds continued to overfly the fleeing men and suppressed enemy activity until, at 0630 hrs, the leading vehicles reached the Pakistani base at Mogadishu Stadium. 'By 0700 hrs, the last runner had reached safety at an aid station inside the stadium.'[14] Incredibly, the runners had not suffered either a fatality or a serious injury. However, all were mentally and physically exhausted.

Inside the stadium the grassed pitch was covered in wounded men, and unwounded survivors walked among them looking for friends. The doctors were overwhelmed but had to prioritise their patients, some of whom were surviving Somali prisoners, depending on the gravity of their injuries. Clothes were cut off to expose the wounds, some of which were life changing. The dead had already started to putrefy, and the rising sun accelerated that awful process.

The men of 10th Mountain Division and who had not participated in the operation helped where they could, but others not so occupied sat in the stands, smoked and chatted.

Chapter 19

4 October, Aftermath

Bashir Haji Yusu, a lawyer by profession, early in the morning of 4 October took his video camera to survey the damage to his city. The streets of Mogadishu were littered with dead donkeys; walls and road surfaces were bloodstained. There were a few corpses, but most had been removed by family members. Bashir recorded the still smouldering wreck of a Humvee and the silent and empty, damaged APCs.

Bashir could see a gathering of people who seemed to be excited about something. He approached and was appalled to see the body of an American soldier 'draped backwards over a wheelbarrow. The body wore only undershorts; it was covered with dry blood and there were bullet holes in the chest and arm.'[1] It was a sad and gruesome sight.

The wheelbarrow was pushed down the street and spectators spat and struck the body. The hatred in the air was palpable and Bashir was disgusted at this abandonment of normal Islamic conduct in which the dead are accorded appropriate dignity. The body was one of the several Americans that had been killed in and around the wreck of *Super Six-Four*.

Elsewhere, a similar scene was playing out around the K4 roundabout. Here another near naked American body was being dragged through the street. A small UN patrol of Saudi Arabian soldiers approached. The Saudis were not perceived to be the 'enemy', not least because they too were Muslims. The exchange between the two groups was chronicled by Bowden:

> 'What are you doing?' one of the soldiers asked.
>
> 'We have Animal Howe,' answered an armed young man, one of the ringleaders.
>
> 'This is an American soldier,' supplied another.
>
> 'If he is dead, why are you doing this? Aren't you a human being?' the Saudi soldier asked the ringleader, insulting him.
>
> One of the Somalis pointed his gun at the Saudi soldier. 'We will kill you too,' the gunman said.

Hideous behaviour by a Somali mob on 4 October 1993. An image seen around the world.

People at the back of the crowd shouted at the Saudi, 'Leave it, leave it alone! These people are angry. They might kill you.'

'But why do you do this?' the Saudi persisted. 'You can fight, and they can fight, but this man is dead. Why do you drag him?'

More guns were pointed at the Saudis. The disgusted soldiers drove off.[2]

There was universal disgust at this grotesque Somali behaviour and, although it cannot be condoned, an explanation was provided by Captain Haad of the Somali National Alliance – albeit twenty-nine years later. He claimed that the bodies of the US soldiers had been dragged through the streets by enraged civilians/irregulars who had lost dozens of friends and family, and that the actual SNA soldiers had not partaken in the incident.[3] In this interview, he referred to Bloody Monday (12 July 1993) and said:

> Wouldn't you be very sorry? About 73 of our elder men, our religious leaders, our most prominent people, having their bodies mutilated – we collected parts of their bodies from the building in which they were attacked. If you were a son of one of those people killed on that day, what would be your situation, how would you feel?

Several days after the incident, the SNA issued a public appeal, stating that despite the 'wanton destruction and suffering beyond human comprehension' inflicted by UNOSOM II and US forces, the alliance urged respect towards the deceased, injured, and prisoners of war, in accordance with Islamic principles.[4]

The fighting had ceased, and it was time to count the cost in human terms. The US lost eighteen killed and between eighty-four and ninety-seven wounded in the Battle of Mogadishu. During its stay in Somalia, 26 Americans were killed and 170 wounded. Nations contributing to UNOSOM I and II lost fifty confirmed dead but there were probably several more. Wounded were not accounted for.

Scott Peterson addressed the issue of Somali casualties at the hands of UNOSOM and II and the USA. He confirmed that determining an accurate audit was dependent on the provision of the unvarnished truth and that was scarce. He wrote, contemporaneously:

> Aidid told me that 13,000 Somalis had died at the hands of UN 'peacekeepers'. After regular denials of any significant Somali casualties from other officials US envoy Oakley estimated 6,000 to 10,000 casualties but made no breakdown of dead and wounded. Two thirds of these were said to be women and children.[5]

In the Battle of Mogadishu, Somali casualties are poorly defined. Robert Oakley was questioned on TV and asked to comment on the Somali casualties on 3 October. He replied:

> My own personal estimate is that there must have been 1,500 to 2,000 Somalis killed and wounded that day, because that battle was a true battle. And the Americans, and those who came to their rescue, were being shot at from all sides … a deliberate war battle, if you will, on the part of the Somalis. And women and children were being used as shields and in some cases women and children were actually firing weapons and were coming from all sides. Sort of a rabbit warren of huts, houses, alleys, and twisting and turning streets, so those who were trying to defend themselves were shooting back in all directions. Helicopter gunships were being used as well as all sorts of automatic weapons on the ground by the US and the United Nations. The Somalis, by and large, were using automatic rifles and grenade launchers and it was a very nasty fight, as intense as almost any battle you would find.[6]

The consensus is that the number killed was somewhere in the range 315–700 killed and 812–1,000 wounded.[7] This author favours the higher number of killed. The rationale is on the basis, mentioned by Oakley, of the number of occasions high-calibre automatic, quick-firing weaponry was directed into crowds.

Chapter 20

The Imprisonment of CWO 3 Michael Durant, 4–14 October

There remained the unfinished business of Michael Durant, the imprisoned pilot of *Super Six-Four*. Very badly injured and in persistent pain, Durant had feared for his life from the moment of his capture. His incarceration and the loudly expressed demands by the US Government that he be released was international news.

Mohammed Gait was assigned briefly as Durant's companion and it was he who brought him indifferent food and then told the pilot that the rest of his crew were dead. He said:

> Your friends had no pain. They are not living. But some of their bodies were beaten, dragged in these streets of Mogadishu. Some, they were cut into parts and pulled along. I saw this. Many Somalis very angry with the UN and the Americans. Many, many Somalis die in the fighting. Our women, they are the most angry. They are also the most cruel. A Somali woman must make her revenge upon a person who kills her son or husband. She must take something from the guilty person. There is no trial, no jury. This is justice in our world.[1]

Mohammed, seeing the horror on Duran's face, added quickly, 'You must understand, but the people have not control. They were very, very angry. No one could stop them.' Durant did not know, but the images of his friends had been viewed around the world and had served to alter perceptions of who had committed atrocities in Somalia.

A little later, Mohammed remarked, 'The people look for you. They know you are a prisoner somewhere and want to kill you. You have much luck, to be a prisoner of the militia.'

Durant was aware that it was not just Somalis who were looking for him; so too were his comrades. He had not been abandoned, as he could hear the loudspeakers broadcasting in the sky above his prison. Their constant message was, 'We have not forgotten you, Michael.' It was good for morale but did nothing to improve his condition.

4 October (Day 2): It was on this day that Durant first met Mr Abdi, who, judging from his demeanour and the deference of the companioning Somalis, was obviously a man of some consequence. Abdi's English was modulated and fluent.[2] He enquired as to Durant's needs and the wounded man said that he needed a doctor. Abdi asked Durant to make a video, clearly for propaganda purposes. He declined but realised that he could not prevent himself being videoed. He was pressed for information on his unit and, showing as much respect as he could summon, declined to give that too.

Soon after, and much to Durant's surprise, a doctor came into his cell and introduced himself as Dr Abdullah Hashi Kediye. The doctor, who had attended medical school in California, spoke fluent English. He examined Durant's leg and pronounced, 'This leg looks very bad.' He explained that he had come from Digfer Hospital, where they were treating hundreds of Somali wounded, and observed, 'This is not California; we have few supplies and virtually no surgical equipment.'[3]

The parlous state of the Somali medical organisation was exemplified by the provision of just four aspirin and a handful of antibiotic tablets. Durant was given a warm can of Pepsi-Cola and then the interrogators returned. They manhandled him into a sitting position and by so doing, they caused him excruciating pain. A team arrived with lights and video cameras. The prisoner was asked the same questions, and again he refused to give more than his name and rank. The interrogator was irritated, and it showed. He said to Durant:

> We have brought a doctor for you. This doctor say [*sic*] your wounds are very serious. You would like us to invite him again, no? We take care of you and then you see your family again. You only must answer questions. It is so very simple.

Durant was under enormous physical and mental pressure, and he admitted to being a soldier. He was asked, 'Why did you kill innocent people?' and he responded, 'Innocent people being killed is not good.'[4] It was what they wanted. The lights were turned off. Four heavily armed men arrived and told Durant that he needed to be moved for his own safety.

The move into a vehicle ramped his pain up to a new dreadful level. The team leader, he learned later, was called Abdullah Hassan Mohamed Firimbi and he became Durant's constant companion for the remainder of his imprisonment. He ate and slept in the same room.

The video was shown around the world and Durant's face featured on the cover of any number of news magazines. Three examples are below.

The doctor reappeared and having donned surgical gloves and taken a pair of forceps, he commented to his patient, 'This is going to hurt you a bit.' It did and, as he sought to clean and sanitise the wound, he probed for the ends of the broken bone. It was an agonising process although it occurred to Durant that if the Somalis were prepared to give him some of their very scarce medical care, then the probability was that they did not want to kill him.

5 October (Day 3): Robert Oakley was at a drinks party when he received a phone call from Anthony Lake, the National Security Adviser to President Clinton. The call was to arrange a meeting.

Oakley, a career diplomat, was a quick-witted and outspoken man but of considerable intellect. He was also well acquainted with Somalia and its culture and had represented President George Bush throughout Operation RESTORE HOPE. He had handed over his diplomatic responsibilities to Admiral Jonathan Howe back in March 1993. Since then, he had watched with dismay the increasing mayhem in Somalia and the faltering efforts of the UN to stem the chaos. He was at a loss to think what, if anything, he could do to help – especially after the crushing debacle of the Battle of Mogadishu.

Leslie Aspin had been grilled by members of the House, who echoed the anger felt by their constituents. 'How could this happen?' (page 180) was being asked, and the answers were inadequate. The intelligence failures, a factor in the humiliating defeat of the 'best army in the world' by a civilian mob, was difficult to stomach. 'The size, scope and ferocity of Aidid's counterattack on 3 October had stunned members of Congress.'[5]

Oakley met with President Clinton, Vice President Al Gore, Anthony Lake and his deputy, Samuel Berger. US Ambassador to the UN Madeleine Albright and a representative of Chairman of the Joint Chiefs of Staff were also present. The meeting lasted six long hours as Clinton ruminated on how he was to ameliorate a political, diplomatic, domestic and military disaster.

American diplomat Robert B. Oakley (1931–2014), photographed in Somalia in 1993.

It was conceded by the advisory group that Aidid had won a major victory. Clinton decided that the US would discontinue military action, negotiate with Aidid and withdraw all its troops from Somalia by March 1994. Oakley was charged to deliver the message but also to warn Aidid of the cataclysmic military action that would follow if Durant was not released.

6 October (Day 4): Durant's food looked as if it had improved when he was given an American-issue 'Meal, Ready-to-Eat' (MRE). However, in this case the packaging was weather-beaten, the lettering faded and the contents only edible to a very hungry man with no other options. Firimbi was playing the part of guardian and nurse. He helped Durant to wash himself and Durant wrote that Firimbi:

> was methodical and thorough taking care not to cause me any additional pain as he worked over my limbs. The task didn't appear to be subservient to him, just an assignment that he had been given and intended to carry out well.[6]

Minister Abdi swept in to ask if Durant would welcome a visit by a representative of the International Red Cross. However, the *quid pro quo* was that Durant would talk to journalists. Durant's instant refusal irritated Abdi but he said that he would send a radio. Durant expressed his gratitude for the radio but then he asked, 'Mr Minister, when will I be allowed to see my family?' The subtext was, 'When will I be released?'

Abdi's response was specific. He said, 'You will be released, Mr Durant, when the United Nations releases the twenty-four Somalis who were captured by your task force. One prisoner for twenty-four. I think that is a fair exchange, don't you?'[7]

The radio was delivered and thereafter, having searched all the available wavelengths, Durant was able to listen to the BBC World Service, US Armed Forces Network and Radio Mogadishu. Through these means Durant learned that the original targets of Operation GOTHIC SERPENT were Abdi Qeybdiid Hasan Awale and Omar Salad Elmi.

7 October (Day 5): The radio continued to provide Durant with updates on the current situation and a US spokesman confirmed many of Durant's fears about the fate of his friends. He took comfort from the fact that his imprisonment was mentioned. He also took comfort from a further visit by the doctor, who announced that he was going to apply a splint to his broken leg. The doctor left a bottle of aspirin and another of antibiotics.

When the doctor left, Durant found that the splint was not a success. He experienced great pain when he made any movement of his leg. He resolved to get the doctor to remove his handiwork.

He lay on his back, tried to keep his leg still and heard a voice. It was an amplified voice but still instantly recognisable as that of his old friend Dan Jollota. The voice boomed: 'Mike Durant ... we will not leave without you.' The message was repeated and, as the Black Hawk flew away, so the voice faded.

8 October (Day 6): There was a sudden and significant change in the atmosphere. A bed was delivered, complete with mattress and flowered cotton sheets. Durant was lifted from the floor onto this bed, a painful process. A bedside cabinet was added and upon this were placed more of the degraded MREs, the radio, aspirin and antibiotics.

Durant recorded:

> Firimbi brought in a yellow plastic bottle and my dog bowl. Filled with water. He then proceeded to give me a full-up 'whore's bath' from toes to nose, including shampooing my hair in the bowl and drying me off with a towel.

The largess did not stop there. The room was sprayed with a rose-scented mist and then one of the guards arrived bearing a tin of talcum powder and a can of deodorant. Durant was dusted all over with the talc and then comprehensively sprayed with the deodorant. He commented, 'I smelled like a French hooker.' He was offered a suit of blue hospital pyjamas but all the attention he had been given had inadvertently caused him pain, and he declined the pyjama offer, although he did accept the gift of a fly swatter.[8]

The reason for all that close attention became clear when a young, mid-thirties European woman with shoulder-length blonde hair and deep blue eyes entered the room. She gave Durant a bewitching smile and he noted that 'her face glowed with a deep tan'.

To be confronted by this vision who 'looked like an angel' was all a bit much for Durant and he thought he was 'dreaming'. The young woman took Durant's hand and said in a soft Scandinavian accent, 'Hello, Michael. I'm Suzanne Hofstetter from the International Committee of the Red Cross.'[9]

The very presence of this attractive young woman was viewed by Durant as 'a gift from God'. However, she deflated him when she said that he was not being released immediately but that release might come 'very soon'. When she enquired about his treatment, Durant pulled his punches because it was evident that the Somali men who accompanied her all spoke English. He did not criticise his medical treatment but limited himself to saying, 'I'm concerned about my survival.' Ms Hofstetter got the message, and she replied, as much for the benefit of her escorts as for Durant:

> I understand your concern. Well, I can tell you that everything that could possibly be done to get you released is being done and now that the Red Cross is involved the Somalis know that they are fully accountable for you.[10]

She gave Durant the opportunity to write a letter to his wife and family, a letter later scrutinised at length by the intelligence service. She also gave him the chance to write to his comrades, and in that letter, he said that he had heard the message broadcast by Dan Jollota.

Suzanne Hofstetter's very welcome visit had lasted about an hour, but her escorts had told her she was at risk and so she had to leave. The moment she departed, she left an unfillable void. Durant acknowledged that his head was spinning. He had 'not been released but he was overcome with emotion. Happiness, sadness, hope and despair all rolled into one.'[11]

Suzanne Hofstetter (1958–2017), the representative of the International Red Cross.

Almost immediately after Ms Hofstetter had gone, two Caucasian men entered Durant's room. They were journalists and their presence was the *quid pro quo* for the IRC visit. Durant was furious but stipulated that he would not answer any questions about his unit or their mission. However, he was lured into saying, 'Americans are good people by nature. We normally want to help when we see people in need. We did *try* [Durant's emphasis] to help. Something has gone wrong here.'

It was a mistake, but the journalists had what they wanted and left the pilot to rue his incautious remark. The simple fact, widely acknowledged, was that a lot had gone 'wrong' in Somalia. But it was not Durant's remit to make such a judgement.

His comrades could not have cared less and their support for him was reflected on subsequent radio programmes in which there were many requests for music to be played for him. The Somalis realised that perhaps Ms Hofstetter or the journalists might reveal the location of his now much more comfortable prison and Firimbi announced that he was to be relocated – again.

Durant was told that he had to be moved but he said that he could not face a move sitting in a car. He had to lay flat, and so he explained he had to travel in a truck. In the event, no truck was available, and he was moved in a car anyway. His splinted leg was the site of extreme pain of a quality that almost made him pass out. He thought he was going to die.

At the new location, a single-storey building he described as a 'ranch house', he was once more laid on the floor. There was no bed, no radio, no aspirin but there was constant, unbearable pain, which he had to bear. He made it clear to Firimbi that he needed the doctor – and very soon. The doctor did attend, and Durant demanded that the splint be removed. The doctor demurred but Durant insisted. His leg still hurt like hell, but a little less than before.

Firimbi started to talk of a ceasefire. His English was very limited, but he got across the fact that Aidid was no longer going to shoot, and neither was the UN. Durant realised that a cease in hostilities was to his advantage.

9 October (Day 7): Durant acknowledged that 'there are no atheists in foxholes' and, on day 7 of his captivity, he reverted to the strict Catholicism he had set aside some years before. His revived faith gave him comfort and strength. Overnight, a box had been deposited in his cell, a gift presumably from Suzanne Hofstetter. The box contained all manner of riches: a disposable razor, shaving cream, a toothbrush and toothpaste. There were three paperback novels, a tablet of writing paper, two pens, a recently issued MRE, a bottle of water and a roll of toilet paper. Enclosed was a first aid kit, but its contents were sparse. Some Tylenol antibiotics and, strangely, a bottle of children's vitamins. Finally, and at the bottom of the box were two small wooden crosses on beaded neck chains, a pack of playing cards and a US Army Bible.

Durant felt sure that all these mundane gifts must contain something more significant, a weapon perhaps. He examined each item in forensic detail, but all his new possessions were just what they purported to be.[12]

Firimbi arrived with a bowl of hot water and Durant was afforded the luxury of a shave. He cleaned his teeth and his morale soared. However, the MRE had woken his digestive system and, for the first time since his capture, he had to defecate. He communicated this to Firimbi, who 'helped me to maneuvre my butt [over a bowl] … but let's just say that the man earned his combat pay that morning.'

The Bible contained several blank pages, and Durant saw that it might well serve as a record of his confinement. He wrote a succession of single words, each of which was designed to refresh his memory if he was ever released and given the chance to tell his story.

Over the next four days, items from his previous cell arrived. The bed was warmly welcomed, and the radio once again provided a link to the big world outside. Nevertheless, it was a time of extreme boredom enlivened only by the music requests being played for his benefit and at the request of his Night Hawk colleagues.

Durant was quite unaware of the high-level activity that his captivity had engendered nor of the pace of the negotiations to free him.

13 October (Day 11): Durant continued to make notations in his Bible but as one uneventful day merged into the next, there was little or nothing worthy of note other than yet another agonising move. By now, the pain generated by the broken leg was awful but it was something he had to live with. He noted:

> The two broken bones overlapped by more than two inches, the muscles atrophying and nerves twitching to compensate for the damage. My spine

> was locked stiff, and I'd discovered more shrapnel buried in my leg. The shards of metal cocooned inside knots of swollen flesh. But I still prayed that my buds would show up. They could haul me out of there any way they wanted, and I would welcome the agony.[13]

Durant had given hours of thought as to how he could escape – highly improbable given the severity of his wounds – or how he could signal his location. His army issue T-shirt had been taken from him just after his video interrogation. Durant reasoned that, if he asked for its return having been washed, the possibility was that the T-shirt would be hung out to dry. Clutching firmly on the very thinnest of straws, Durant hoped that the shirt would be spotted from the air and connected to him and his location. Of course, it didn't happen.

On the BBC came news of a meeting of clan elders to discuss Durant's release, but the prisoner dismissed it as being no more than speculation. The doctor paid a visit and announced that he was going to put the injured leg into a full plaster. Durant was having none of that. But he was overjoyed when, just before he left, the doctor handed over two photographs of Durant's wife Lorrie and his son Joey. A new MRE and box of milk were also provided, but drinking all of the milk at a single sitting was far more than Durant's digestion could take. He was comprehensively sick and Firimbi 'earned another combat medic decoration'.

Firimbi, back from his distasteful chores, excitedly told Durant, 'BBC now, BBC now!' Durant tuned in his radio and heard the BBC announcer say in his clipped British accent:

> The former American Ambassador to Somalia, Robert Oakley, has arrived in the Somali capital, Mogadishu, to engage in talks on behalf of the US Government. Ambassador Oakley was apparently dispatched at the behest of President Clinton in order to maintain the tenuous cease-fire presently in effect between Somali militias and UN forces. And perhaps to secure the release of a US helicopter pilot who was shot down and captured on October the third.[14]

Firimbi was enthused and in high good humour, pointing to the radio and repeating 'Oak-a-lee good. Oak-a-lee good!' Two of the guards entered and endorsed the view of Oak-a-lee but added, 'Howe, very Baaddd.' Their opinion of Admiral Howe was shared in other circles. Howe was recognised as being single-minded in his pursuit of Aidid, almost to the point of obsession. He had also been a main player in the Bloody Monday massacre. Little wonder that the Somali called him *Animal* Howe, and that he was a focus for Somali hate.

Oakley was taking a risk, but Aidid would not meet him, and Oakley had to work through intermediaries. Oakley duly delivered the message from Clinton that the US would withdraw from Somalia by the end of March 1994. By any yardstick, this was capitulation, and Aidid had achieved his aim of expelling American troops from Somalia, albeit in six months' time.

Both Bowden and Durant in their books speculate on what Oakley *might* have said. However, the consensus is that he made clear that unless Durant was released, the US would inflict Armageddon and would lay waste to Mogadishu. If Durant was released, US military operations would cease. It would reflect well on Aidid, and reasonable negotiations could follow. Aidid was content with that arrangement, and he agreed to release his prisoners.

The day ran to a close and Durant, unaware of the political activity, was reading his Bible when Minister Abdi appeared at his bedside. Abdi's demeanour was notably calm and relaxed. He muttered to Firimbi, who nodded and slipped out of the door. Abdi said, 'I have some news for you, Mr Durant.' He continued, 'The elders of the National Alliance have convened, they have made a decision.' There was a pause, and then he concluded, 'You will go home tomorrow. Unconditionally.'

Durant was stunned, relieved, ecstatic, and briefly speechless. But he managed to say '*Insh Allah*' (If God wills it). Abdi remarked pragmatically, 'It is no longer in the hands of God. It is in the hands of General Mohamed Farrah Aidid.' Abdi left Durant to his thoughts of home and family.

14 October (Day 12): Durant's last day in captivity started with more music being played for him on the Armed Forces Network. The announcer confirmed his imminent release but gave no details. Firimbi escorted a young African man into Durant's cell.

Durant could see that he was not a Somali; his face had none of the European elements that Somalis had absorbed over generations. This man had a broad, flat nose and a skin colour 'ink black'. The visitor was grinning from ear to ear and Firimbi introduced him, saying, 'This man prisoner, Nigerian.' Durant presumed that he had come to share his meagre facilities but only momentarily, because the man beamed, opened his arms wide and said, 'Free'.

It transpired that the Nigerian was a UN soldier captured about a month earlier. He too had been visited by Suzanne Hofstetter. His imprisonment had been accompanied by frequent, brutal torture. This young man would not have been privy to any information of use to Aidid. His torture was entirely gratuitous.

Durant commented, 'This was when the circus came to town.' Four dignitaries shuffled into the room. They all wore what appeared to be traditional, ethnic silk robes heavily decorated in geometric patterns, worn with flat-sided caps, not unlike a Fez.

They were a colourful sight and had clearly come for a party. They engaged in animated conversation in a language Durant could not identify. Somalis brought in teapots, cups and saucers. The scene bordered on the bizarre as Firimbi passed out snacks from a tray. Quite why the colourfully garbed gentlemen were there and what the purpose of the tea party was were never explained.

At this point, a Red Cross doctor arrived. He produced a form for Durant to sign and advised that he was about to administer some morphine. The morphine produced magical results. Durant recorded, 'It was like taking the first sip of cool clear water after crawling across a broiling desert for eleven days.'[15] The pain management worked but the journey to the American base in a three-vehicle convoy that followed was fraught with unexpected danger. Durant, laying on a litter in the second vehicle, had his feet projecting out of the back. He was very nearly decanted onto the road and into the path of the third vehicle when his driver braked. Firimbi grabbed Durant's hand and held him tightly until journey's end. Several times the litter slid towards oblivion, but each time, Firimbi was steadfast.

Later, Durant regretted that he did not have the chance to thank Firimbi for his care and companionship over the previous, nerve-racking and very painful eleven days. The Somali slipped away during the hectic reception that greeted Durant on friendly territory.

They never met again.

Chapter 21

Analysis

The fighting had stopped, and the dust began to settle. On 6 October 1993, President Clinton had accepted the untenable situation of American forces in Somalia and issued orders for the cessation of all military operations against the Somali National Alliance. The following day, he promulgated a significant defence and political policy change. He ruled that, in future, substantial US forces would be sent to Somalia only as short-term reinforcements. However, all American forces would be withdrawn from the country by the end of March 1994.

Years later, Clinton expressed a measure of surprise that the battle had even occurred and claimed that he had decided on a diplomatic solution before the incident. He was reported to have said:

> It's true that we had made good progress by mid-August through the efforts of former President Carter to reach a diplomatic solution. And by mid-September we thought we could start drawing back a bit. I knew we had good intelligence that indicated we could take some of the people who killed the Pakistani soldiers off the street, but I was surprised when I heard about the raid.[1]

Clinton distanced himself from any responsibility for the military command operating in Somalia, notwithstanding his status as commander-in-chief. He went on to say that Vietnam taught the US that military decisions should not be made in Washington, but from the 'commander on the scene', but he then reiterated that he was as surprised 'as the public' to find out about the raid and 'saddened' by the casualties.[2]

Despite Clinton's belated recollections there had been no direct orders previously given to Task Force Ranger to halt operations against the SNA. The extraction of US forces from anti-SNA operations in Somalia had a knock-on effect on the other UNOSOM II contingents. Thereafter, they all avoided any confrontation with the SNA. The practical effect was to terminate UNOSOM patrols in Mogadishu and to cease the manning of the numerous checkpoints in SNA-controlled territory.

Not unreasonably, the Somalis who had opposed the UN and the USA, and had shed copious amounts of blood in the streets of Mogadishu, saw the planned American withdrawal and the now quiescent UN as an outright victory. The international view was similar. The USA had suffered a humiliating defeat at the hands of an irregular force of partially armed civilians.

The question still to be answered was, 'Who was to blame?' The simple answer is the commander on the day. In this case, the first, and most obvious, target for critics was Major General William Garrison. Cohen and Gooch opined:

> At first sight, the idea that a solitary, highly placed individual can, by his own incompetence and stupidity, create a military disaster is desperately attractive. It is at one with the traditional idea that a commander carries the responsibility for everything that that happens in, and therefore to, his command.[3]

In this case the blame was distributed among the pundits all the way up the command chain to the President himself. Garrison, an honourable man, readily acknowledged the shortcomings of a mission he had planned and led. He wrote in his own hand a *mea culpa* to President Clinton, in which he tabulated his failings and offered explanations for his actions. Bowden reproduced the text but did not identify his source.

I. The authority and accountability for the Op rests here, in MOG with the TF Ranger commander and not in Washington.
II. Excellent intelligence was available on the target.
III. Forces were experienced in area as a result of six previous operations.
IV. Enemy situation was well known. Proximity to Bakaara Market [SNA strongpoint]. Previous reaction times of bad guys.
V. Planning for the Op was bottom up and not top down. Assaulters were confident it was a doable operation. Approval of plan was retained by TF commander.

VI. Techniques, tactics and procedures were appropriate for mission/targets.
VII. Reaction forces were planned for contingency (A) CSAR on immediate standby (B) UH69 with medics and security.
VIII. Loss of first Helo was supportable. Pilot pinned in wreckage presented a problem.
IX. 2nd Helo crash required response from the 10th Mtn QRF. The area of the crash was such that SNA were there nearly immediately, so we were unsuccessful in reaching the crash site in time.
X. Rangers on 1st crash site were not pinned down. They could have fought their way out. Our creed would not allow us to leave the body of the pilot pinned in the wreckage.
XI. Armor reaction force would have helped but casualty figures may or may not have been different. The type of men in the task force simply would not be denied in their mission of getting to their fallen comrades.
XII. The mission was a success. Targeted individuals were captured and extracted from the target.
XIII. For this particular target, President Clinton and Sec Aspin need to be taken off the blame line.[4]

This is a comprehensive list, but items IV and VII are open to challenge. The speed of the previous SNA reactions had been noted and were assumed to be unchanged. Patently a miscalculation. The contingency planning (note VII) was proved to be inadequate.

President Clinton met relatives of those killed, among whom was Lieutenant Colonel James Smith, the father of Corporal Jamie Smith. The colonel had been a Ranger himself and had lost a leg in Vietnam. Another was the father of Medal of Honor winner Randy Shughart, who 'insulted the President by telling him he was not fit to be the commander in chief'.[5] Certainly, Clinton did not appear to have a solid grasp on affairs in Somalia and provided a dearth of leadership.

General Colin Powell put the Battle of Mogadishu into perspective when he judged that the deaths of eighteen soldiers in Vietnam would not even have warranted a press conference.[6] This engagement was in effect little more than a skirmish, but its proportions were as nothing compared to its symbolism.

This skirmish, small as it was, nevertheless was of similarly symbolic importance as the much larger Battle of Dien Bien Phu thirty-nine years earlier. There, a French garrison of only 4 per cent of that nation's total force in Vietnam, and which had successfully tied down 60 per cent of the enemy Viet Minh, surrendered in May 1954. That single, humiliating defeat led directly to the flight of France from Vietnam.

The Battle of Mogadishu, although very much smaller in scale, resulted in the humiliation of the USA and had a vastly disproportionate effect on Somalia, US defence policy and the standing of the USA in the international community. In both cases, sophisticated Western armies were soundly defeated by an irregular, Third World enemy.

There have been hosts of critics of Operation GOTHIC SERPENT. Among these was Major Roger Sangvic, who studied the topic while a student at the Command and General Staff College. He concluded that the defeat was due to 'a system failure'. He distributed blame all the way up the command chain and, like Mr Shughart, included President Clinton. Nevertheless, Sangvic concluded that Secretary Aspin (who resigned on 15 December 1993) was the recipient of a disproportionate share of that blame.

A feature of the post-operation analysis, by some, was a focus on the tanks that were *not* in Somalia. On that basis, they could not have been a factor in the result. It had been Aspin's decision not to send tanks to Somalia but, as a civilian, he depended on his senior military advisors – in this case, Generals Powell and Hoar – to guide him.

> Neither of these generals strongly advocated the deployment to Aspin even though the worsening situation on the ground merited their strong support. Both Hoar and Powell's approval recommendations can be characterized as lukewarm. Aspin's real failure was of not being more critical of the conduct of the TFR operations.[7]

Had General Garrison's force been equipped with tanks it may well have altered the balance. However, he had no armour and, just like every general in recorded history, he had to fight with the assets he had, and not those on a distant 'wish list'. He planned accordingly.

Across the world, military operations are analysed after the event. Command structures, tactical doctrine and logistic measures are reviewed and adapted to ameliorate what are perceived to be failings. A good example of that process was the steps taken after the American invasion of Grenada in 1983. Operation URGENT FURY was 'a master class in political and military ineptitude'.[8] In the 'after action report', the command, control and intelligence deficiencies were noted and corrected. US operations, after Grenada, were significantly more effective as a result of those corrections.

The causes for the debacle in Mogadishu are easily identified, not least the similarities with the defeat suffered by the USA in Vietnam. The mistakes made there were replicated in Somalia. The libraries at West Point and in the Pentagon are both equipped with books on military strategy but, clearly, they are unread. The great von Clausewitz, whose book is in both libraries, addressed the fundamentals when he wrote:

> The first, the supreme, the most far-reaching act of judgement that the statesman and commanders have to make is to establish … the kind of war on which they are embarking, neither mistaking it for, nor not trying to turn it into something alien to its true nature. This is the first of all strategic questions and most comprehensive.

In Vietnam, the USA was drawn into a guerrilla war that it decided to fight along conventional lines, and it based its entire strategy on the Vietnamese body count. It did not adopt the British tactic used to defeat a guerrilla enemy in Malaya, albeit on a very much smaller scale. The British method was to infiltrate the forest to fight and kill the enemy in his base. This was complemented by an effective 'hearts and minds' policy.

In Vietnam, the USA, like the French before them, treated the indigenous civilian population with insensitivity and earned the undying hatred of many. Any US entry into the rain forest was made in very large helicopter-borne numbers. Then, the Viet Cong could only be engaged when the Viet Cong was compliant. General Westmoreland, the commander, was unaware that his adversary would spend as many lives as it took to expel him and his forces. The American forces assumed an entirely false, all-embracing superiority over its enemy, and paid a high price for their arrogance.

In Somalia, the same arrogant and ill-judged superiority was again in place. When General Garrison did his 'appreciation of the situation', he was fully aware of his strengths but significantly did not call to an immediate readiness state elements of 10th Mountain Division. He was content to conduct his operation with TFR but underestimated his enemy and gave little or no credence to the intelligence, motivation and armament of the SNA. In combination, these failings were absolutely critical.

Somalia too was a guerrilla war, albeit in a very difficult urban setting. Given the unquenchable hatred of the civil population and the impossibility of any 'hearts and minds' approach, the US had to adopt innovative and flexible tactics. Instead, Garrison replicated operations, in the face of well-established military principles. His replications presumed that he had an enemy devoid of imagination, skill or commitment. He was militarily naïve, and this invited disaster and ultimately, national humiliation.

The massacre on Black Monday had assured Americans of unqualified hatred and it had motivated civilians to give their lives at the Battle of Mogadishu. The US faced an armoury of RPGs, all of which could and would destroy low-flying helicopters. Despite this evident threat, the aviators did not alter their tactics as a counter.

This author recognises that William Garrison was a high-grade, experienced, courageous and skilled leader. However, I can only conclude that, notwithstanding Garrison's personal attributes, as the architect and commander of GOTHIC SERPENT he bears the responsibility for its failure. The absence of tanks is a military red herring, best ignored.

In summary, the US intervention in Somalia failed due to mission overreach, fragmented command structures, underestimation of local complexities, operational setbacks and political pressures. The experience underscored the challenges of military involvement in complex humanitarian crises without clear objectives and understanding of local dynamics.

Mogadishu left a scar, and the USA was reluctant to take on any further direct involvement in African affairs after October 1993 for what has been referred to as the 'Somalia Syndrome'.[9]

* * *

Thirty years after the Battle of Mogadishu, Mark Bowden, the acknowledged subject matter expert on the topic, penned an article in the *New York Times* in which he revealed that, before the debacle in Mogadishu, one wise man

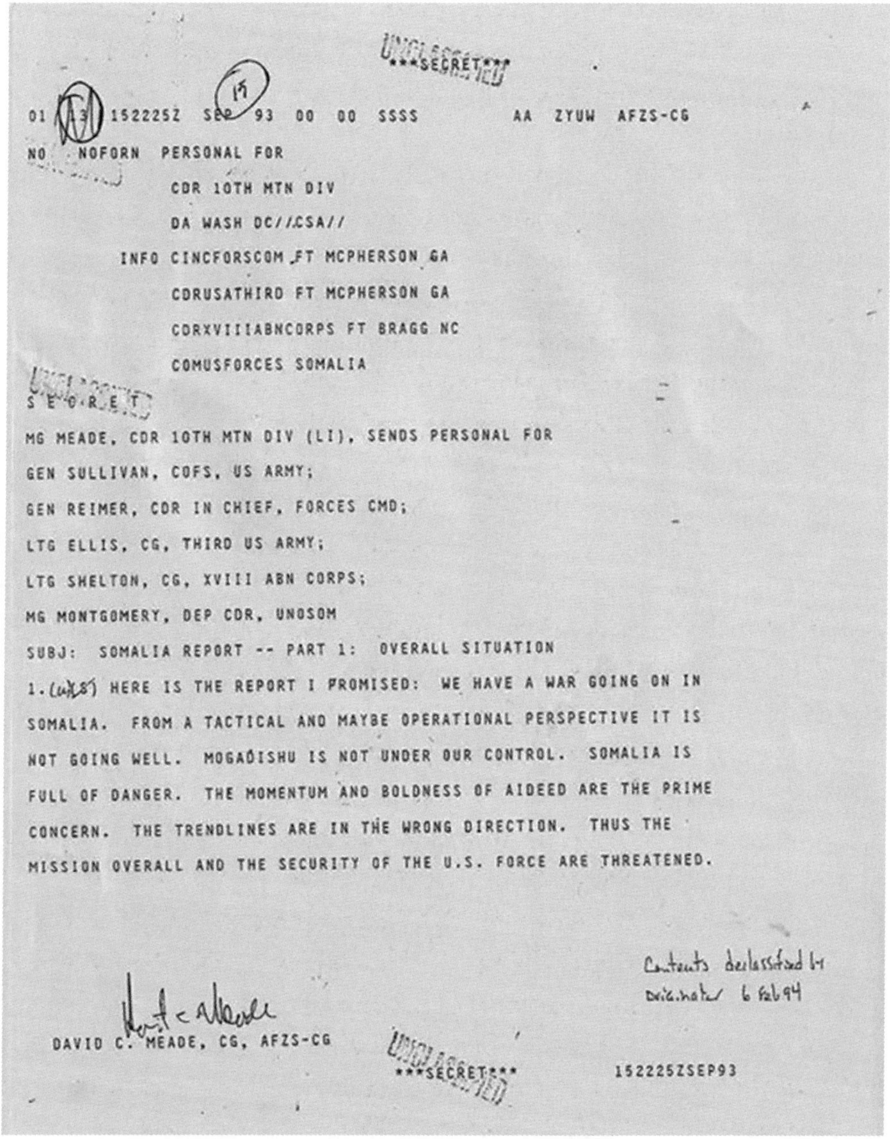

UNCLASSIFIED ***SECRET***

01 13 152225Z SEP 93 00 00 SSSS AA ZYUW AFZS-CG

NO NOFORN PERSONAL FOR
CDR 10TH MTN DIV
DA WASH DC//CSA//
INFO CINCFORSCOM FT MCPHERSON GA
CDRUSATHIRD FT MCPHERSON GA
CDRXVIIIABNCORPS FT BRAGG NC
COMUSFORCES SOMALIA

UNCLASSIFIED
S E C R E T

MG MEADE, CDR 10TH MTN DIV (LI), SENDS PERSONAL FOR
GEN SULLIVAN, COFS, US ARMY;
GEN REIMER, CDR IN CHIEF, FORCES CMD;
LTG ELLIS, CG, THIRD US ARMY;
LTG SHELTON, CG, XVIII ABN CORPS;
MG MONTGOMERY, DEP CDR, UNOSOM

SUBJ: SOMALIA REPORT -- PART 1: OVERALL SITUATION

1. (U)(S) HERE IS THE REPORT I PROMISED: WE HAVE A WAR GOING ON IN SOMALIA. FROM A TACTICAL AND MAYBE OPERATIONAL PERSPECTIVE IT IS NOT GOING WELL. MOGADISHU IS NOT UNDER OUR CONTROL. SOMALIA IS FULL OF DANGER. THE MOMENTUM AND BOLDNESS OF AIDEED ARE THE PRIME CONCERN. THE TRENDLINES ARE IN THE WRONG DIRECTION. THUS THE MISSION OVERALL AND THE SECURITY OF THE U.S. FORCE ARE THREATENED.

Contents declassified by Dec. note 6 Feb 94

DAVID C. MEADE, CG, AFZS-CG

UNCLASSIFIED ***SECRET*** 152225ZSEP93

The original memo from General Meade that was ignored but, in effect, ended his career. (New York Times, *2 October 2023*)

urged caution and that if his advice had been accepted, the battle would probably never have taken place.[10]

Major General David Mead, the commander of 10th Mountain Division, the major US formation in Somalia, had appraised the situation. He was aware of the volatility of the atmosphere in Mogadishu and recognised the extraordinary level of hostility being directed at all his countrymen serving in the country. He was sufficiently concerned that he breached army protocol on 15 September 1993 by sending a signal directly to General Gordon Sullivan, the Army Chief of Staff.

In his memo Meade said, 'You're likely to have a big fight over some period of time with considerable casualties, and, in the end, you're going to turn over the city to the Somalis.' He sent on to say, 'We have a war going on in Somalia. From a tactical and maybe operational perspective, it is not going well. Mogadishu is not under our control. Somalia is full of danger.' Mead noted the 'momentum and boldness' of Mohamed Farrah Aidid and concluded, 'The trend lines are in the wrong direction. Thus, the mission overall and the security of the US Force are threatened.'

It is a characteristic of the US Armed Forces that not even well-argued courteous dissent is encouraged. The command chain is impermeable, and the primacy and judgement of the senior officer is sacrosanct. General Sullivan ignored Meade's advice, as was his privilege, and GOTHIC SERPENT was duly launched. However, Meade paid a high price for his conscientious memo, which must have been judged to be insubordinate. His career went no further and he retired two years later.

General Meade had his prescient cable declassified shortly before he retired in 1995, and while he never made it public, he wanted history to know about it. He gave a sealed copy to his friend Charles Krohn, a retired lieutenant colonel, who locked it away with a sheaf of other professional papers.

David Meade died in 2019. Soon after, Colonel Krohn, when cleaning out his safe, read the memo for the first time. He then telephoned Mark Bowden and said, 'It shows he did his best to prevent what was going to happen. He must have known the risk he was taking going directly to the chief of staff.'

Bowden commented, 'But just because General Meade's plea did not provoke immediate action may not mean that no one listened. It's just as likely that it was considered and simply rejected. Prescience shows only in history's rear-view mirror.'

Chapter 22

Education or Indoctrination?

American children are required to swear fealty to their nation's flag each morning and they are taught that, by merely being an American citizen, they are superior to all lesser beings. This indoctrination is also the norm in North Korea, China and other totalitarian states. It is designed to breed a citizen's unwavering and unquestioning adherence to the state.

Most Americans have, to some degree, the arrogance that their early indoctrination produces. It is to be seen in the presumption that the American way is the only way and that America is 'the best' at everything and the font of all wisdom. This absurd presumption is viewed by the rest of the world with distain, incredulity, amusement or a combination of all three.

The assertion that the US Army is 'the best in the world' is frequently voiced, but that is an entirely subjective view, unsupported by the evidence. The training of US forces, in this specific case for the USN, was a:

> formula [that] primarily involved classical conditioning and systematic desensitization using violent movies but also integrated cultural distance processes in order to get the men to think of the potential enemies they will have to face as inferior forms of life [with films] biased to present the enemy as less than human: the stupidity of local customs is ridiculous. Local personalities are presented as evil demigods.[1]

Given that mindset in the training organisation, the effects are predictable. There is no doubt that American soldiers form one of the largest armies in the world, serving the needs of the richest and most powerful nation on the planet. These men are well trained, the best equipped and have the most sophisticated and all-embracing logistic support. However, man for man, they are matched by the soldiers of other nations, because skill-at-arms, courage and commitment are human characteristics that cannot be measured and are not in the sole possession of the USA.

The US Army is at its very best when it engages in conventional warfare and can commit its armour and overpowering air power against, usually, Third World countries such as Iraq. It is much less successful when it is engaged by an irregular or guerrilla enemy and suffered defeats in Vietnam, Somalia and Afghanistan.

This author would argue that the reason why the US was defeated in Somalia was because Garrison and the men around him – all who had been indoctrinated from birth and desensitised by training – assumed, arrogantly and mistakenly, a superiority over the SNA. Accordingly, Garrison underestimated the depth of the hatred they faced. He also miscalculated the commitment of the citizens of Mogadishu and, more importantly, the speed with which they could assemble.

Similarly, Garrison knew that the SNA had rocket-propelled grenades, but he set aside the possibility that it had ample supplies of this potent weapon. In the event, three aircraft were lost and two badly damaged. It was the loss of *Super Six-One* and *Four* that sealed the fate of GOTHIC SERPENT.

Chapter 23

Whatever Happened to Old …?

Aidid, Mohamed Farrah (1934–96)

After hostilities ended, Admiral Howe was replaced as the UN representative by Guinean Lansana Kouyaté. Productive discussions followed with Mohamed Farrah Aidid and the last of the UN forces left Somalia in 1995. Curiously, with the withdrawal of all foreign troops, Aidid's importance in Somali life was reduced. Unabashed, he declared himself to be President of Somalia in June 1995. This grandiose measure fell flat as his self-appointed status was not recognised by other states, all of whom deferred to Ali Mahdi Muhammad, who had been elected president back in 1991.

On 24 July 1996, Aidid and his armed supporters engaged with those of the president, who by now had recruited Osman Ali Ato to his cause. Ato had previously been a staunch supporter of Aidid, but he had 'turned his coat'.

During the exchange of fire, Aidid was badly wounded. It did not kill him, but a heart attack did, on 2 August 1996, while he was undergoing surgery.[1]

Aspin, Leslie (1938–1995)

After his resignation as Secretary of Defense, Leslie Aspin was appointed to chair the President's Foreign Intelligence Advisory Board (under Clinton; in 2008, this was renamed the President's Intelligence Advisory Board). It was a committee with a mandate to scrutinise US intelligence agencies.

Aspin was not a well man and struggled with hypertrophic cardiomyopathy for several years. He died in May 1995 after suffering a stroke.

Awale, Abdi Qeybdiid Hasan (1948–)

Hasan Awale was a close associate of Aidid and filled the role of interior minister in the SNA's clashes with UN forces during the ill-fated 'nation-building' phase of UNOSOM II. His house was the site of the Bloody Monday massacre, and he was one of the two high-value captives taken on 3 October.

After the withdrawal of the UN, he continued at the top of the SNA. In 2001, as part of the new 'Transitional National Government', he was chief of police in Mogadishu for two years.

He participated in the complex political chaos that resulted in the second Battle of Mogadishu, in 2006. He supported the 'Alliance for the Restoration of Peace and Counter-Terrorism' (ARPCT) against the 'Islamic Courts Union' (ICU). Disillusioned by the ARPCT, he abandoned it later that same year.

On 26 December 2006, he took the leadership of the 'Transitional Federal Government' and, backed by Ethiopian soldiers, fought and won the Battle of Bandiradley. This was when Galmudug forces fought ICU militants. The fighting pushed the Islamists out of Bandiradley and over the border south into Adado district. He was elected on 1 August 2012 as the new president of Galmudug state, a semi-autonomous federal state within the larger Federal Republic of Somalia.

Boutros-Ghali, Boutros (1922–2016)

Boutros Boutros-Ghali's tenure as Secretary-General of the United Nations was marked by controversy and crisis, which included the Somali, Rwandan and Angolan civil wars. He was criticised over the UN's inaction in Angola and later during the genocide in Rwanda.

In 1996, Boutros-Ghali ran unopposed for a second term as Secretary-General, but the United States, long dissatisfied with his leadership, opposed his bid by exercising its Security Council veto and ensured the termination of his tenure in Somalia.

After leaving the UN, Boutros-Ghali served as the first secretary-general of La Francophonie, from 1997 to 2002. He then became chairman of the South Centre, an intergovernmental think tank for developing countries. He died in 2016, in Cairo, at the age of 93.

Durant, Chief Warrant Officer Michael (1961–)

After being freed, and recovering, Michael Durant resumed flying with the 160th SOAR. He retired from the army in 2001 with more than 3,700 flight hours. On retirement, Durant began offering seminars to military personnel about helicopter manoeuvring and Combat Search and Rescue operations. He also lectures on the Battle of Mogadishu and, in 2003, published a book, oft quoted in this one. He is pictured here lecturing in 2002.

Durant is well educated and is the recipient of a BSc in Aeronautics and an MBA in Aviation Management. In 2008, he moved to Huntsville, Alabama, and bought and ran an engineering company called Pinnacle Solutions. Among his clients were the US Navy, the US Marine Corps and NASA.

In 2021, and in order to pursue a political ambition to win election to the US Senate, Durant gave over control of Pinnacle Solutions to its employees by way of an Employee Stock Ownership plan. However, his election bid failed.

Durant and his wife, Lisa (who is also a former army aviator), now live in Madison, Alabama. They have six children and three grandchildren. Durant's previous marriage to his first wife, Lorrie, whose voice heard on the radio during his incarceration was so very welcome, sadly ended in divorce.

Eversmann, Sergeant Matt (1967–)

In 2006, Matt Eversmann deployed to Iraq as a company first sergeant with the 10th Mountain Division. He left the army in 2008, and spent a decade in the healthcare, non-profit and data management sectors before exploring his entrepreneurial spirit.

He lectures on the Somali campaign. He and his wife Tori started Eversmann Advisory to help young leaders compete in the business sector. They live 3 miles from the Atlantic Ocean and spend every moment they can in the sand and surf.

Garrison, Major General William F. (1944–)

After William Garrison accepted responsibility for the failure of GOTHIC SERPENT, he was moved to command the US Army John F. Kennedy Special Warfare Center and School (USAJFKSWCS).

This is the US Army's premier institution for training and educating personnel in Special Operations, including Special Forces, Civil Affairs, and Psychological Operations. However, Garrison's career was at an end, and he retired two years later.

He is an honourable man and a fine officer. He was admired and respected by those under his command, perhaps best expressed by Staff Sergeant Dan Schilling, who took part in Operation GOTHIC SERPENT, and who shared his feelings about Garrison in Bowden's book (p. 187):

> I should pause here for a moment to say a few words about General Garrison. Many know his record and command history. I'm not the person to expound on his exploits; in fact I don't know the man very well. But I will say he is the finest general officer I have ever worked for and probably ever will. He understood his men and how we thought, what we wanted and needed, and understood the situation anywhere he was, immediately and completely. He is the finest leader an operator could ask for. It wasn't a shame that his career was derailed after our deployment; it was a criminal act committed by political cowards.

Notwithstanding his many fine attributes, this author believes that it was Garrison, and his flawed plan, that led to the debacle of Mogadishu.

Harrell, Lieutenant Colonel Gary (1951–2023)

In October 1993, Gary Harrell was severely wounded by enemy mortar fire, just after the Battle of Mogadishu. He recovered and attended the United State Army War College, graduating in 1995.

Thereafter, he was Deputy Commander Delta Force and took command from 1998 to 2000. His next appointment was Director, Joint Security Directorate in Central Command until 2002. The war in Afghanistan brought him command of Special Forces Task Force 'Bowie' and was Assistant Division Commander of 10th Mountain Division. From 2003 to 2005, Harrell was assigned as commanding general, Special Operations Command Central.

During Operation IRAQI FREEDOM, Harrell commanded special operations forces that were responsible for combat operations to prevent Scud missiles from being launched from western Iraq and for stability operations in northern Iraq.

In his last post, he served as Deputy Commanding General of the Army Special Operations Command. He retired as a major general in 2008.

Howe, Admiral (Rtd) Jonathan (1935–)

Jonathan Howe's tenure in Somalia was not a success and his support and justification for the Bloody Monday massacre earned him the unbridled hatred of many Somalis. His single-minded determination to capture or kill Aidid failed. He was replaced by Lansana Kouyaté in late 1993.

He was a submariner and an engineer who served in the early nuclear boats. It was during this period that, in 1971, he authored *Multicrises: Sea Power and Global Politics in the Missile Age*. In 2025, he published *Opportunity*

Lost or Mission Impossible? My Year in Somalia as Special Representative of the UN Secretary-General, 1993–1994.

After his retirement from the USN, Howe was chairman of the board of the World Affairs Council of Jacksonville from 2006 to 2012. He served as chairman of the board of Fleet Landing and was a past president of the Rotary Club of Jacksonville.

Admiral Howe was married to Dr Harriet Mangrum Howe, whom he met in high school. Harriet was an assistant professor of sociology at the University of Florida. Admiral Howe has six children and currently resides in Florida.

Hofstetter, Suzanne (1958–2017)

In November 2014, the International Committee of the Red Cross's delegation in Washington tracked down Michael Durant and invited him to record a conversation about his time as a prisoner in Somalia as part of a wider history project. Inevitably, he made mention of Suzanne Hofstetter, the woman who brought him reason to hope that he might be released … sometime.

On 8 May 2015, Mike Durant was reunited for the first time in twenty years with the ICRC delegate, Suzanne Hofstetter.

Howe, Sergeant First Class Paul (1959–)

Paul Howe provided much of the information about Delta Force operations for the writing of the 1999 book *Black Hawk Down: A Story of Modern War*. In 2000, Howe graduated with an MIS (Masters of Interdisciplinary Studies) from Stephen F. Austin State University.

He left the army after twenty years' service to become an instructor specialising in high-risk training for law enforcement. In 2011, he published a book entitled *Leadership and Training for the Fight (Using Special Operations Principals to Succeed in Law Enforcement, Business and War)*. He has a facility in Nacogdoches, Texas, where he provides professional instruction on Combat Shooting & Tactics (CSAT). He teaches 'hostage rescue' for several law enforcement agencies.

Howe is married to Constance 'Connie' (née Beckwith), a former Army Reserve major and the daughter of Delta Force founder Colonel Charles Beckwith. Howe lives and works in Nacogdoches, Texas.

McKnight, Lieutenant Colonel Danny R. (1951–)

Danny McKnight participated in the US invasion of Panama in 1989 and subsequently took command of 3rd Ranger Battalion of the 75th Ranger Regiment. He left the army after twenty-nine years' service in 2002, having risen to the rank of colonel.

He lectures as a motivational speaker.

Miller, Captain Austin Scott (1961–)

Austin Scott Miller is now a retired four-star general in the US Army and is a former Delta Force commander. He served as the final commander of NATO's Resolute Support Mission and United States Forces – Afghanistan from September 2018 to July 2021.

He previously served as the commander of Joint Special Operations Command from March 2016 to 2018. Since 2001, he has seen active service in Iraq and Afghanistan. He retired from the army after relinquishing command in July 2021.

Miller currently serves on the Board of Advisors for Striveworks and sits on the board of directors of for Workhorse.

Montgomery, Major General Thomas M. (1941–)

After the Battle of Mogadishu, Thomas Montgomery was designated commander of Joint Task Force Somalia and given command of the American withdrawal from the country. Due to the hazardous situation, Montgomery pressed to keep a significant US force in Somalia through the final date of redeployment, emphasising that the last element to depart should be 'an Abrams tank with its gun tube pointed toward Mogadishu'.

Montgomery was promoted to lieutenant general and from 1994 to 1997, he served as the United States representative to the NATO Military Committee. At the conclusion of his tenure in that appointment, Montgomery retired from the US Army.

In the years following his retirement from active military service, Montgomery was involved in mentoring Reserve Officer Training Corps cadets at his *alma mater*, Indiana University, and also served on the board of trustees of the Command and General Staff College Foundation.

Muhammad, Ali Mahdi (1939–2021)

Ali Mahdi Muhammad was the long-term opponent of Aidid and served as president of Somalia from 1991 until 2000. His status was confirmed by the Cairo Agreement of December 1997. In 2000, Muhammad participated in another conference in Djibouti, where he lost a re-election bid to Barre's former interior minister, Abdiqasim Salad Hassan. Muhammad conceded his defeat and, speaking after the result, was promulgated. He indicated that he respected the outcome of the election and would support and work with the new president-elect.

Ali Mahdi Muhammad died on 10 March 2021 in Nairobi, Kenya. He had contracted Covid-19, which was sweeping through Kenya at the time.

Oakley, Robert B. (1931–2014)

Before Robert Oakley was co-opted to negotiate with Aidid he had been rewarded with numerous State Department distinctions. He served in Somalia from October 1993 until March 1994. In January 1995, he joined the Institute for National Strategic Studies at the National Defense University. In 2000, Oakley claimed in an interview with the *Washington Post* that the Clinton administration's 'obsession with Osama' was making Bin Laden stronger.

He is pictured here with Aidid after the cessation of hostilities. Oakley died in McLean, Virginia, from Parkinson's disease on 10 December 2014, aged 83.

Rierson, Sergeant First Class Matt (1960–93)

Matt Rierson had survived the rigours and stress of the Battle of Mogadishu and had distinguished himself by his professionalism and courage. A few days after the battle, on 6 October Matt Rierson was killed by a random mortar shell that landed near him as he chatted with other soldiers near the airport hangar. He was posthumously awarded the Silver Star by President Clinton. The citation for the decoration reads:

> for conspicuous gallantry and intrepidity in action against hostile enemy forces while serving with the 1st Special Forces Operational Detachment – Delta, Task Force RANGER, Special Operations Command, during combat

operations in Mogadishu, Somalia, on 3 and 4 October 1993. Sergeant Rierson was part of the assault force which conducted an air assault raid deep into the enemy sector.

Following the successful apprehension of two key militia officials and twenty-two enemy soldiers, Sergeant Rierson accompanied the detainees and wounded personnel to his base in the vehicular convoy. This convoy came under intense enemy fire, during which time, numerous friendly casualties were suffered. With total disregard for his own personal safety Sergeant Rierson repeatedly dismounted his vehicle, exposing himself to enemy fire, in order to direct the drivers through enemy roadblocks and ambushes. It was due in part to his exceptional leadership that the convoys were able to reach the base safely.

Sergeant Rierson then immediately accompanied the relief element headed for two downed helicopters. Once again, Sergeant Rierson demonstrated calm, effective leadership under fire that allowed the stalled convoy to fight its way to the crash site. At the crash site, Sergeant Rierson directed his team in a security position while the body of the pilot was recovered. His team provided security throughout the night as the enemy repeatedly tried to overrun the site. Sergeant First Class Rierson's heroic actions saved the lives of fellow comrades and reflect great credit on himself and the United States Army.

Steele, Captain Mike (1960–)

Mike Steele was awarded a Bronze Star with Valour Device for the part he played in the Battle of Mogadishu. It was as a colonel that he commanded the 3rd Brigade (Rakkasan) of the 101st Airborne Division from June 2004 until November 2006.

During his command, he oversaw the transformation of the unit from a traditional three-battalion infantry brigade into a six-battalion infantry brigade combat team composed of two infantry battalions, a reconnaissance squadron, a field artillery battalion support battalion, and a special troops battalion.

Steele and his brigade deployed to Iraq in late 2005, and in March 2006, the brigade planned and executed Operation SWARMER, which was a joint US–Iraqi air assault operation targeting insurgents in the desert area to the north-eastern province of Samarra. In addition to Operation SWARMER, the brigade conducted numerous other brigade- and battalion-sized operations, including Operation IRON TRIANGLE.

Steele's career foundered when, for the killings of unarmed combatants during Operation IRON TRIANGLE (2006), four soldiers were indicted. They testified that Steele had told them to 'kill all military-age males'.[2] Steele refused to testify at the hearing for the accused soldiers, which is considered unusual for a commanding officer.

He was investigated in connection with the incident and stated that he did not use 'specific language' to order his soldiers to kill all military-age males, and said, 'We don't shoot people with their hands up.' He was not charged but was later formally reprimanded by (then) Lieutenant General Peter Chiarelli, the commander of the Multi-National Corps – Iraq.[3]

The reprimand effectively ended Steele's future chances of promotion in the army. The content of the reprimand has not been made public, but two anonymous Defense Department officials identified by the *New York Times* have said that the reprimand was 'for not reporting the deaths and other details of the raid'.

It was alleged that Steele also instigated the use of 'kill boards' to track how many Iraqis each company in his battalion had killed, while one of Steele's battalion commanders, Lieutenant Colonel Nathaniel Johnson, Jr., has written that 'Colonel Steele constantly articulated his judgment and displeasure that my battalion was not being aggressive enough toward the insurgents.'

Annexure A

Timeline of Events in Somalia, 1989–94

1989

January: The Somali National Movement (SNM) intensifies its insurgency against Siad Barre's government in the north of the country.

July: The Somali Patriotic Movement (SPM) is formed, mainly composed of the Ogaden clan, to oppose Siad Barre's regime.

October: Barre's government forces launch a brutal crackdown on insurgencies, costing massive civilian casualties in the northern regions.

1990

July: Various rebel groups, including the SNM and the United Somali Congress (USC), liberate significant territory in their fight against the government.

December 1990–January 1991: The forces of USC, led by Major General Mohamed Farrah Aidid, close in on Mogadishu, accelerating the collapse of Siad Barre's regime.

1991

26 January: President Siad Barre is forced from power and flees Mogadishu. There he forms the Somali National Front (SNF) and a three-division strong army. Siad bases himself in the Somali 'breadbasket' between the rivers. His army runs amok.

27 January: The USC enters Mogadishu, and Ali Mahdi Muhammad is declared interim president, but factional fighting within the USC leads to the onset of clan-based conflict.

April–May: The SNM declares the independence of Somaliland in the north. This is not internationally recognised.

July: Mogadishu descends into mayhem as factional fighting between Ali Mahdi Muhammad and General Mohamed Farrah Aidid intensifies.

November–December: The civil war spreads across Somalia, with various clans and militias vying for control.

1992

January: Famine worsens in southern Somalia, exacerbated by the ongoing civil war. The result is a humanitarian crisis.

April: The United Nations establishes the 'United Nations Operation in Somalia' (UNOSOM I). The aim is to provide humanitarian aid and monitor the ceasefire in Mogadishu.

August: The situation deteriorates further, prompting more international attention and an ineffective peace conference.

9 December: The United States leads a multinational coalition to launch Operation RESTORE HOPE (UNITAF), aimed at securing humanitarian aid deliveries.

1993

January–March: UNITAF secures key areas in Somalia, particularly that of Mogadishu, and food distribution improves.

26 March: The United Nations Operation in Somalia II (UNOSOM II) is established, with a broader mandate to help rebuild Somalia and disarm militias.

Proactive UN military action commences after a deadly ambush of UN forces by Aidid's militia, leading to increased tensions.

12 July, Black Monday: US forces attack a peace conference and kill about seventy unarmed participants. This was, by any yardstick, a war crime and a factor in the defeat of the USA three months later.

July–October: From this point, a war situation develops and the USA heads military operations against the Somalia National Alliance (SNA) and, specifically, efforts to kill or capture Mohamed Farrah Aidid. These operations cause significant 'collateral damage' and many more non-combatant Somali citizens are killed in the process. Resistance to the UN hardens and hatred of the USA is commonplace.

3–4 October: The Battle of Mogadishu is fought on 3–4 October as the USA mounts Operation GOTHIC SERPENT. This was a further attempt to capture Aidid's top lieutenants. This operation was depicted in the book and film *Black Hawk Down*. The operation is an abject failure as the US did not make allowance for the armament of the SNA nor for its capacity to activate the civilian population.

The battle results in the deaths of eighteen US soldiers and hundreds of Somali fighters and civilians. The USA was humiliated, and the US Secretary of Defense, Les Aspin, resigned, leading to a shift in US policy.

1994–95

January–March: The US begins to withdraw its forces from Somalia, scaling down its involvement in the conflict.

March: The UN continues its peacekeeping efforts, but on a small scale and with limited success as Somalia remains divided by clan warfare.

October: The US completes its withdrawal from Somalia, leaving the country in a state of ongoing civil conflict and without a central government.

UNOSOM II is not viable without American logistic and financial support. The United Nations is defeated and withdraws from Somalia.

Annexure B

The Clan System in Somalia and its Effect on Social, Humanitarian and Military Activity

Somali society is organised around a clan system that predates colonialism and the modern state. Clans are patrilineal, meaning lineage is traced through the male line, and they form the basis of social identity, political allegiance and economic relationships. The major clans are:

Dir: One of the oldest and with several subclans such as **Issa** and **Gadabuursi**.

Darod: A large clan with significant supporting subclans among them, which are the **Ogaden, Marehan** and **Harti**.

Hawiye: Predominantly in central and southern Somalia, with significant subclans like the **Abgaal** and **Habar Gidir**.

Isaaq: Predominantly to be found in Somaliland (north-western Somalia), the Isaaq clan is a major player in the region.

Rahanweyn (Digil-Mirifle): Located primarily in southern Somalia, the Rahanweyn are agriculturalists and have subclans like the **Geledi** and **Hadame**.

Minority clans include the **Bantu, Benadiri** and other smaller groups who do not fit into the major clan families and often face discrimination.

Each major clan is divided into subclans, which are further divided into smaller units down to the level of individual extended families. This hierarchical structure affects alliances, conflicts and social organisations.

After the collapse of the Siad Barre government in 1991, Somalia lapsed into a bitter civil war, with clan-based militias fighting for control over territories and resources. The conflict was characterised by shifting alliances and rivalries between different clans and subclans, often driven by historical grievances and competition for power. The absence of a central government led to the dominance of warlords, who were often clan leaders or influential figures within their clans. Not the least of these was Mohamed Farrah Aidid.

The United Nations and other international actors, including the United States, struggled to navigate the complex clan dynamics during their interventions in Somalia. Operation RESTORE HOPE, initiated in December 1992, aimed to provide humanitarian relief but was complicated by the need to negotiate with various clan leaders and factions. The clan system made it difficult to establish a unified national government or a stable peace, as different clans had competing interests and grievances. Clan elders played a crucial role in mediating disputes and maintaining social order at the local level, especially in the absence of a central government.

Traditional forms of governance, such as the *Xeer* (customary law), were based on clan affiliations and were used to resolve conflicts, distribute resources and manage communal affairs.

By 1993, the fragmentation of Somali society had deepened, with some clans and subclans establishing semi-autonomous regions, such as Somaliland (dominated by the Isaaq clan) and Puntland (dominated by the Majeerteen subclan of the Darod).

The clan system in Somalia in 1993 was a double-edged sword. It provided a framework for social organisation and conflict resolution in the absence of a central government, but the downside was that it also fuelled divisions, perpetuated the civil war, and complicated international efforts to restore peace and stability.

The participants in the Somali scene in 1991–93 required an understanding of the intricacies of the clan system. That understanding was essential for any effective intervention or political solution in Somalia.

Annexure C

Starvation

The logistics of warfare are all about bullets, bandages and bread, but often the most important of these is 'bread'. In all campaigns the adversaries seek to disrupt or destroy the other's logistic chain. This is a tactic as old as war itself.[1] However, there are examples when a naturally occurring famine is used to political advantage. An example was the famine in Ukraine in 1932–33, which was ruthlessly exploited by Stalin.

> Any individual denied food dies of nutritional dystrophy, a process whereby once a body has used up all its fat reserves, the muscles are broken down to obtain energy. The small intestine atrophies and it becomes increasingly difficult for the victim to absorb nutrients from what little food he or she can obtain. As a defence mechanism the body reduces the activity of vital organs such as the heart and liver, and the victims suffer not only from muscular debility but from a more general and overpowering fatigue.

In Somalia in 1991–92, the effects of the famine were exacerbated by the thoughtless actions of the competing warlords and those who hindered humanitarian activities of non-governmental aid organisations.

Annexure D

Citation
Medal of Honor
Master Sergeant Gary Ivan Gordon

Master Sergeant Gary Ivan Gordon, United States Army, distinguished himself by actions above and beyond the call of duty on 3 October 1993, while serving as Sniper Team Leader, United States Army Special Operations Command with Task Force Ranger in Mogadishu, Somalia. Master Sergeant Gordon's sniper team provided precision fire from the lead helicopter during an assault and at two helicopter crash sites, while subjected to intense automatic weapons and rocket-propelled grenade fires.

When Master Sergeant Gordon learned that ground forces were not immediately available to secure the second crash site, he and another sniper unhesitatingly volunteered to be inserted to protect the four critically wounded personnel, despite being well aware of the growing number of enemy personnel closing in on the site. After his third request to be inserted, Master Sergeant Gordon received permission to perform his volunteer mission. When debris and enemy ground fires at the site caused them to abort the first attempt, Master Sergeant Gordon was inserted one hundred meters south of the crash site. Equipped with only his sniper rifle and a pistol, Master Sergeant Gordon and his fellow sniper, while under intense small arms fire from the enemy, fought their way through a dense maze of shanties and shacks to reach the critically injured crew members.

Master Sergeant Gordon immediately pulled the pilot and the other crew members from the aircraft, establishing a perimeter which placed him and his fellow sniper in the most vulnerable position. Master Sergeant Gordon used his long-range rifle and side arm to kill an undetermined number of attackers until he depleted his ammunition. Master Sergeant Gordon then went back to the wreckage, recovering some of the crew's weapons and ammunition. Despite the fact that he was critically low on ammunition, he provided some of it to the dazed pilot and then radioed for help.

Master Sergeant Gordon continued to travel the perimeter, protecting the downed crew. After his team member was fatally wounded and his own rifle ammunition exhausted, Master Sergeant Gordon returned to the wreckage, recovering a rifle with the last five rounds of ammunition and gave it to the pilot with the words, 'good luck.' Then, armed only with his pistol, Master Sergeant Gordon continued to fight until he was fatally wounded.

His actions saved the pilot's life. Master Sergeant Gordon's extraordinary heroism and devotion to duty were in keeping with the highest standards of military service and reflect great credit upon him, his unit and the United States Army.

The citation for Sergeant First Class Randall David Shughart was similar.

Notes

Chapter 1

1. Durant, M.J. with Hartov, S., *In the Company of Heroes* (New York, Bantam Press, 2003), p. 7.

Chapter 2

1. Stevenson, J., *Losing Mogadishu: Testing U.S. Policy in Somalia* (Maryland, Naval Institute Press, 1995), p. 3.
2. History of Somalia: events, people, dates (Britannica.com).
3. Ibid.
4. Peterson, S., *Me Against My Brother: At War in Somalia, Sudan, and Rwanda* (London, Routledge, 2000), p. 11.
5. Ayele, Negussie, 'Adwa 1896: Who was Civilized & Who was Savage?' (*Ethiopian Review*, Vol. 7, No. 2, 30 April 1997), p. 50.
6. Lewis, I.M., *A Pastoral Democracy: A Study of Pastoralism and Politics among the Northern Somali of the Horn of Africa* (Oxford University Press, for the International African Institute, 1961), pp. 15–16.
7. Lewis, I.M., 'In the Land of the Mad Mullah' (London, *Sunday Times*, 30 August 1992), pp. 15–16.
8. Hanley, G., *Warriors and Strangers* (London, Hamish Hamilton, 1971), p. 19.
9. Lewis, *A Pastoral Democracy*, p. 1.
10. Stevenson, *Losing Mogadishu*, pp. 1–2.
11. Britannica.com.
12. Baker, A.I., *From Biplane to Spitfire: The Life of Air Chief Marshal Sir Geoffrey Salmond KCB RCMC DSO* (Barnsley, Pen & Sword, 2003), pp. 161–2.
13. Ibid.
14. Archer, Sir G., *British Somaliland and its Tribes* (historical notes issued by HMG in January 1945), p. 1. Quoted by Peterson, *Me Against My Brother*, p. 10.
15. Del Boca, A., *Gli italiani in Africa Orientale: II. La Conquista Dell'impero* (Cles, Arnoldo Mondadori, 1992), pp. 244–53.
16. Britannica.com.

Chapter 3

1. Metz, H.C. (ed.), 'Siad Barre and Scientific Socialism' in *Somalia: A Country Study* (Washington, D.C., Library of Congress, Federal Research Division, 1992).
2. Abdullahi, Mohamed Diriye, *Culture and Customs of Somalia* (London, Bloomsbury Academic, 2001).
3. Stevenson, J., *Losing Mogadishu: Testing U.S. Policy in Somalia* (Maryland, Naval Institute Press, 1995), p. 5.

4. Peterson, S., *Me Against My Brother: At War in Somalia, Sudan, and Rwanda* (London, Routledge, 2000), p. 12.
5. Wiles, P. (ed.), *The New Communist Third World: An Essay in Political Economy* (London, Routledge, 1982), p. 279.
6. Metz, 'Siad Barre and Scientific Socialism'.
7. Mohamed Diriye Abdullahi.
8. Peterson, *Me Against My Brother*, p. 12.
9. Mohamed Diriye Abdullahi.
10. De Waal, A., African Rights and Mines Advisory Group, *Violent Deeds Live On: Landmines in Somalia and Somaliland* (London, African Rights, December 1993), p. 15.
11. Kapteijns, L., *Clan Cleansing in Somalia: The Ruinous Legacy of 1991* (University of Pennsylvania Press, 2013), pp. 81–3.
12. Ibid., pp. 84–8.
13. 'Somalia – No Mercy in Mogadishu: The Human Cost of the Conflict & The Struggle for Relief' (New York, Africa Watch and Physicians for Human Rights, 1992), p. 49.
14. Patman, R.G., *The Soviet Union in the Horn of Africa: The diplomacy of intervention and disengagement* (Cambridge, Cambridge University Press, 1990), p. 287.
15. 'Somalia – No Mercy in Mogadishu', p. 44.
16. Stevenson, *Losing Mogadishu*, p. 5.
17. Refugee Policy Group (RPG), *Hope Restored? Humanitarian Aid in Somalia 1990–94* (US Office of Foreign Disaster Assistance, November 1994), p. 7.
18. De Waal et al., *Violent Deeds Live On*, p. 15.
19. Johns, M., *Preserving American Security Ties to Somalia* (Washington, D.C., Heritage Foundation, December 1989), p. 2.
20. De Waal et al., *Violent Deeds Live On*, p. 21.
21. Drysdale, J., *Whatever Happened to Somalia?* (London, Haan Publishing, 1994), p. 27.
22. Ibid., p. 20.
23. Peterson, *Me Against My Brother*, p. 15.
24. Richburg, K., 'Aidid: Warlord in a Famished Land' (*Washington Post*, 8 September 1992).
25. Peterson, *Me Against My Brother*, pp. 31–2.
26. Ibid., p. 24.
27. Drysdale, *Whatever Happened to Somalia?*, pp. 41–2.
28. Ibid., pp. 45–7.
29. Roberts, G., 'Food Shipment-Related Security Incidents for the period 17 June 1992–20 June 1992' (interview at CARE International Headquarters, 5 August 1992).
30. 'The Price of Charity' (London, *The Economist*, 12 September 1992).
31. Quoted by Peterson, *Me Against My Brother*, p. 33.

Chapter 4

1. 'The Price of Charity' (London, *The Economist*, 12 September 1992), p. 33.
2. Compagnon, D., 'Politial Decay in Somalia: From Personal Rule to Warlordism' (*Refuge: Canada's Journal on Refugees*, 1992), pp. 8–13.
3. Andersen, L., Møller, B. and Stepputat, F., *Fragile States and Insecure People? Violence, Security, and Statehood in the Twenty-First Century* (London, Palgrave Macmillan, 2007), pp. 88–9.
4. Hilaire, M., *Waging Peace: The United Nations Security Council and Transnational Armed Conflicts* (Logos Verlag Berlin GmbH, 2015), p. 219.

5. Lewis, I.M., *A Modern History of Somalia* (London, Longman Group, 1987), pp. 76–7.
6. De Waal, A., *Famine Crimes: Politics & the Disaster Relief Industry in Africa* (Indiana University Press and the International African Institute in association with James Currey, 2007), p. 165.
7. Clarke, W. and Herbst, J. (eds.), *Learning from Somalia: The Lessons of Armed Humanitarian Intervention* (Boulder, CO, Westview Press, 1997), pp. 124–5.
8. De Waal, *Famine Crimes*, pp. 159–61.
9. Ibid., p. 168.
10. Sahnoun, M., *Somalia: The Missed Opportunities* (Washington, D.C., United States Institute of Peace Press, 1994), p. 33.
11. Maren, M., *The Road to Hell: The Ravaging Effects of Foreign Aid and International Charity* (New York, The Free Press, 1997), p. 214.
12. Drysdale, J., *Whatever Happened to Somalia?* (London, Haan Publishing, 1994), p. 86.
13. Stevenson, *Losing Mogadishu: Testing U.S. Policy in Somalia* (Maryland, Naval Institute Press, 1995), p. 7.
14. Ibid., p. 11.
15. Ibid.
16. Elmi, A.S., 'The chewing of khat in Somalia' (*Journal of Ethnopharmacology*, August 1983), pp. 163–76.
17. Bartholet, J., 'The Road to Hell' (*Newsweek*, 21 September 1992).
18. Stevenson, *Losing Mogadishu*, p.12.
19. Jama, Abdinur, 'Somalia's Billion-Dollar Miraa Addiction: A Nation Bleeding Cash to Kenya' (*Wardheer News*, 17 February 2025).
20. Davies, J.L., *The Liberation Movements of Somalia* (Wayback Machine, August 1994).
21. De Waal, *Famine Crimes*, p. 167.
22. 'Barre' (Nairobi, *The Daily Nation*, 15 May 1992).
23. Sahnoun, *Somalia: The Missed Opportunities.*
24. Wilhelm, Major General C.C., 'In a memorandum referring to "the 30-day Attitude Adjustment"' (*HQ UNITAF*, 12 January 1993).
25. Peterson, S., *Me Against My Brother: At War in Somalia, Sudan, and Rwanda* (London, Routledge, 2000), p. 23.

Chapter 5

1. 'Somalia: Beyond the Warlords: The Need for a Verdict on Human Rights Abuses' (*News from Africa Watch*, Vol. V, No. 2, 7 March 1993), p. 12.
2. Naylor, P.C., *Historical Dictionary of Algeria* (Oxford, Scarecrow Press, 2006), p. 400.
3. Stevenson, J., *Losing Mogadishu: Testing U.S. Policy in Somalia* (Maryland, Naval Institute Press, 1995), p. 47.
4. Sahnoun, Mohamed, *Somalia*: *The Missed Opportunities* (Washington, D.C., United States Institute of Peace Press, 1994).
5. Drysdale, J., *Whatever Happened to Somalia?* (London, Haan Publishing, 1994), p. 1.
6. Ibid., p. 55.
7. Levin, D.H., 'When Great Power Gets a Vote: The Effects of Great Power Electoral Interventions on Electoral Results' (*International Studies Quarterly*, June 2016), pp. 198–200.

8. Malis, M., Querubin, P. and Shanker, S., 'Persistent Failure? International Interventions Since World War II' (*The Handbook of Historical Economics*, San Diego, CA, January 2021), pp. 642–73.
9. Drysdale, *Whatever Happened to Somalia?*, p. 41.
10. Clarke, W. and Herbst, J. (eds.), *Learning from Somalia: The Lessons of Armed Humanitarian Intervention* (Boulder, CO, Westview Press, 1997), p. 155.
11. Stevenson, *Losing Mogadishu*, p. 45.
12. Peterson, S., *Me Against My Brother: At War in Somalia, Sudan, and Rwanda* (London, Routledge, 2000), p. 52.
13. Drysdale, *Whatever Happened to Somalia?*, pp. 52–3.
14. Polybius, *Histories* (*c.* 125 BC) (*Familiar Quotations from Greek Authors*, trans. C.T. Ramage, published in 1895).
15. Afrah, M.M., *Mogadishu: A Hell on Earth – A Journalist's Diary about the War in Mogadishu* (Nairobi, Copos Ltd, 1993), p. 2.
16. Peterson, *Me Against My Brother*, pp. 21–2.
17. Chapter VII of the UN Charter.
18. UN Security Council resolution 794, 3 December 1992.
19. *The Guardian*, 5 December 1992.
20. 'CIA Warns Bush on Somali Mission' (*International Herald Tribune*, 3 December 1992).
21. Peterson, *Me Against My Brother*, p. 51.
22. Ibid., p. 58.
23. Ibid., p. 55.
24. *Los Angeles Times*, 28 December 1992.
25. Di Prizio, R.C., *Armed Humanitarians: U.S. Interventions from Northern Iraq to Kosovo*, (Baltimore, Johns Hopkins University Press, 2002), p. 46.
26. Refugee Policy Group, 'Hope Restored: Humanitarian Aid in Somalia' (Washington, D.C., Centre for Policy, Analysis and Research on Refugee Issues, November 1994), pp. 2, 5.
27. Elmi, A.A., *Understanding the Somalia Conflagration: Identity, Political Islam and Peacebuilding* (London, Pluto Press, 2010), pp 58–9, 77–8.
28. In an interview, 14 December 1992.
29. Interviewed by Jonathan Stevenson at HQ, 2e Régiment Étranger de Parachutistes, 16 December 1992.
30. Sheehan, N., *A Bright Shining Lie* (London, Jonathan Cape, 1989), p. 713.
31. Stevenson, J., 'Will Bungle Turn into Betrayal?' (London, *Evening Standard*, 6 January 1993), p. 16.
32. Stevenson, *Losing Mogadishu*, p. 53.
33. Ibid.
34. Stewart, R.W. *United States Forces, Somalia After Action Report and Historical Overview: The United States Army in Somalia, 1992–1994* (Center of Military History United States Army, Washington, D.C., 2003), p. 6.
35. 'United Nations Operations in Somalia' (UNOSOM II *Peacekeeping.un.org*, retrieved 16 September 2021. Ramsbotham and Woodhouse, 1999), p. 225.
36. Stewart, R.W., *The United States Army in Somalia* 1992–1994 (Centre of Military History United States Army, Washington, D.C., 1994), p. 13.
37. Stevenson, *Losing Mogadishu*, p. 62.

38. In an interview at World Food Programme headquarters on 15 January 1993 with Jonathan Stevenson.
39. In an interview with Jonathan Stevenson, 18 December 1992.
40. Stevenson, *Losing Mogadishu*, p. 57.
41. Stevenson, K. and Whitmore, J., 'When is quitting time?' (*Newsweek*, International Edition, 18 January 1993), p. 31.
42. Kraft, S, 'U.S. Soldiers Surprise Robbers, Kill 6 Somalis: Africa: Three of dead are known to be victims of robbery …' (*Los Angeles Times*, 17 January 1993).
43. Stewart, *The United States Army in Somalia* 1992–1994, p. 14.
44. 'Summary of UN activity in Somalia' (*Peacekeeping.un.org*, UNITAF, UNOSOM II as at March 1993).
45. Stewart, *The United States Army in Somalia* 1992–1994, p. 18.

Chapter 6

1. Bradbury, M., *The Somali Conflict: Prospects for Peace* (Oxfam Military Library, 1994), pp. 271–3.
2. Ibid.
3. Trama, G.A., *Rules of Engagement* (Buenos Aires, Joint Staff College, 2016), pp. 25–6.
4. 'CIA warns Bush on Somali Mission' (*International Herald Tribune*, 3 December 1992).
5. Drysdale, J., *Whatever Happened to Somalia?* (London, Haan Publishing, 1994), p. 115.
6. Thakur, Ramesh, 'From Peacekeeping to Peace Enforcement: The UN Operation in Somalia' (Cambridge University Press, *The Journal of Modern African Studies*, 1994) pp. 387–410.
7. Peterson, S., *Me Against my Brother: At War in Somalia, Sudan, and Rwanda* (London, Routledge, 2001).
8. '"Briefcase admiral" blamed in Somalia crisis: American UN envoy lambasted for "personal vendetta" against Aideed and for deploying gunships over Mogadishu' (London, *The Independent*, 8 October 1993).
9. Ibid.
10. The person or group who has true control or a great influence on the individual in control but is not officially, or publicly, in charge.
11. Bradbury, *The Somali Conflict*, pp. 271–3.
12. 'The UN's Greatest Failure' (*The Baltimore Sun*, 10 October 1993).

Chapter 7

1. *New York Times*, 14 June 1997.
2. Ibid.

Chapter 8

1. Hirsch, J.L. and Oakley, R.B., *Somalia and Operation Restore Hope: Reflections on Peacemaking and Peacekeeping* (Washington, D.C., United States Institute of Peace Press, 1995), pp. 115–21.
2. Drysdale, J., *Whatever Happened to Somalia?* (London, Haan Publishing, 1994), p. 181.
3. Ibid., p. 182.
4. Lorch, D., 'U.N. Moves Troops to Somali City and Vows Punishment for Attack' (*New York Times*, 8 June 1993).

5. *UN Commission of Inquiry Established under Security Council Resolution 885 to Investigate Armed Attacks on UNOSOM II* (Secretary-General, 1 June 1994).
6. Hirsch and Oakley, *Somalia and Operation Restore Hope.*
7. Ngulube, M.S.W., Hagglund, G. and Erskine, E.A., 'Report of the Commission of Inquiry Established Pursuant to Security Council Resolution 885 (1993) to Investigate Armed Attacks on UNOSOM II Personnel which led to Casualties Among Them' (Security Council Report, 24 February 1994).
8. Cockburn, A., 'Somalia Slips From Hope to Quagmire: In Monday's attack, the peacekeepers looked more like warlords' (*Los Angeles Times*, 13 July 1993).
9. Pouligny, B., *Peace Operations Seen from Below: UN Missions and Local People*, (Bloomfield, CT, Kumarian Press, 2006), p. 179.
10. Durch, W.J. (ed.), *Introduction to Anarchy: Humanitarian Intervention and 'State-Building' in Somalia* (New York, St Martin's Press, 1996), p. 334.
11. Sangvic, Major R.N., *Battle of Mogadishu: Anatomy of a Failure* (Fort Leavenworth, KS, US Army Command and General Staff College, 1998), p. 8.
12. Durch., *Introduction to Anarchy*, p. 344.

Chapter 9

1. Peterson, S., *Me Against My Brother: At War in Somalia, Sudan, and Rwanda* (London, Routledge, 2000), p. 118.
2. Sanjeeh, in an interview with Peterson. Date unspecified. Quoted by Peterson, *Me Against My Brother*, p. 118.
3. Peterson, *Me Against My Brother*, pp. 3–166.
4. Richburg, K.B., 'In War on Aidid, UN Battled Itself' (*Washington Post*, 6 August 1993).
5. 'Somalia: Building Human Rights in the Disintegrated State' (*Amnesty International*, November 1995), p. 6.
6. Peterson, *Me Against My Brother*, p. 118.
7. Ibid., p. 119.
8. Bowden, M., *Black Hawk Down: A Story of Modern War* (New York, Atlantic Monthly Press, 1999), p. 73.
9. Ibid., p. 120.
10. Pouligny, B., *Peace Operations Seen from Below: UN Missions and Local People* (Bloomfield, CT, Kumarian Press, 2006), p. 179.
11. Ibid.
12. Richburg, K.B., (*Washington Post*, 14 July 1993).
13. Kimber, C., 'Why Somalis hit back against US forces' (*Socialist Worker*, 19 January 2002).
14. Peterson, *Me Against My Brother*, p. 118.
15. Hartley, A., *The Zanzibar Chest: A Story of Life, Love, and Death in Foreign Lands* (Open Road & Grove/Atlantic, 2016), p. 263.
16. Baumann, R.F. and Yates, L.A., with Washington, V.F., *My Clan Against the World: US and Coalition Forces in Somalia 1992–1994* (Fort Leavenworth, KS, Combat Studies Institute Press, 2003).
17. Doe, C., 'US Forces Attack Somali Warlord's Forces' (*United Press International*, 12 July 1993).
18. Peterson, *Me Against My Brother*, pp. 121–2.
19. Megas, N., 'Did the U.S. Cover Up a Civilian Massacre Before Black Hawk Down?' (*The Daily Beast*, 6 January 2019).

20. Peterson, *Me Against My Brother*, pp. 133–4.
21. Stewart, R.W, *The United States Army in Somalia 1992–1994* (US Army Center of Military History, 1994), p. 16.
22. 'News Groups Pull Staff from Somalia' (*The Press of Atlantic City*, 17 July 1993).
23. 'Bombe su Mogadiscio, è strage' (*l'Unità*, 13 July 1993), p. 1.
24. 'U.N. Troops Kill Eighty' (*Evening Herald*, 12 July 1993), pp. 1–2.
25. Peterson, *Me Against My Brother*, p. 133.
26. Binet, L., *Somalia 1991–1993: Civil War, Famine Alert and UN 'Military Humanitarian' Intervention* (Médecins Sans Frontières, 2013), pp. 191–2.
27. Rollins, P.C. and O'Connor, J.E. (eds.), *Why We Fought: America's Wars in Film and History* (Lexington, KY, University Press of Kentucky, 2008).
28. Aroma, Cabdulqaadir, *Hadimadii Gumeysiga* (in Somali), (Mogadishu: Aroma Publications, 2005), pp. 250–3.
29. Salih, M.A. Mohamed and Wohlgemuth, L. (eds.), *Crisis Management and the Politics of Reconciliation in Somalia: Statements from the Uppsala Forum, 17–19 January 1994*, (Uppsala, Nordiska Afrikainstitutet, 1994), pp. 126–8.
30. Richburg, K.B., *Out of America: A Black Man Confronts Africa* (New York, Basic Books, 1997), pp. 79–8.
31. Aroma, Cabdulqaadir, *Hadimadii Gumeysiga*, pp. 250–3.
32. Pouligny, *Peace Operations Seen from Below*, p. 177.
33. Peterson, *Me Against My Brother*, p. 127.
34. Schofield, J., *Silent Over Africa: Stories of War and Genocide* (Australia, Harper Collins 1996), p. 101.
35. Husband, M., 'UN Somali action comes under fire' (*The Guardian*, 5 August 1993), p. 20.
36. Gleis, J.L., *Withdrawing under Fire: Lessons Learned from Islamic Insurgencies* (Washington, D.C., Potomac Books, 2011), p. 7.
37. Pouligny, *Peace Operations Seen from Below*, p. 179.
38. Policy Review, 'African Atrocities and the "Rest of the World"' (*Hoover Institution*, 6 December 2008).
39. Remer, T., 'Somalia: The Next Test; Bringing Democracy to a Chaotic Country is a Tougher Task than Bringing Humanitarian Aid' (*Edmonton Journal*, 24 July 1993).
40. Keane, F., 'Good News: The United States has decided to cross the Mogadishu line' (*The Economist*, 5 July 2003).
41. Tilford, Dr E.H., Tucker, Dr D. and Oakley, AMB R.B., *Two Perspectives on Interventions and Humanitarian Operations* (US Army War College Press, 1997), p. 15.
42. 'Long among most obliging allies, Italy challenges Washington, UN: Somali crisis prompts call for greater say in world order' (*The Globe and Mail*, 16 July 1993).
43. Petty, T., 'Fight in Somalia Worries Germans' (*Philadelphia Daily News*, 17 July 1993), p. 7.
44. Pick, H., 'Three Strikes; UN operation in Bosnia, Somalia and Iraq in shambles' (*The Gazette*, 17 July 1993).
45. 'Pakistanis Fire on Somali Civilians; U.N. Renews Raids ...' (*Los Angeles Times*, 14 June 1993).
46. Watson, P., 'Pakistani Troops Kill Somali Protesters' (*Chicago Tribune*, 14 July 1993).
47. Dempsey, G. and Fontaine, R.W., *Fool's Errands: America's Recent Encounters with Nation Building* (Washington, D.C., Cato Institute, 2001), pp. 38–3.
48. Peterson, *Me Against My Brother*, p. 127.
49. Megas, 'Did the U.S. Cover Up a Civilian Massacre Before Black Hawk Down?'

50. Peterson, *Me Against My Brother*, p. 127.
51. 'UN Counts on US Rangers to Find Warlord' (*New York Times*, 26 August 1993).
52. Montgomery, Major General T., in an interview with PBS radio. Date unknown, but probably mid-1994.

Chapter 10

1. Chapman, F.S. DSO, *The Jungle is Neutral* (London, W.W. Norton & Company, 1949).
2. West, R., *War and Peace in Vietnam* (London, Sinclair Stevenson, 1995), p. 31.
3. Lawrence T.E., 'The Science of Guerrilla Warfare' (Contribution to *Encyclopaedia Britannica* 1929).
4. Smith, S., 'Mogadiscio, les premiers morts américains' (Paris, *Libération*, 9 August 1993).
5. Gellman, B., 'The Words behind a Deadly Decision: Secret Cables Reveal Maneuvering over Request for Armor in Somalia' (*Washington Post*, 30 October 1993).
6. 'Afrique Contemporaine 4th Quarter 1993' (Paris, *Libération*, 25 August 1993).
7. Drew, E., *On the Edge: The Clinton Presidency* (New York, Touchstone, 1994), p. 321.
8. US Senate, Committee on Armed Services, Memorandum for Senator Thurmond and Senator Nunn, from Senator Warner and Senator Levin, subject: 'Review of the Circumstances Surrounding the Ranger Raid on October 3–4, 1993 in Mogadishu, Somalia' (Washington, D.C., GPO, 29 September 1995), pp. 39–40.
9. Trevithick, J., 'These Secret Helicopters were Flown by A Shadowy Unit During the Battle of Mogadishu' (*The Drive*, 2 May 2019).
10. Durant, M., *In the Company of Heroes* (New York, Bantam Press, 2003), p. 148.
11. Ibid.
12. Ibid., p. 149.
13. Nash, N.S., *Caribbean Crisis: The Invasion of Grenada* (Barnsley, Pen & Sword, 2025).
14. Stewart, *The United States Army in Somalia 1992–1994* (US Army Center of Military History, 1994), p. 18.
15. *Los Angeles Times*, 6 September 1993.
16. Richburg, K.B., 'US Helicopters fire on Somalis: Last Ditch Action as Crowds Attack UN Peacekeepers' (*Washington Post*, 9 September 1993).
17. Powell, General C., *My American Journey* (New York, Ballantine Books, 2003).

Chapter 11

1. *La Presse*, 11 September 1993. *The Independent*, 11 September 1993.
2. *La Presse*, 23 September 1993.
3. Agence France-Presse, 21 September 1993.
4. In an interview with the BBC, Ato indicated that many aspects of the movie are factually incorrect. He took exception with the ostentatious character chosen to portray him; Ato does not look like the actor who portrayed him, smoke cigars, or wear earrings – facts that were later confirmed by SEAL Team Six sniper Howard E. Wasdin in his 2012 memoirs. Wasdin also indicated that whilst the character in the movie ridiculed his captors, Ato in reality seemed concerned that Wasdin and his men had been sent to kill rather than apprehend him.
5. 'Ambush in Mogadishu', interview with Captain Haad, (*FRONTLINE*, pbs.org), retrieved 5 December 2019.
6. Gelleman, B., 'The Words behind a Deadly Decision' (*Washington Post*, 30 October 1993).

7. RPG-7, Rocket-Propelled Grenade Launcher, history, spec and pictures, Military Security and Civilian Guns and Equipment (militaryfactory.com, 21 November 2013).
8. Connor, S., 'Ground Wars' (*New Scientist*, Reed Business Information, 23 July 1987).
9. Ibid., 28 September 1993.
10. Willbanks, J.H., *America's Heroes: Medal of Honor Recipients from the Civil War to Afghanistan* (Bloomsbury Publishing, ABC-CLIO, 2019), p. 308.
11. Carney, Colonel J.T. and Schemmer, B.F., *No Room for Error: The Story Behind the USAF Special Tactics Unit* (London, Random House, 2007), p. 250.
12. Baumann, R.F. and Yates, L.A., with Washington, V.F., *My Clan Against the World: US and Coalition Forces in Somalia 1992–1994* (Fort Leavenworth, KS, Combat Studies Institute Press, 2003), p. 173.
13. *The Sabre & Lance: Journal of the Pakistan Armoured Corps* (Nowshera, The School of Armour & Mechanised Warfare, 1997).

Chapter 12

1. Napoleon in a letter dated 9 November 1816 and sent from St Helena.
2. Durant, M.J. with Hartov, S., *In the Company of Heroes* (New York, Bantam Press, 2003), p. 8.
3. Wheeler, E. & Roberts, R., *Doorway to Hell: Disaster in Somalia* (Barnsley, Frontline Books, 2012), pp. 113–16.
4. '3 Killed as U.S. Chopper is Shot Down in Somalia' (*New York Times*/Reuters, 25 September 1993).
5. Chun, C.K.S., *Gothic Serpent: Black Hawk Down, Mogadishu 1993* (Oxford, Osprey Publishing 2012), p. 32.
6. Richburg, K.B., '3 GIs Killed as Somalis Down Helicopter' (*Washington Post*, 26 September 1993).
7. Atkinson, R., 'Night of a Thousand Casualties' (*Washington Post*, 31 January 1994).
8. Atkinson, R., 'The Raid That Went Wrong' (*Washington Post*, 30 January 1994).
9. Sun Tzu, *The Art of War* (*c.* 500 BC).
10. R. Gosende to US Government in Washington. Bowden, M., *Black Hawk Down: A Story of Modern War* (New York, Atlantic Monthly Press, 1999), p. 17.
11. Garrison to Hoar, 15 September 1993, quoted by Bowden, M., *Black Hawk Down*, p. 26.
12. Bowden, *Black Hawk Down*, p. 7.
13. Durant, *In the Company of Heroes*, p. 8.
14. Garrison to Hoar, memo entitled 'To keep you informed', 3 October 1993.

Chapter 13

1. Bowden, *Black Hawk Down: A Story of Modern War* (New York, Atlantic Monthly Press, 1999), p. 13.
2. Durant, M. with Hartov, S., *In the Company of Heroes* (New York, Bantam Press, 2003), p. 4.
3. *Fast Rope Inspection Manual* (Western Australia, *Jeyco*, 1992 Pty Ltd). Archived from the original (PDF) on 3 July 2014.
4. A chalk is a military passenger detail in an aircraft.
5. Atkinson, R., 'Night of a Thousand Casualties' (*Washington Post*, 31 January 1994).
6. Blackburn survived his fall and was evacuated to Germany. There he spent almost a month in a hospital, before being transferred to Walter Reed Medical Center in

Washington, D.C. His recovery was a lengthy process: it took over two years and when completed, he was medically discharged from the army. He became a policeman in his hometown of Pensacola.

7. Bowden, *Black Hawk Down*, p.18.
8. Ibid., p. 31.
9. Ibid.
10. Ibid., p. 20.
11. Ibid., p. 13.
12. Ibid., p. 35.
13. Ibid., pp. 145–6, 357.
14. 'On this day, October 3, 1993, Battle of Mogadishu', *SOFREP*, sofrep.com, retrieved 25 May 2020.
15. 'Black Hawk Down' (*The Philadelphia Inquirer*, archived from the original on 13 May 2018, retrieved 25 August 2013).
16. Atkinson, R., 'Night of a Thousand Casualties'.
17. Peterson, S., *Me Against My Brother: At War in Somalia, Sudan, and Rwanda* (London, Routledge, 2000), p. 140.
18. Ibid., pp. 3–166.
19. Bowden, *Black Hawk Down*, p. 40.
20. www.huey.co.uk/m60.php.
21. Bowden, *Black Hawk Down*, pp. 45–6.
22. Ibid., p. 48
23. Ibid., p. 46.

Chapter 14

1. Bowden, *Black Hawk Down: A Story of Modern War* (New York, Atlantic Monthly Press, 1999), p. 81.
2. Durant, M. with Hartov, S., *In the Company of Heroes* (New York, Bantam Press, 2003), p. 19.
3. Atkinson, R., 'Night of a Thousand Casualties' (*Washington Post*, 31 January 1994).
4. Durant, *In the Company of Heroes*, p. 20.
5. Atkinson, 'Night of A Thousand Casualties'.
6. Durant, *In the Company of Heroes*, p. 21.
7. Eversmann, M. and Schilling, D. (eds.), *The Battle of Mogadishu: Firsthand Accounts from the Men of Task Force Ranger* (Novato, CA, Presidio, 2004), p.129.

Chapter 15

1. Atkinson, R., 'Night of a Thousand Casualties' (*Washington Post*, 31 January 1994).
2. Eversmann, M. and Schilling, D. (eds.), *The Battle of Mogadishu: Firsthand Accounts from the Men of Task Force Ranger* (Novato, CA, Presidio, 2004), pp, 34–6.
3. Durant, M. with Hartov, S., *In the Company of Heroes* (New York, Bantam Press, 2003), pp. 22–3.
4. Ibid., p. 13.
5. Ibid., pp. 21–4.
6. Bowden alleges that Durant was on his 'fourth or fifth circle' (p. 103); he was not there to count, but Durant was!
7. Durant, *In the Company of Heroes*, pp. 25–6.

8. Ibid., p. 27.
9. Ibid., p. 28.
10. Ibid., p. 34.
11. Ibid., p. 37.
12. Ibid., p. 39.
13. Ibid., p. 43.

Chapter 16

1. 'On this Day. October 3, 1993. Battle of Mogadishu', (*SOFREP*, sofrep.com, retrieved 25 May 2020.
2. US Department of Defense Archive. Quoted by Bowden, *Black Hawk Down*, p. 101,
3. Bowden, *Black Hawk Down: A Story of Modern War* (New York, Atlantic Monthly Press, 1999), p. 113.
4. Ibid., p. 114.
5. Ibid., p. 112.
6. Ibid., pp. 120–1.
7. Nash, N.S., *Caribbean Crisis: The Invasion of Grenada*, 1983 (Barnsley, Pen & Sword, 2025).
8. Bowden, *Black Hawk Down*, p. 122.
9. Ibid., p. 123.
10. Wheeler, E. and Roberts, C., *Doorway to Hell: Disaster in Somalia*, (Barnsley, Frontline Books, 2021), pp. 113–16.
11. Peterson, S., *Me Against My Brother: At War in Somalia, Sudan, and Rwanda* (London, Routledge, 2000), p. 141.
12. US Department of Defense Archive. Quoted by Bowden, *Black Hawk Down*, p. 124.
13. Ibid.
14. Bowden., *Black Hawk Down*, pp. 125–6.
15. Ibid., pp. 126–7.
16. Ibid., p. 128.
17. Ibid.
18. US Department of Defense Archive. Quoted by Bowden, *Black Hawk Down*, p. 130.
19. Bowden, *Black Hawk Down*, p. 130.
20. Ibid., pp. 212–13.
21. Ibid., p. 217.
22. Ibid.
23. National Museum of the United States Air Force.
24. Bowden, *Black Hawk Down*, p. 228.

Chapter 17

1. Chun, C.K.S., *Gothic Serpent: Black Hawk Down, Mogadishu 1993* (Oxford, Osprey Publishing, 2012).
2. Atkinson, R., 'Night of a Thousand Casualties' (*Washington Post*, 31 January 1994).
3. Peterson, S., *Me Against My Brother: At War in Somalia, Sudan, and Rwanda* (London, Routledge, 2000), p. 142.
4. Bowden, *Black Hawk Down: A Story of Modern War* (New York, Atlantic Monthly Press, 1999), p. 263.

Chapter 18

1. Drysdale, J., *Whatever Happened to Somalia?* (London, Haan Publishing, 1994), p. 211.
2. Bowden, *Black Hawk Down: A Story of Modern War* (New York, Atlantic Monthly Press, 1999), p. 271.
3. Wheeler, E. and Roberts, C., *Doorway to Hell: Disaster in Somalia* (Barnsley, Frontline Books, 2012), pp. 113–16.
4. Neville, L., *Day of the Rangers* (London, Osprey Publishing, 2018), pp. 219–24.
5. Bowden, *Black Hawk Down*, p. 284.
6. Ibid., p. 285.
7. Ibid, p. 286.
8. Peterson, S., *Me Against My Brother: At War in Somalia, Sudan, and Rwanda* (London, Routledge, 2000), pp. 141–3.
9. Bowden, *Black Hawk Down*, p. 287.
10. Biddle, S.D., *Nonstate Warfare: The Military Methods of Guerillas, Warlords, and Militias* (Council on Foreign Relations, Princeton, Princeton University Press, 2021), pp. 182–224.
11. Ibid.
12. Ibid., p. 289.
13. Wellington on being asked his view of the Battle of Waterloo, 1815.
14. Chun, C.K.S., *Gothic Serpent: Black Hawk Down, Mogadishu 1993* (Oxford, Osprey Publishing, 2012).

Chapter 19

1. Bowden, *Black Hawk Down: A Story of Modern War* (New York, Atlantic Monthly Press, 1999), p. 291.
2. Ibid., p. 292.
3. 'Ambush in Mogadishu', interview with Captain Haad (*FRONTLINE*, www.pbs.org), retrieved 22 August 2022.
4. 'SNA Official Urges Respect for Prisoners' (Foreign Broadcast Information Service, Daily Report, Sub-Saharan Africa, 7 October 1993).
5. Peterson, S., *Me Against My Brother: At War in Somalia, Sudan, and Rwanda* (London, Routledge, 2000), p. 88.
6. Robert Oakley interviewed on *Frontline*, a PBS radio programme.
7. Dauber, C.E., *The Shot Seen Round the World: The Impact of the Images of Mogadishu on American Military Operations* (Michigan State University Press, Rhetoric & Public Affairs, 2001), pp. 653–87.

Chapter 20

1. Durant, M.J. with Hartov, S., *In the Company of Heroes* (London, Bantam Press, 2003), p. 93.
2. A search of the internet has not revealed any of 'Minister Abdi's personal details. It may be that he gave Durant a false name. He is not to be confused with Abdi Qeybdiid Hasan Awale, who was in American captivity at this time, and had been since 3 October.
3. Durant, *In the Company of Heroes*, p. 114.
4. Ibid., p. 117.
5. Bowden, *Black Hawk Down: A Story of Modern War* (New York, Atlantic Monthly Press, 1999), p. 310.
6. Durant, *In the Company of Heroes*, p. 175.

7. Ibid., p. 177.
8. Ibid., p. 243.
9. Ibid., p. 244.
10. Ibid., p. 246.
11. Ibid., p. 250.
12. Ibid., p. 267.
13. Ibid., p. 308.
14. Ibid., p. 314
15. Ibid., p. 325.

Chapter 21

1. Hughes, D., 'Bill Clinton "Surprised" at Black Hawk Down Raid' (ABC News, 18 April 2014).
2. Ibid.
3. Cohen, E.A. and Gooch, J., *Military Misfortunes: The Anatomy of Failure in War* (New York, The Free Press, 1990), p. 6.
4. Bowden, M., *Black Hawk Down: A Story of Modern War* (New York, Atlantic Monthly Press, 1999), pp. 337–8.
5. Ibid., p. 343.
6. Ibid., p. 341.
7. Sangvic, Major R.N., *Battle of Mogadishu: Anatomy of a Failure* (Fort Leavenworth, KS, US Command and General Staff College, 1998).
8. Nash, N.S., *Caribbean Crisis: The Invasion of Grenada 1983* (Barnsley, Pen & Sword, 2025).
9. Patman, R.G., 'Strategic Shortfall: The Somalia Syndrome and the March to 9/11' (*International Politics*, 23 December 2014), pp. 89–109.
10. Bowden, M., 'The Secret Memo from the General Who Foresaw Black Hawk Down' (*New York Times*, 6 September 2023).

Chapter 22

1. Watson, P., *War on the Mind: The Military Uses and Abuses of Psychology* (New York, Basic Books, 1978). Quoted by D. Grossman in *On Killing* (New York, Back Bay Books, 1995), p. 161.

Chapter 23

1. Serrill, M., 'Dead by the Sword' (*Time Magazine*, 12 August 1996).
2. AP, 'Soldiers in Iraq Say They Were Ordered to Kill All Adult Males' (*Editor & Publisher*, editorandpublisher.com, 21 July 2006).
3. 'Army Says Improper Orders by Colonel Led to 4 Deaths' (*New York Times*, 21 January 2007).

Annexure C

1. Nash., N.S., *Hunger: Food Deprivation as a Military Weapon* (Barnsley, Pen & Sword, 2023), p. 1.

Bibliography

'3 Killed as U.S. Chopper is Shot Down in Somalia' (*New York Times*/Reuters, 25 September 1993).

Abdullahi, Mohamed Diriye, *Culture and Customs of Somalia* (London, Bloomsbury Academic, 2001).

Afrah, M.M., *Mogadishu: A Hell on Earth – A Journalist's Diary about the War in Mogadishu* (Nairobi, Copos Ltd, 1993).

'Afrique Contemporaine 4th Quarter 1993' (Paris, *Libération*, 25 August 1993).

Agence France-Presse (21 September 1993).

'Ambush in Mogadishu', interview with Captain Haad (*FRONTLINE*, pbs.org, retrieved 5 December 2019 and 22 August 2022).

Andersen, L., Møller, B. and Stepputat, F., *Fragile States and Insecure People? Violence, Security, and Statehood in the Twenty-First Century* (London, Palgrave Macmillan, 2007).

Archer, Sir G., *British Somaliland and its Tribes* (historical notes issued by HMG in January 1945).

'Army Says Improper Orders by Colonel Led to 4 Deaths' (*New York Times*, 21 January 2007, Aroma, Cabdulqaadir, *Hadimadii Gumeysiga* (in Somali), (Mogadishu: Aroma Publications, 2005).

Associated Press, 'Soldiers in Iraq Say They Were Ordered to Kill All Adult Males' (*Editor & Publisher*, editorandpublisher.com, 21 July 2006).

Atkinson, R., 'Night of a Thousand Casualties' (*Washington Post*, 31 January 1994).

Atkinson, R., 'The Raid That Went Wrong' (*Washington Post*, 30 January 1994).

Ayele, Negussie, 'Adwa 1896: Who was Civilized & Who was Savage?' (*Ethiopian Review*, Vol. 7, No. 2, 30 April 1997).

Baker, A.I., *From Biplane to Spitfire: The Life of Air Chief Marshal Sir Geoffrey Salmond KCB RCMC DSO* (Barnsley, Pen & Sword, 2003).

Barre (Nairobi, *The Daily Nation*, 15 May 1992).

Bartholet, J., 'The Road to Hell' (*Newsweek*, 21 September 1992).

Baumann, R.F. and Yates, L.A, with Washington, V.F., *My Clan Against the World: US and Coalition Forces in Somalia 1992–1994* (Fort Leavenworth, KS, Combat Studies Institute Press, 2003).

Biddle, S.D., *Nonstate Warfare: The Military Methods of Guerillas, Warlords, and Militias* (Council on Foreign Relations, Princeton, Princeton University Press, 2021).

Binet, L., *Somalia 1991–1993: Civil War, Famine Alert and UN 'Military Humanitarian' Intervention 1991–1993* (Médecins Sans Frontières, 2013).

'Bombe su Mogadiscio, è strage' (*l'Unità*, 13 July 1993).

Bowden, M., *Black Hawk Down: A Story of Modern War* (New York, Atlantic Monthly Press, 1999).

Bradbury, M., *The Somali Conflict: Prospects for Peace* (Oxfam Military Library, 1994).

'"Briefcase admiral" blamed in Somalia crisis: American UN envoy lambasted for "personal vendetta" against Aideed and for deploying gunships over Mogadishu' (London, *The Independent*, 8 October 1993).

Britannica.com. History of Somalia: events, people, dates.

Carney, Colonel J.T. and Schemmer, B.F., *No Room for Error: The Story Behind the USAF Special Tactics Unit* (London, Random House, 2007).

Chapman, F.S. DSO, *The Jungle is Neutral* (London, W.W. Norton & Company, 1949).

Chapter VII of the UN Charter.

Chun, C.K.S., *Gothic Serpent: Black Hawk Down, Mogadishu 1993* (Oxford, Osprey Publishing, 2012).

'CIA warns Bush on Somali Mission' (*International Herald Tribune*, 3 December 1992).

Clarke, W. and Herbst, J. (eds.), *Learning from Somalia: The Lessons of Armed Humanitarian Intervention* (Boulder, CO, Westview Press, 1997).

Cockburn, A., 'Somalia Slips From Hope to Quagmire: In Monday's attack, the peacekeepers looked more like warlords' (*Los Angeles Times*, 13 July 1993).

Cohen, E.A. and Gooch, J., *Military Misfortunes: The Anatomy of Failure in War* (New York, The Free Press, 1990).

Compagnon, D., 'Political Decay in Somalia: From Personal Rule to Warlordism' (*Refuge: Canada's Journal on Refugees*, 1992).

Connor, S., 'Ground Wars' (*New Scientist*, Reed Business Information, 23 July 1987).

Dauber, C.E., *The Shot Seen Round the World: The Impact of the Images of Mogadishu on American Military Operations* (Michigan State University Press, Rhetoric & Public Affairs, 2001).

Davies, J.L., *The Liberation Movements of Somalia* (Wayback Machine, August 1994).

De Waal, A., *Famine Crimes: Politics & the Disaster Relief Industry in Africa* (Indiana University Press and the International African Institute in association with James Currey, 2007).

De Waal, A., African Rights and Mines Advisory Group, *Violent Deeds Live On: Landmines in Somalia and Somaliland* (London, 1993).

Del Boca, A., *Gli Italiani in Africa Orientale: II. La Conquista Dell'impero* (Cles, Arnoldo Mondadori, 1992).

Dempsey, G. and Fontaine, R.W., *Fool's Errands: America's Recent Encounters with Nation Building* (Washington, D.C., Cato Institute, 2001).

Di Prizio, R.C., *Armed Humanitarians: U.S. Interventions from Northern Iraq to Kosovo* (Baltimore, Johns Hopkins University Press, 2002).

Doe, C., 'US Forces Attack Somali Warlord's Forces' (*United Press International*, 12 July 1993).

Drew, E., *On the Edge: The Clinton Presidency* (New York, Touchstone, 1994.).

Drysdale, J., *Whatever Happened to Somalia?* (London, Haan Publishing, 1994).

Durant, M.J. with Hartov, S., *In the Company of Heroes* (New York, Bantam Press, 2003).

Durch, W.J. (ed.), *Introduction to Anarchy: Humanitarian Intervention and 'State-Building' in Somalia* (New York, St Martin's Press, 1996).

Elmi, A.A., *Understanding the Somalia Conflagration: Identity, Political Islam and Peacebuilding* (London, Pluto Press, 2010).

Elmi, A.S., 'The chewing of khat in Somalia' (*Journal of Ethnopharmacology*, August 1983).

Eversmann, M. and Schilling, D. (eds.), *The Battle of Mogadishu: Firsthand Accounts from the Men of Task Force Ranger* (Novato, CA, Presidio, 2004).

Garrison to Hoar, memo entitled 'To keep you informed', 3 October 1993.

Gellman, B., 'The Words behind a Deadly Decision: Secret Cables Reveal Maneuvring over Request for Armor in Somalia' (*Washington Post*, 30 October 1993).

Gleis, J.L., *Withdrawing under Fire: Lessons Learned from Islamic Insurgencies* (Washington, D.C., Potomac Books, 2011).

Hanley, G., *Warriors and Strangers* (London, Hamish Hamilton, 1971).

Hartley, A., *The Zanzibar Chest: A Story of Life, Love, and Death in Foreign Lands* (Open Road & Grove/Atlantic, 2016).

Hilaire, M., *Waging Peace: The United Nations Security Council and Transnational Armed Conflicts* (Logos Verlag Berlin GmbH, 2015).

Hirsch, J.L. and Oakley, R.B., *Somalia and Operation Restore Hope: Reflections on Peacemaking and Peacekeeping* (Washington, D.C., United States Institute of Peace Press, 1995).

Hughes, D., 'Bill Clinton "Surprised" at Black Hawk Down Raid' (ABC News, 18 April 2014).

Husband, M., 'UN Somali action comes under fire' (*The Guardian*, 5 August 1993).

Jama, Abdinur, 'Somalia's Billion-Dollar Miraa Addiction: A Nation Bleeding Cash to Kenya' (*Wardheer News*, 17 February 2025).

Johns, M., *Preserving American Security Ties to Somalia* (Washington, D.C., Heritage Foundation, December 1989).

Kapteijns, L., *Clan Cleansing in Somalia: The Ruinous Legacy of 1991* (University of Pennsylvania Press, 2013).

Kaus, M., 'What Black Hawk Down Leaves Out' (*Slate*, 21 January 2002).

Keane, F., 'Good News: The United States has decided to cross the Mogadishu line' (*The Economist*, 5 July 2003).

Kimber, C., 'Why Somalis hit back against US forces' (*Socialist Worker*, 19 January 2002).

Kraft, S., 'U.S. Soldiers Surprise Robbers, Kill 6 Somalis: Africa: Three of dead are known to be victims of robbery …' (*Los Angeles Times*, 17 January 1993).

La Presse, 11 and 23 September 1993.

Lawrence, T.E., 'The Science of Guerrilla Warfare' (contribution to *Encyclopaedia Britannica*, 1929).

Levin, D.H., 'When Great Power Gets a Vote: The Effects of Great Power Electoral Interventions on Electoral Results' (*International Studies Quarterly*, June 2016).

Lewis, I.M., 'In the Land of the Mad Mullah' (London, *Sunday Times*, 30 August 1992).

Lewis, I.M., *A Modern History of Somalia* (London, Longman Group, 1987).

Lewis, I.M., *A Pastoral Democracy: A Study of Pastoralism and Politics among the Northern Somali of the Horn of Africa* (Oxford University Press, for the International African Institute, 1961).

'Long among most obliging allies, Italy challenges Washington, UN: Somali crisis prompts call for greater say in world order' (*The Globe and Mail*, 16 July 1993).

Lorch, D., 'U.N. Moves Troops to Somali City and Vows Punishment for Attack' (*New York Times*, 8 June 1993).

Los Angeles Times, 28 December 1992.

Malis, M., Querubin, P. and Shanker, S., 'Persistent Failure? International Interventions Since World War II' (*The Handbook of Historical Economics*, San Diego, CA, January 2021).

Maren, M., *The Road to Hell: The Ravaging Effects of Foreign Aid and International Charity* (New York, The Free Press, 1997).

Megas, N., 'Did the U.S. Cover Up a Civilian Massacre Before Black Hawk Down?' (*The Daily Beast*, 6 January 2019).

Metz, H.C. (ed.), 'Siad Barre and Scientific Socialism' in *Somalia: A Country Study* (Washington, D.C., Library of Congress, Federal Research Division, 1992).

Nash, N.S., *Caribbean Crisis: The Invasion of Grenada 1983* (Barnsley, Pen & Sword, 2025).

Nash. N.S., *Hunger: Food Deprivation as a Military Weapon* (Barnsley, Pen & Sword, 2023).
National Museum of the United States Air Force.
Naylor, P.C., *Historical Dictionary of Algeria* (Oxford, Scarecrow Press, 2006).
Neville, L., *Day of the Rangers* (London, Osprey Publishing, 2018).
'News Groups Pull Staff from Somalia' (*The Press of Atlantic City*).
Ngulube, M.S.W., Hagglund, G. and Erskine, E.A., 'Report of the Commission of Inquiry Established Pursuant to Security Council Resolution 885 (1993) to Investigate Armed Attacks on UNOSOM II Personnel which led to Casualties Among Them' (Security Council Report, 24 February 1994).
'No Mercy in Mogadishu: The Human Cost of the Conflict & The Struggle for Relief' (New York, Africa Watch and Physicians for Human Rights, 1992).
'Pakistanis Fire on Somali Civilians; U.N. Renews Raids …' (*Los Angeles Times*, 14 June 1993).
Patman, R.G., 'Strategic Shortfall: The Somalia Syndrome and the March to 9/11' (*International Politics*, 23 December 2014).
Patman, R.G., *The Soviet Union in the Horn of Africa: The diplomacy of intervention and disengagement* (Cambridge, Cambridge University Press, 1990).
Peterson, S., *Me Against My Brother: At War in Somalia, Sudan, and Rwanda* (London, Routledge, 2000).
Petty, T., 'Fight in Somalia Worries Germans' (*Philadelphia Daily News*, 17 July 1993).
Pick, H., 'Three Strikes; UN operation in Bosnia, Somalia and Iraq in shambles' (*The Gazette*, 17 July 1993).
Policy Review, 'African Atrocities and the "Rest of the World"' (*Hoover Institution*, 6 December 2008).
Polybius, *Histories* (*c.* 125 BC), (*Familiar Quotations from Greek Authors*, trans. C.T. Ramage, 1895).
Pouligny, B., *Peace Operations Seen from Below: UN Missions and Local People* (Bloomfield, CT, Kumarian Press, 2006).
Powell, General C., *My American Journey* (New York, Ballantine Books, 2003).
Refugee Policy Group, 'Hope Restored: Humanitarian Aid in Somalia' (Washington, D.C., Centre for Policy, Analysis and Research on Refugee Issues, November 1994).
Remer, T., 'Somalia: The Next Test; Bringing Democracy to a Chaotic Country is a Tougher Task than Bringing Humanitarian Aid' (*Edmonton Journal*, 24 July 1993).
Richburg K.B., *Out of America: A Black Man Confronts Africa* (New York, Basic Books, 1997 and Washington, D.C., New Republic, 2009).
Richburg, K.B., '3 GIs Killed as Somalis Down Helicopter' (*Washington Post*, 26 September 1993).
Richburg, K.B., 'In War on Aidid, UN Battled Itself' (*Washington Post*, 6 August 1993).
Richburg, K.B., (*Washington Post*, 14 July 1993).
Richburg, K.B., 'Aidid: Warlord in a Famished Land' (*Washington Post*, 8 September 1992).
Richburg, K.B., 'US Helicopters Fire on Somalis: Last Ditch Action as Crowds Attack UN Peacekeepers' (*Washington Post*, 9 September 1993).
Robert Oakley interviewed on *Frontline*.
Roberts, G., 'Food Shipment-Related Security Incidents for the period 17 June 1992–20 June 1992' (interview at CARE International Headquarters, 5 August 1992).
Rollins, P.C. and O'Connor, J.E. (eds.), *Why We Fought: America's Wars in Film and History* (Lexington, KY, University Press of Kentucky, 2008).

RPG-7, Rocket-Propelled Grenade Launcher, history, spec and pictures, Military Security and Civilian Guns and Equipment (militaryfactory.com, 21 November 2013).
Sahnoun, Mohamed, *Somalia: The Missed Opportunities* (Washington, D.C., United States Institute of Peace Press, 1994).
Salih, M.A. Mohamed and Wohlgemuth, L. (eds.), *Crisis Management and the Politics of Reconciliation in Somalia: Statements from the Uppsala Forum, 17–19 January 1994* (Uppsala, Nordiska Afrikainstitutet, 1994).
Sangvic, Major R.N., *Battle of Mogadishu: Anatomy of a Failure* (Fort Leavenworth, KS, US Army Command and General Staff College, 1998).
Schofield, J., *Silent Over Africa: Stories of War and Genocide* (Australia, Harper Collins, 1996).
Sheehan, N., *A Bright Shining Lie* (London, Jonathan Cape, 1989).
Smith, S., *Mogadiscio, les premiers morts américains* (Paris, *Libération*, 9 August 1993).
'SNA Official Urges Respect for Prisoners' (Foreign Broadcast Information Service, Daily Report, Sub-Saharan Africa, 7 October 1993).
'Somalia: Beyond the Warlords: The Need for a Verdict on Human Rights Abuses' (*News from Africa Watch*, Vol. V, No. 2, 7 March 1993).
'Somalia: Building Human Rights in the Disintegrated State' (*Amnesty International*, November 1995).
Stevenson, J., *Losing Mogadishu: Testing U.S. Policy in Somalia* (Maryland, Naval Institute Press, 1995).
Stevenson, J., 'Will Bungle Turn into Betrayal?' (London, *Evening Standard*, 6 January 1993).
Stevenson, K. and Whitmore, J., 'When is quitting time'? (*Newsweek*, International Edition, 18 January 1993).
Stewart, R.W., *United States Forces, Somalia: After Action Report and Historical Overview: The United States Army in Somalia, 1992–1994* (Center of Military History, United States Army Washington, D.C., 2003).
Stewart, R.W., 'Summary of UN Activity in Somalia' (peacekeeping.un.org, UNITAF, UNOSOM II, as at March 1993).
Sun Tzu, *The Art of War* (*c.* 500 BC).
Thakur, Ramesh, 'From Peacekeeping to Peace Enforcement: The UN Operation in Somalia (Cambridge University Press, *The Journal of Modern African Studies*, 1994).
'The Price of Charity' (London, *The Economist*, 12 September 1992).
The Sabre & Lance: Journal of the Pakistan Armoured Corps (Nowshera, The School of Armour & Mechanised Warfare, 1997).
'The UN's Greatest Failure' (*The Baltimore Sun*, 10 October 1993).
Tilford, Dr E.H., Tucker, Dr D. and Oakley, AMB R.B., *Two Perspectives on Interventions and Humanitarian Operations* (US Army War College Press, 1997).
Trama, G.A., *Rules of Engagement* (Buenos Aires: Joint Staff College, 2016).
Trevithick, J., 'These Secret Helicopters were Flown by a Shadowy Unit During the Battle of Mogadishu' (*The Drive*, 2 May 2019).
'UN Commission of Inquiry Established under Security Council Resolution 885 to Investigate Armed Attacks on UNOSOM II' (Secretary-General, 1 June 1994).
'UN Counts on US Rangers to Find Warlord' (*New York Times*, 26 August 1993).
UN Security Council resolution 794, 3 December 1992.
'United Nations Operations in Somalia' (UNOSOM II, peacekeeping.un.org, Ramsbotham and Woodhouse, 1999).
'U.N. Troops Kill Eighty' (*Evening Herald*, 12 July 1993).

US Department of Defense Archive.

US Senate, Committee on Armed Services, Memorandum for Senator Thurmond and Senator Nunn, from Senator Warner and Senator Levin, subject: 'Review of the Circumstances Surrounding the Ranger Raid on October 3–4,1993 in Mogadishu, Somalia' (Washington, D.C., GPO, 29 September 1995).

Watson, P., 'Pakistani Troops Kill Somali Protesters' (*Chicago Tribune*, 14 July 1993).

Watson, P., *War on the Mind: The Military Uses and Abuses of Psychology* (New York, Basic Books, 1978).

West, R., *War and Peace in Vietnam* (London, Sinclair Stevenson, 1995).

Wheeler, E. and Roberts, C., *Doorway to Hell: Disaster in Somalia* (Barnsley, Frontline Books, 2012).

Wiles, P. (ed.), *The New Communist Third World: An Essay in Political Economy* (London, Routledge, 1982).

Wilhelm, Major General C.C., 'In a memorandum referring to "the 30-day Attitude Adjustment"' (*HQ UNITAF*, 12 January 1993).

Willbanks, J.H., *America's Heroes: Medal of Honor Recipients from the Civil War to Afghanistan* (Bloomsbury Publishing, ABC-CLIO, 2019).

www.huey.co.uk/m60.php.

Index